A Family Guide to Childhood Glaucoma and Cataracts

A Family Guide to Childhood Glaucoma and Cataracts

by
Alex V. Levin, MD, MHSc, FAAP, FAAO, FRCSC

with
Christopher M. Fecarotta, MD

Edited by
Sharon F. Freedman, MD,
Andrea Osborn, and
Ian Hubling

Shadow Fusion LLC
Anchorage

Published by Shadow Fusion LLC.

Library of Congress Control Number: 2014943907

ISBN 978-1-935964-14-8

Address for Correspondence:
Alex V. Levin, MD, MHSc, FAAP, FAAO, FRCSC
Pediatric Ophthalmology and Ocular Genetics
Wills Eye Hospital, 840 Walnut Street, Philadelphia, PA, 19107
Phone: 215-928-3914 Fax: 215-928-3983
E-mail: alevin@willseye.org

Supported in part by Visteon Corporation and The Foerderer Fund

This book is dedicated to my wife and two sons, who are and always will be the central focus of my life, and to the patients and families who have made my career joyous.
     Alex V. Levin

CONTENTS

IMPORTANT NOTICE

The purpose of this book is to educate. It is sold with the understanding that the authors and publisher shall have neither liability nor responsibility for any injury caused or alleged to be caused, directly or indirectly, by the information contained in this book. While every effort has been made to ensure its accuracy, this book's contents should not be construed as medical advice. Each person's health needs are unique. To obtain recommendations appropriate to you or your child's particular situation, please consult a qualified healthcare provider.

ACKNOWLEDGMENTS

The authors would like to thank all of the parents, children, and professionals who contributed to the writing of this book. In particular, we pay tribute to all of the parents who have, at one time or another, served on the Board of the Pediatric Glaucoma and Cataract Family Association (PGCFA). Founding Board Members are indicated by an asterisk (*). Current Board Members are indicated by a dagger (†).

Dawn Atwell, Past Co-Chair
Mike Atwell, Past Co-Chair
Barbara Bartlett*
Ross Bartlett*
Lidia Beiforte
Barbara Burton
Paul Burton
Brenda Cadieux
Dennis Cadieux
Ann Carvalho
Rosemary Cescolini
Christine Clark
Jeff Greenspan*
Thea Greenspan*
Casey Harshman†
Molly Harshman†
Ian Hubling†, Webmaster
Diane Iliadis
Greg Josey
Susan Josey*
Rachel Kraljevik
Mike Taitz
Anne Lenarduzzi*
Frank Lenarduzzi*
Alex Levin*†, Chair, Scientific Advisory Committee
Robert Lewis†, Fundraising Chair
Cheryl MacDonald
Peter McCormick
Liz McManus, Past Newsletter Editor
Richard Mirtic*
Ray Mistry†
Monika Mistry†
Anne-Marie Mohler*
John Mohler*
Gary Montgomery†
Jill Montgomery†
Leslie Mowat*, Founding President
Jan Ong
Andrea Osborn†, Newsletter Editor
Enza Perruzza

Seetha Proban
David Prowten†, Chair
Edye Rome-Webster
Jodi Roul
Yolanda Runinsztjn
Art Samuel
Russell Schildkrau
Lucy Spivak
Bill Stevenson
Rosie Stevenson
David Van†, Treasurer
Joany Verschuurren
Janice Vogtle†
Patty Weizenberg
Brian Worth*
Jane Worth*

The following professionals deserve special mentions as they assisted us with the answers to several specific questions. We are grateful for their participation.

Beverley Griffiths, RN
Yasmin Shariff, RN
Nasrin Tehrani, MBBCh, MSc, FRCS Ed(Ophth), FRCSC
Alissa Ulster, MSW, RSW
Terri L. Lewis, PhD
Bruno Bissonette, MD, FRCSC
Susan Edmonds, OD
Norman B. Medow, MD
George Holliday

The contributors to the PGCFA's newsletter, *MORINformation*, should also be mentioned, but unfortunately the list is much too long to include here. (To read archived newsletter issues, please visit our website: *http://www.pgcfa.org.*) These contributors include physicians from around the world, other health care professionals, Board Members, readers from various walks of life including, most importantly, children and adults affected by childhood glaucoma and/or cataract. In particular, we thank all of the members of the Department of Ophthalmology and Vision Sciences, the Eye Clinic staff at The Hospital for Sick Children in Toronto, and many people throughout Wills Eye Hospital in Philadelphia who not only support the PGCFA by contributing to *MORINformation*, but also have cared for many of our children, supported our families, hosted and attended our annual Education Day, and were there whenever we needed them. Our Scientific Advisory Board members, Drs. David Walton, Sharon Freedman, Ken Nischal, Asim Ali, and Norm Medow, also provide invaluable professional and personal support. They are international experts and we are proud to have them working with us.

The PGCFA survives purely on the basis of private donations. We appreciate the early financial support we received from Allergan, Inc., and the grant from Visteon Corporation that helped make this book a reality. Many other private individuals and corporations have provided financial support over the years. We are also thankful for the vision of Dr. M. Sara Rosenthal, from Sarahealth Press, and her staff, who believed in this effort and worked with us to construct the first draft of this manuscript. We regret that we were unable to finish the project under her direction. Many thanks also to Dr. Levin's Administrative Assistant, Karen Scannapieco, who makes all things possible, and Research Assistants Rizwan Alvi and William Aultman, who kept this project on task.

Many thanks to William Aultman, who, in his role as Research Assistant, was the glue that helped keep the multiple pieces of this complex project together. His efforts allowed it to come to fruition. Thanks also to Jack Scully and Roger Barone. Their photographic skills made many of the images used herein come alive.

We hope that, in the future, no family will ever be left in isolation with their unanswered questions. With this goal in mind, we are extremely grateful for the support of the Robison D. Harley, MD Fund of the Wills Eye Society Trust. Its contribution will allow us to make a number of books available to those families that might not otherwise be able to afford to purchase one.

This book would never have been possible without the able leadership and guidance of our publisher, Justin Oldham, and editor, Beth Hartt, of Shadow Fusion LLC. Mr. Oldham brings a unique perspective to this project. He is a patient with aniridia, cataract, and glaucoma, who knows the world of low vision, multiple surgeries, eyedrops, and much of what this book is about. For those of you who may have low vision or eye loss concerns, please also consult his company's publications *Being Legally Blind: Observations for Parents of Visually Impaired Children* and *Your Ocular Prosthetic*. Mr. Oldham's deep understanding of the information from a patient's perspective has been poignant and invaluable, enhancing his skills as a thoughtful publisher. Beth's rigorous editing and stewardship have been simply outstanding. No detail was left unattended. Her hard work is greatly appreciated.

The high quality of this book was guaranteed not only by the assistance of pediatric ophthalmologist Dr. Chris Fecarotta, who became involved as a resident in training at Wills, but also by our editors. Dr. Sharon Freedman is one of the premier pediatric glaucoma specialists in the world. Ian Hubling is a parent of a delightful boy with glaucoma caused by Sturge-Weber syndrome. Andrea Osborn is the former editor of the PGCFA newsletter and parent of a lovely child who has done beautifully after cataract surgery and patching for amblyopia. In addition, the entire PGCFA Board and Scientific Advisory Board have offered guidance and support in many ways as this book came to life over the years.

Most of all, we acknowledge the plight of the children affected by pediatric glaucoma and cataract, the tribulations of their families, and the warm, caring, and compassionate care given to them by Dr. J. Donald Morin, to whom this effort is dedicated.

Alex V. Levin, MD, MHSc, FAAP, FAAO, FRCSC
Chief, Pediatric Ophthalmology and Ocular Genetics
Robison D. Harley, MD Endowed Chair in Pediatric Ophthalmology and Ocular Genetics
Wills Eye Hospital
Jefferson Medical College of Thomas Jefferson University

HISTORY OF THE PGCFA

Inspired by Dr. Alex Levin, the Pediatric Glaucoma Family Association (PGFA) was formed in November 1993 to fulfill a need for interaction and information between parents and children with glaucoma. Dr. Levin asked the first ten parents he had scheduled on a particular day if they would be interested. Each parent asked that day accepted and the PGFA was born.

The first meeting was held in the office of Dr. Levin at The Hospital for Sick Children (HSC). The goal the group established was to promote the quality of life for children with glaucoma and their families by providing information, resources, education, and support.

The first item on the agenda was how the association could honor the memory of Dr. J. Donald Morin. Dr. Morin was a former Ophthalmologist-in-Chief at HSC and passed away in June of 1993. He was an internationally acclaimed expert in pediatric glaucoma, had one of the largest pediatric glaucoma practices in the world, and was loved by his patients. The first newsletter, aptly named *MORINformation* by the PGFA's first President, Leslie Mowat, was published the summer of 1994. In October 1994, the PGFA held the first open house and education evening for parents at HSC.

The focus of the PGFA changed as people became more aware of the group. The mailing list for the newsletter grew, with people from all over the world asking to be added. A Scientific Advisory Board was established and met in October 1999. The Board was comprised of Dr. David Walton of the Massachusetts Eye and Ear Infirmary in Boston, MA; Dr. Sharon Freedman of Duke University Eye Centre in Durham, NC; and Dr. Alex Levin of Wills Eye Hospital in Philadelphia, PA.

In January 2000, the PGFA expanded to include parents of children with cataracts who were also in need of information, education, and support. Cataract surgery is the most common cause of pediatric glaucoma, and many glaucoma patients have cataracts. The two groups have much in common. With a committed and united organization, more people could be helped. A family picnic was held to celebrate and became an annual event. The group's name was officially changed to the Pediatric Glaucoma and Cataract Family Association (PGCFA) in September 2000.

This was an important time for the group. The PGCFA secured its own domain name *(http://www.pgcfa.org)* and developed a website. Having a website has given the PGCFA a much higher profile. People from around the world access the site for education and family support. It offers dialogue opportunities between families, access to old newsletters, links to other related sites, medical information about cataracts and glaucoma, and an *Ask the Doctor* feature.

Through active fundraising activities, the organization and its supporters have been able to purchase diagnostic equipment for the benefit of families dealing with glaucoma and cataracts. The PGCFA has also been able to support research into these medical conditions.

As parents with children dealing with glaucoma and/or cataracts, we wished for a place where we could go to get our questions answered in an easy-to-read format. Many of us have the same questions about the care and future of our children. This parents' handbook, set up in a question and answer format, has always been a very important project of the PGCFA. It is a common resource where our common questions, fears, and anxieties can be answered. The goal has been to be able to make this handbook available to all newly diagnosed families. This would not be possible without continued support from corporations and friends. Thanks to the inspiration of the founding members and the dedication of the current members of the PGCFA, this book is finally a reality. If you are inspired to help the children see the sun, the moon and the stars, please support the PGCFA. We continue to grow, thanks to the volunteers on the Board, parents, and friends.

Michael and Dawn Atwell
Past Co-Chairs, PGCFA Board

PREFACE

Dr. J. Donald Morin was one of my heroes and mentors. I trained under him during my fellowship in pediatric ophthalmology at The Hospital for Sick Children (HSC) in Toronto, where he was Ophthalmologist-in-Chief and Fellowship Director. His expertise in the field of pediatric glaucoma was legendary. He assembled the largest pediatric glaucoma practice in Canada and certainly one of the largest in the world.

Dr. Morin seemed to know "everything" about pediatric glaucoma, and when patients had gone from doctor to doctor with no answer, they often turned to him for advice, care, and surgery. I saw him operate on some of the most difficult and diseased eyes, sometimes with success and sometimes not. He was a last chance for many patients. Despite Dr. Morin's expertise, he also struggled with the difficulty of managing these eye diseases in children. He was an innovator and often pushed the boundaries of pediatric ophthalmic care long before such efforts required the oversight of Research Ethics Boards or detailed *informed consent* discussions. He charted rough waters, yet I never saw him lose composure. He consistently maintained his professorial style as he led his trainees to a higher level of understanding and skill.

Dr. Morin was not loved by everyone. He was sometimes short, tough, condescending, or curt. Some trainees feared his wrath, should they not have the right answer to one of the questions he asked as he peered down at them through the *bifocals* perched on the end of his nose. I never did see that wrath for real. It was probably more fiction than fact. He inspired us to learn, to do better, but we rarely saw his compassion, or the hours he invested and the struggles he fought on behalf of his patients. There was a hidden heart of gold beneath that professorial air that I would only come to appreciate later in my career.

I was a staff member in the Department of Ophthalmology at HSC at the time of his death in 1993. Dr. Morin and his successor as Departmental Chief, Dr. J. Raymond Buncic, had recruited me to this position. I jumped at the opportunity to work at the hospital affectionately known as "SickKids."

I'll never forget one of the first times I saw Dr. Morin after my fellowship ended. Still in the recruitment process, I ran into him at a pediatric ophthalmology conference, and he asked me to call him "Don." I told him I couldn't imagine doing so; as a budding pediatric ophthalmologist, I felt this giant simply loomed too large in my mind. But, over time, our friendship grew.

Dr. Morin was my mentor as I began my practice at SickKids, giving advice, and ensuring that both my professional and personal life were in order. I came to know the "other side" of Don Morin: warm, caring, and compassionate.

The last time I saw him was on his deathbed, there at an age much too young with a life stolen by cancer. He drew me down to him and gave me a hug, and then whispered in my ear, "Take good care of my patients."

I was left with the awesome responsibility of trying to fill his enormous shoes; a task I feel I will forever be struggling to achieve. Perhaps the greatest challenge in assuming this task was fulfilling the expectations of his patients, almost every one of whom expressed deep sorrow about his untimely passing. Parents would cry on hearing the news of his death. Hoping to find some clues to improve my own abilities as a pediatric ophthalmologist, I would ask them, "What made Dr. Morin so special?" Time and time again, they would talk about his compassion, reliability, expertise, availability, and the confidence he instilled. I will forever be awestruck by the true love these families had for this great man. From those who had successful treatment to those who went blind despite his best efforts, Dr. Morin represented hope, concern, and caring.

As I began to care for this huge population of patients and families afflicted by pediatric glaucoma, I came to realize that their needs extended beyond the medical realm. They had to cope with a disease they could not see, one that often forced their children to have multiple surgeries, take many medications, and in some, caused a partial or complete loss of vision. Sometimes patients are left feeling isolated and uninformed.

Glaucoma in children is definitely an uncommon disorder. Most ophthalmologists will see very few cases in their careers. It is not a topic that could be raised at a cocktail party with the hopes of having multiple people chime in with their own experiences. Often, people have never even heard of glaucoma. Those who know of it as a disease that occurs in adults never thought a child could be afflicted with it. Families need information and they need each other.

Inspired by Dr. Morin's concern for his patients, which I could see in the eyes of the families who were now left under my care, I wanted to do something to both fulfill their needs and honor Dr. Morin's memory. It seemed a support group might be a viable option. But how can one start a support group without people to offer their support? I knew I needed an organizing committee, so I asked the next ten parents who came into my office with a child with glaucoma if they would be on the Board of an organization that had not yet formed. The response rate was 100 percent. All were happy to volunteer their time, likely due to their strong feelings for Dr. Morin.

The first meeting was held in 1995 in the waiting room of my office. The parents of ten children attended, and some of them stayed on the Board for over a decade. They decided to call themselves The Pediatric Glaucoma Family Association (PGFA), and the organization was born. We hoped to put the word out about pediatric glaucoma so families would not be left feeling isolated and stranded when they received a diagnosis. We wanted parents to have a place to turn and someone to talk to when their children were diagnosed or when challenging crossroads appeared in their children's care, such as surgery or failing vision.

The founding President of the Board, Ms. Leslie Mowat, was an inspiration to all of us. She led the formation of this group, which quickly set to work. There was fundraising to do and information to gather.

The PGFA decided to publish a newsletter, to be circulated to my patients and also someday to other families not under my care. We racked our brains to find a catchy title for it. For weeks I ran various permutations through my head. Eventually, I turned to my father, a lawyer who always had a secret love for advertising and catchy slogans, hoping that together we could come up with something fancy. But my creativity proved useless. I was completely outmatched by Ms. Mowat, who came up with the fantastic idea of honoring Dr. Morin with the name *MORINformation*. The group instantly accepted the name and the newsletter was born with the financial assistance of Allergan, Inc. At first, we were concerned about the involvement of a pharmaceutical company. In exchange for the company's assistance, we stipulated that there would be no advertising, no access to mailing lists, and only a small by-line acknowledging the company's support. Allergan boldly agreed to our requests. Obviously, the company wanted to help, as well.

The years went by and the PGFA grew. The newsletter became an international publication, circulated around the globe. The group raised funds and contributed significantly to the purchase of equipment for the care of children with glaucoma at HSC, but it wanted to do more. Eventually, a website was born under the guidance of our webmaster, Ian Hubling, catapulting us to a new level of information provision.

The leading cause of glaucoma in children is cataract surgery (aphakic glaucoma), while one of the most common complications of cataract surgery is glaucoma. It became obvious to the group that it would be natural to pair the two, and the organization expanded to become the Pediatric Glaucoma and Cataract Family Association (PGCFA). Now, both groups of patients could benefit from the information and support provided by the group.

Over the years, the group has collected many questions from enquiring families. At first, we made up questions in an *Ask the Doctor* column in our newsletter. Later, the same format was repeated on the website, allowing families to send in questions to be answered by a physician. The PGCFA Scientific Advisory Board, comprised of internationally acclaimed pediatric glaucoma specialists, Dr. David Walton in Boston (one of the fathers of pediatric glaucoma treatment in the United States) and Dr. Sharon Freedman at Duke University in North Carolina, with me as Chair, answered these questions, sometimes with the assistance of *nurses*, social workers, *opticians*, and other physician experts from various fields. As time has passed, many questions have been answered. The Scientific Advisory Board grew to include Dr. Asim Ali in Toronto, Dr. Norman Medow in New York City, and Dr. Ken Nischal, initially in London, England, and now in Pittsburgh. Eventually the PGCFA decided to bring the information together in the form of a book—this book—which has been developed over the past several years.

To begin the process, the members of the Board, who at the time were all parents of children with glaucoma or cataracts, brainstormed. They wrote down every question they thought a parent might ask over the course of the raising of a child with either pediatric glaucoma or cataract. The questions were pooled and grouped in chapters. Eventually, we set out to provide the answers to the questions with the expert help of many consultants.

This book has truly been a labor of love. It required enormous dedication from so many people—too many to mention here. I remain deeply grateful to the patients and families who have contributed to this effort. It is for them, and for patients and families around the world, that this book exists. The information, of course, is powerful. The knowledge that no one needs to go through the process alone is even more critical. Your continued support and donations (which can be made through the PGCFA website at *http://www. pgcfa.org*) will assist us in this effort. The PGCFA website will also make the book available for purchase online.

Our goal is to get the answers to the people who need them most—the parents and children affected by these diseases. Though we know that it is impossible to be completely comprehensive, we hope this book will provide you with "everything you wanted to know about pediatric glaucoma and cataract but were afraid to ask." New questions come in every week through the *Ask the Doctor* section of our website, and I am sure the book will go through revisions as more questions are added.

Information is not enough to make these children see again. Research continues on many fronts in the fields of pediatric glaucoma and pediatric cataract. As we struggle and strive to improve our care for these children and perhaps someday find cures for these disorders, we do so with the realization that the start was made by Dr. Morin years ago. There is a very powerful partnership that can be forged between patients, families and their physicians. Inspired by the deep personal link his families felt towards Dr. Morin, we continue to work, in his memory, to bring vision to affected children so they can indeed see the sun, the moon, and the stars for the rest of their lives.

Alex V. Levin, MD, MHSc, FAAP, FAAO, FRCSC
Chair, PGCFA Scientific Advisory Board

AN INTRODUCTION TO THE EYE

The eye functions like a camera (see Figure 1). Just as a camera uses a lens to focus a picture on film, the eye uses its domed clear covering (*cornea*) and a *lens* situated behind the *pupil* to focus light on the *retina*, which lines the inside of the back of the eye. Retinal blood vessels supply nutrients and oxygen to keep the retina healthy. The retina takes the light rays and converts them into electric messages, which are passed along the *optic nerve* that connects the eyeball to the brain. These electric messages are decoded into perceptions of images known to us as vision. A special focusing point in the center of vision, called the *fovea*, gives us our best straight ahead vision, for example, when we are reading. The fovea is surrounded by the *macula*, another specialized area of retina, which gives us color vision and the ability to see in brightly lighted conditions.

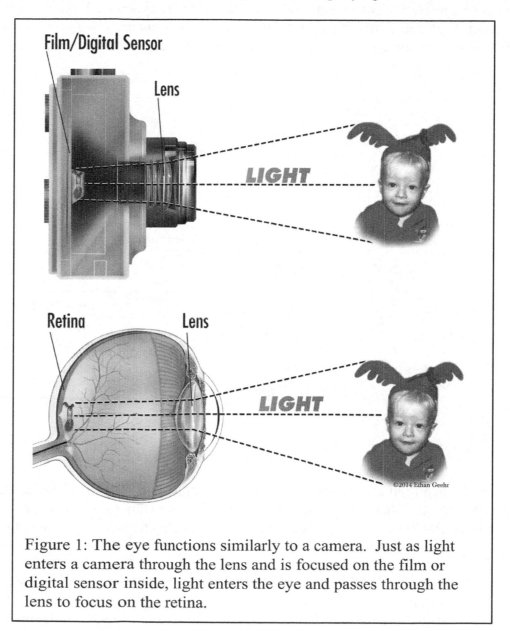

Figure 1: The eye functions similarly to a camera. Just as light enters a camera through the lens and is focused on the film or digital sensor inside, light enters the eye and passes through the lens to focus on the retina.

The colored part of the eye (*iris*) surrounds the black pupil, which is simply a hole in the iris through which light can pass. The **pupil** is able to become smaller (constrict) in response to bright light or become larger (*dilate*) in dim illumination. Pupil constriction (*miosis*) is due to activation of the *pupil sphincter muscle*. Enlargement (*mydriasis*) of the pupil is governed by the *pupil dilator muscle*.

Immediately behind the iris, invisible from external view, is a ring of folded tissue (*ciliary processes* or *pars plicata*) that encircles the inside of the eye. This ring produces fluid that travels through the pupil to fill the front of the eye between the cornea and the iris (*anterior chamber*). This fluid (*aqueous humor*) is then continuously drained through the tissue in the front part of the eye that allows excess aqueous humor to drain (*trabecular meshwork*, also known as the *angle of the eye*), which is located around the edges of the iris. From there, fluid flows into a tiny circumferential canal (*Schlemm's canal*) located just underneath the white of the eye (*sclera*) near the outer edge of the cornea (for 360 degrees around). From there, the fluid enters the bloodstream via vessels on the surface of the eye (*episcleral veins*) connected to the rest of the body's bloodstream. Taken together, the cornea, anterior chamber, iris, pupil, and lens make up the *anterior segment* of the eye. The structures further back in the eye (vitreous, retina, and optic nerve) constitute the *posterior segment.*

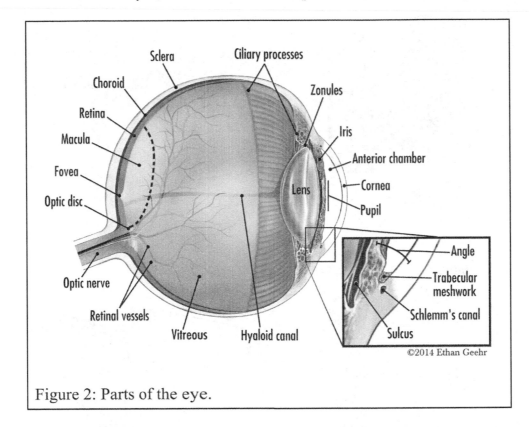

Figure 2: Parts of the eye.

Glaucoma occurs when fluid cannot drain out of the eye as fast as it is made. This causes a backup of pressure inside the eye that can damage the optic nerve and sometimes other parts of the eye, especially in young children. A *cataract* refers to any type of cloudiness or opacity in the lens of the eye.

The optic nerve is made up of millions of nerve fibers that collect the electronic messages from the retina. It is attached to the back end of the eye, bringing with it the blood vessels that nourish the retina lining the inside wall of the eye. The blood vessels travel in the center of the optic nerve until they enter the eye. This canal, which is an empty space in the optic nerve surface, is called the *cup of the optic nerve* or *optic cup.*

Eye doctors can look through the pupil into the eye and see the optic nerve as it enters (see Figure 3). The optic nerve stops at its entrance point inside the eye and forms a circular area with blood vessels coming out of its center. This disc is referred to as the *optic nerve head*, *optic disc*, or simply as the disc.

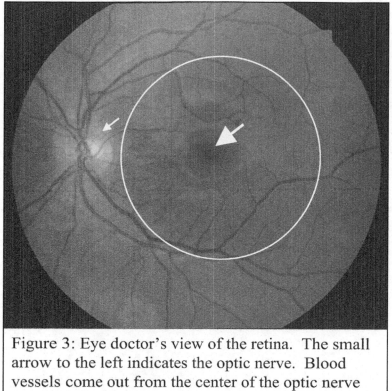

Figure 3: Eye doctor's view of the retina. The small arrow to the left indicates the optic nerve. Blood vessels come out from the center of the optic nerve and course along the retina. The larger arrow points to the fovea in the center of the macula (the area within the circle). The fovea is the specialized spot for straight ahead vision.

The lens is contained in and surrounded by a continuous membrane (called either the *bag* or the *lens capsule*). During cataract surgery, the front of the bag (*anterior capsule*) is opened to allow the surgeon access to the lens itself, which is then removed. Depending on the age of the child and the type of the surgery, the rear wall of the bag (*posterior capsule*) may or may not be opened. If the posterior capsule is left intact, it will almost always become cloudy at a later date. Additional surgery, either with instruments or with a laser, may be necessary to restore clear vision by making an opening in this cloudy posterior capsule.

The lens is held in place by tiny fibers (*zonules*) that run from the edge of the lens to the front part of the ciliary processes (*ciliary body*) all the way around the lens. They hold the lens in place behind the pupil. If these zonules are too stretchy, break due to *trauma*, or are missing or defective due to *congenital* disease, then the lens can drift out of its central position behind the pupil. This condition is called *ectopia lentis* or a *subluxed lens*. If the lens goes through the pupil into the anterior chamber or backwards so that it is lying on the retina, it is called a *dislocated lens*. Unfortunately, the terms subluxed and dislocated are often incorrectly used interchangeably.

Alex V. Levin, MD, MHSc, FRCSC, with Christopher M. Fecarotta, MD

The area behind the lens and in front of the retina contains a jelly-like, clear, viscous fluid called the *vitreous humor*, or simply vitreous. This fluid allows the eye to maintain its shape and provides support for its various structures.

PART I: GENERAL QUESTIONS

A. EYE HEALTH PROFESSIONALS

Q. What is an ophthalmologist?
A. *Ophthalmologists* are medical doctors (also called MDs or physicians) who have gone to college, graduated from medical school, and taken a minimum of four years of residency training in the medical subspecialty of *ophthalmology* (the medical and surgical care of the eye). In medical school, they learned many aspects of medicine and surgery, including all subdisciplines. The ophthalmology residency is specific to the specialty of ophthalmology. After residency, some ophthalmologists take one or more years of subspecialty training, such as pediatric ophthalmology or glaucoma. Ophthalmologists are sometimes called "eye doctors."

Q. What is an optometrist?
A. An *optometrist* is an eye care professional (sometimes called an "eye doctor") who is not a medical doctor (not a physician) and is not trained to perform any kind of surgery. In some locations, optometrists are able to prescribe certain medications. After a training period that is shorter than what is required of an ophthalmologist, an optometrist is able to diagnose problems of the eye, although he/she may need to refer a patient to an ophthalmologist for further care. Optometrists are particularly well-trained to prescribe glasses and contact lenses, and assist individuals with low vision.

Q. What is an orthoptist?
A. *Orthoptists* are eye care professionals who assist ophthalmologists in measuring eye misalignment (*strabismus*) and diagnosing *binocular vision* disorders. They are particularly skilled at evaluation and treatment of problems involving eye muscles, including *nystagmus* and muscle paralysis. Treatments used by orthoptists include lenses, eye exercises, eye patches, or eyedrops. If surgery is needed, they may also help the ophthalmologist determine surgical plans. Some even assist during surgery. Orthoptists may sometimes be involved in other eye care activities, including vision screening, assessment of special needs, low vision assessment, instruction of patients in the use and care of contact lenses, and *refraction*. Orthoptists typically undergo two to four years of training after college.

Q. What is an optician?
A. An optician is an individual who makes and sells glasses, contact lenses, and other vision aids. While opticians in some countries may be able to prescribe glasses or contact lenses, or even perform some diagnostic screening, they cannot do so in Canada or the United States.

Q. What is an ocularist?
A. An *ocularist* is an individual who specializes in making *prosthetic* (artificial or "fake") eyes for individuals who have had an eye removed or have an unsightly small eye (*microphthalmia*, *phthisis*). Ocularists are not otherwise medically trained, and are not able to prescribe glasses or contact lenses, dispense glasses or contact lenses, or diagnose or treat eye diseases.

Q. What is a nurse?
A. A nurse is a professional who has been educated and trained to care for the sick, help patients achieve good health, and prevent disease. Nurses provide care for patients at all stages of life and in all states of health, from normal functioning to crisis. A registered nurse (RN) has graduated from a

university or college and passed a national licensing exam. Licensed practical nurses (LPNs) often provide basic bedside care, including measuring vital signs, keeping patients comfortable, administering medications, or dressing wounds. Nursing aides often work under the supervision of RNs or LPNs and assist in taking care of patients. In some countries, specially trained nursing professionals called nurse anesthetists assist in administering general *anesthesia* to patients during surgery.

Nurses have many different roles, including inpatient care, outpatient clinic care, administration, teaching, and research. They work in many different settings—hospitals, community health centers, clinics, long-term care facilities, outpost and aboriginal communities, patient homes, industries, and schools. In an outpatient eye clinic, a nurse may also provide care for sedated patients.

Q. What are the differences between medical residents, fellows, and students?
A. A medical student is not yet a fully licensed physician. He/she is in the process of learning to be a doctor.

Residents are licensed physicians. They are able to prescribe medications, care for patients, and assist or perform surgery, all under supervision. In most countries, these new doctors enter residency training programs designed to give them skills in a particular specialty after graduating from medical school. In some specialties, the first year of the residency is called an internship. Residencies may last anywhere from one to eight years. The length of the residency depends on the specialty and the country.

After completing a residency, a physician may choose to undertake further sub-specialty training in the form of a fellowship. Fellowships usually last between one and three years. Fellowships are offered in all areas of ophthalmology: pediatric ophthalmology and strabismus, cornea, pathology, iritis, glaucoma, neurophthalmology, retina, oculoplastics, and ocular genetics. Some residencies and fellowships have a research component, while others are purely clinical.

Physicians in North America wishing to specialize in ophthalmology undertake a four (U.S.) or five (Canada) year residency after medical school. Once they complete this residency, they are fully trained ophthalmologists who can go into general practice.

If an ophthalmologist decides to further specialize in pediatric ophthalmology or glaucoma, additional fellowship training is required. Although there is no specific training program in pediatric glaucoma, some glaucoma centers and pediatric ophthalmology centers have a special interest in pediatric glaucoma and provide strong training in this area. Rarely, a pediatric ophthalmologist will first train in pediatrics before completing training in ophthalmology and pediatric ophthalmology. There are very few pediatric ophthalmologists who are also trained as pediatricians.

B. YOUR FIRST VISIT TO THE EYE DOCTOR

Q. What is asked in the first visit?
A. As with most other initial visits to medical providers, you will likely be asked to fill out a number of forms. Some are to provide basic information, such as address, phone numbers, insurance coverage, and general medical history. You are also likely to see informed consent documents at this point. These grant permission for the doctor to treat your child, for the doctor or medical office to share information with other health care providers, and possibly permission to take photographs.

Once you and your child are shown into the examining room, the physician or another designated person will ask detailed questions about your child's medical history. This discussion will include questions about when the eye problem was first noted, symptoms, previous doctor's visits, previous eyedrops and/or surgery, changes that may have been noted in your child's vision, other previous eye problems, other previous or ongoing medical problems, allergies, relevant prior medical tests, and family history. Using this information, the doctor will attempt to determine the nature of the eye problem, decide what testing might be needed, and consider what would be the best treatment plan to pursue.

During the examination, a variety of tests and assessments will be conducted. These may include measuring your child's sharpness of vision at certain predetermined distances (*visual acuity*); inspecting the facial tissues around the eye or eyes for any abnormalities; assessing pupil reactivity, the range of eye movements, and the alignment of the eyes; measuring the pressure of the fluid inside the eye (*intraocular pressure* or *IOP*); and examining the front part of the eye using a flashlight or slit lamp biomicroscope (commonly shortened to *slit lamp*). Depending on the age of the child and the nature of the problem, the doctor may apply a special handheld contact lens to the surface of the eye to look at the trabecular meshwork. Next, eyedrops are then usually instilled to dilate the pupils. The eyedrops cause the iris to contract, enlarging the pupil to allow the doctor to more easily examine the structures inside the eye, including the retina and optic nerve. It is also possible that photographs of the optic nerve or other parts of the eye may be taken.

Q. Should I tell the doctor about other medical problems? Should I tell my child's other doctors about any conditions the eye doctor diagnoses or treats?
A. Absolutely! It is important that the eye doctor knows not only about the other medical conditions, but also medications that may be used to treat those problems, as they may have an effect on your child's eye condition and options for treatment. Your child's other health care providers need to be aware of his/her eye problems and medications for similar reasons. The presence or absence of other medical problems may also be useful in determining exactly why the cataract or glaucoma occurred or in adjusting *anesthesia* in such a way as to make surgery safer.

Q. What questions should I ask my child's eye doctor?
A. What questions you choose to ask are up to you. Here are some suggestions that may help you. These questions may be asked during your first visit with the doctor, on a visit where surgery is being scheduled, or at any other time when the issues come to your mind:

- How is the overall health of my child's eyes?
- How well can my child see compared to a child of the same age who has normal eyes?
- How well can my child see compared to other patients of his/her age that have similar cataracts or glaucoma?
- Who will see my child for check-ups in the short- and long-term?
- How often will my child need to see the eye doctor?
- Can an eye doctor closer to my home conduct some of the eye visits?

Q. What does it mean to see 20/20, 20/60, etc.?
A. We live in a world in which a visual acuity measurement of 20/20 is normal vision. This means that a patient with normal vision can see a certain standard-sized letter at 20 feet. A person who sees 20/60 has to stand at 20 feet to see what a normal person would see at 60 feet. A person who sees 20/200 has to stand at 20 feet to see what a normal person can see at 200 feet.

Some eye doctors use the metric equivalent of these distances. Six meters is approximately equivalent to 20 feet, so the equivalent metric measurement would be written as 6/6 instead of 20/20. The equivalent of the non-metric 20/60 would be 6/18, 20/200 would be 6/60, and so on.

Q. How is visual acuity tested?

A. Depending on the age of your child, an appropriate means of testing visual acuity will be selected. Different methods are used for individuals at different ages and levels of development.

When a child is too young to verbally respond by reading a chart projected or posted at the end of the examining room, the doctor will inspect each eye and see if it is able to fixate on a target, such as a toy, and then follow that target. If your child has similar levels of vision in both eyes, the results should also be similar with each. If your child objects when one eye is covered but does not object when the other is covered, then the second eye usually has worse vision.

There are a wide variety of visual acuity tests available for older children. Some involve reading a chart and making a verbal response, while others involve matching objects, letters, or shapes positioned at a distance with items on a *lap board* or other nearby chart to indicate what is being shown at a distance. Examples of this kind of test include the *Sheridan-Gardiner test* and *HOTV test*.

There are several charts that can be posted or projected onto the wall or a computer screen at the end of the examining room for children who can identify letters to read from. The one familiar to most adults is the *Snellen chart*. A large letter (usually "E") is at the top. The test letters on the remaining lines get smaller all the way down to the bottom of the chart. Other styles include the *tumbling E test* (in which the child is asked to indicate whether the letter "E," in progressively smaller sizes, is pointing up, down, to the right, or to the left), *Landolt C test* (in which the letter "C" is presented in various sizes and the child is asked to indicate whether the opening is pointed up, down, left, or right), and various tests that use pictures which the child is asked to identify.

More sophisticated testing may also be available in some centers. One example is the *preferential looking test* (sometimes called a *Teller visual acuity test*). The young or nonverbal child is presented with a card showing two images—a black-and-white striped square on one side and an unstriped, uniformly gray square on the other. The examiner watches the child through a peephole in the card to determine which image the child turns his/her head toward. As the test progresses, the stripes on subsequent cards become narrower and closer together, eventually becoming indistinguishable from the gray card. When the child no longer shows a preference, indicating that he/she is no longer able to see the stripes, the limit of the child's vision has been reached.

Another test, which is used less commonly, is the *visual evoked potential test*. In this testing method, images are presented to the child's eye from a television or computer screen. Electrodes pasted to the child's head read his/her brainwaves, which indicate whether or not the brain is able to recognize a particular image, such as stripes or a checkerboard pattern, at various sizes.

Q. How old must a child be for the ophthalmologist to determine how much he/she can actually see?

A. The best test is to have the child read a chart of pictures or letters at a distance of 20 feet. This test is called *optotype* visual acuity. The letter (Snellen) chart is most commonly used for this type of test, although other variations (numbers, tumbling Es, Landolt Cs) may also be used. Obviously, this method is not useable for very young infants. There are ways to measure infant vision, but they tend to be somewhat subjective, not very accurate, and must be performed by highly skilled professionals familiar with the techniques. Your child's eye doctor can make some general assessments of the visual development, but a very accurate assessment of the actual vision acuity will not be easily possible until your child is old enough to give some verbal feedback. Very young infants see less than older infants, children, or adults see. What the ophthalmologist measures in infancy will not tell you exactly what your child's vision will be like in the future.

Q. Do visual acuity tests hurt? Are they uncomfortable?
A. Visual acuity testing is designed to be completely painless. The examiner's goal is to get this information without upsetting the child at all.

Q. What are intraocular pressure (IOP) tests?
A. These tests are designed to measure the pressure of the fluid inside the eye. The higher the pressure, the more firm the eye will be. These tests function by applying gentle pressure to the eye from the outside to determine how soft or firm the eyeball is. Particular levels of firmness are indicated by a number. Some of the devices used to measure IOP are pictured in Figure 4. There are several ways to conduct this type of test:

- Goldmann applanation *tonometer*: The Goldman applanation tonometer is an IOP measurement device that is attached to the eye doctor's slit lamp. A numbing drop (*topical anesthetic*) is placed in the eye, followed by an orange-colored drop called *fluorescein*. (Sometimes the two types of drops are mixed together and dispensed as one drop.) The child places his/her chin on the chin rest of the slit lamp. The slit lamp is switched to emit a special blue light. The examiner then moves the tonometer tip forward until it gently contacts the cornea and flattens a small circular area. (The child doesn't feel anything because the eye has been numbed.) The blue light causes the orange dye to fluoresce yellow-green. A special prism inside the tonometer tip allows the examiner to see two semicircular lines (*mires*). When aligned properly, the tonometer provides the eye pressure in units called *millimeters of mercury (mm Hg)*. As long as the child is relaxed and comfortable, this tool gives a very accurate pressure reading. This test is commonly considered to be the best measure of IOP. Once a child is old enough for it to be used, it is likely the one that will be most commonly used for the remainder of his/her lifetime.
- Tono-pen®: A Tono-pen® is a long, somewhat narrow, handheld tonometer. Before it is used, the examiner applies a numbing drop to the eye. No other drops are needed. A tiny computer chip inside the device measures the eye pressure and gives a value as to the reliability of the measurement. A Tono-pen® is very portable because of its size and can also be used when a child is under anesthesia or *sedation*.
- Perkins tonometer: A Perkins tonometer functions similarly to the Goldmann applanation tonometer. The same orange dye and blue light are used. The Perkins tonometer is designed to be handheld and portable. This allows it to be used on patients who are unable to sit in the slit lamp, such as those patients who are under anesthesia or sedation.
- Icare rebound tonometer: The Icare rebound tonometer is a handheld device that determines intraocular pressure by bouncing a small, plastic-tipped probe against the cornea. It is relatively easy to use. Unlike the Tono-pen® and the Goldmann tonometers, the Icare does not require a drop of *anesthetic* to be placed onto the cornea. This means that it is particularly useful for measuring eye pressures in young and otherwise uncooperative children. The Icare may also be particularly useful if it

becomes necessary to monitor home eye pressures in exceptionally difficult cases of glaucoma, as some individuals who are not health care professionals may find it possible to learn to use.

- McKay-Marg tonometer: A McKay-Marg tonometer is very similar to the Tono-pen®, and also gives very accurate readings of eye pressure. This device is largely unavailable and very expensive. Its advantage is that it has a very small tip, which allows for very focused measurements to be done. For example, when there is a scar on the cornea, that area may be more rigid and thick, causing an artificially high measurement. A McKay-Marg tonometer can be used to measure the pressure outside the scarred area, allowing for a more accurate measurement.

- Pneumotonometer (sometimes spelled pneumatonometer): A pneumotonometer is another type of tonometer that measures pressure by pushing air through a porous disc, gently indenting cornea. This device is larger than handheld instruments like the Tonopen®, Perkins, or Icare tonometers, but may have an advantage in measuring intraocular pressure when the cornea is very irregular or scarred.

- Air puff tonometer: These devices are sometimes called non-contact tonometers, as they blow a bit of air onto the cornea and register how much is required to indent it. These machines are inexpensive and widely used as screening devices because they can be used without eyedrops and do not require as much cooperation from the patient. They are, however, less accurate than other devices that measure eye pressure..

- Phosphene tonometer: Phosphene tonometers are handheld devices that place pressure on the eye through the closed eyelid, but require the patient to respond when he/she sees flashing lights. Pressure on the eyeball stimulates the retina to cause these flashing lights. This is a difficult test for children to perform, as it requires very good cooperation and understanding. It tends to be less accurate than other tonometers, even in adults.

- Finger tension: This is generally the least accurate type of intraocular pressure test, although an examiner's accuracy often increases with experience. Usually, the child holds his/her eyes gently shut. The examiner takes two fingers and presses them on the eyelids, estimating the pressure based on how firm or soft the eye feels. Some examiners perform this test when the eye is open, though this practice is less common.

Q. Are different pressure tests used depending on the age of the child?
A. The test that is selected depends largely on the child's level of cooperation. In cases where using eyedrops is expected to cause the child to become uncooperative, the Icare tonometer is particularly useful. A Tono-pen® or Perkins tonometer is most commonly used when the child is under anesthesia or sedation. These can sometimes also be used on a calm or feeding infant. While Goldmann applanation tonometry is the preferred test method, most children are unable to cooperate sufficiently for it to be administered until they are at least 7 years old. Some children as young as 3 years old, particularly those who have had cataract surgery and are used to having contact lenses inserted, may be capable of undergoing this test.

Q. Do pressure tests hurt? Are they uncomfortable?
A. Finger tension measurement is painless. For certain tests in which a tonometer actually touches the eye (e.g., Tono-pen®, Perkins, Goldmann), an anesthetic drop is used to numb the cornea so no

pain is felt when the test is done. Numbing drops are not necessary when an Icare is used. Minimal discomfort is felt from these devices, even though they touch the cornea, because the touch time is so short.

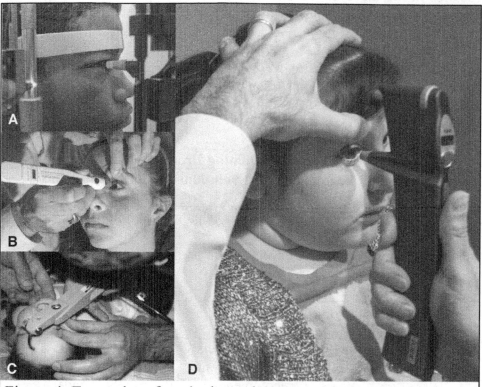

Figure 4: Examples of methods used to measure eye pressure.
A) Goldmann applanation tonometer. B) Tono-pen®. C) Perkins tonometer. D) Icare rebound tonometer.

C. DILATING DROPS

Q. Why must my child have his/her eyes dilated?
A. Dilating drops (also called *mydriatics*) are used to enlarge the pupil during eye examinations. Without using dilating drops, the pupils are usually too small for the doctor to see into the eye well enough to view the retina and optic nerve. In addition, dilating drops make measuring visual acuity for glasses prescriptions for children more accurate.

Q. How do the dilating drops work?
A. Dilating drops work either by temporarily paralyzing the pupil sphincter muscle (the muscle that makes the pupil smaller) or by stimulating the pupil dilator muscle. The eyes of patients with lighter eye colors (blue, green, or hazel) are generally more sensitive and dilate faster than those of patients with darker eyes (brown).

Q. Is dilation painful or uncomfortable?
A. There is usually very little discomfort when the eyes are dilated. The drops will likely sting a bit. Your child will likely be sensitive to bright lights and his/her vision may be blurry until the dilation wears off. The drops are unlikely to impair his/her ability to go about normal play activities. Older children will find reading to be difficult.

Q. What happens after the dilating drops are used?

A. It takes about 20 to 40 minutes for the drops to work. The doctor will then examine the eyes again. When the child is called back into the examination area, the doctor may use the slit lamp to reexamine structures inside the eye. He/she may also use a special headlamp, called an *indirect ophthalmoscope*, and a magnifying lens or other special instruments to better view the retina and optic nerve.

Q. What are the different types of dilating drops?

A. There are two main groups of dilating drops. Those that act by paralyzing the pupil dilator muscle are called *parasympatholytics*. Those that act by stimulating the pupil sphincter muscle are called *sympathomimetics*.

Table 1: Dilating Drops			
Common Name	**Method of Action**	**Solutions Available**	**Average Duration**
Tropicamide	Parasympatholytic	0.5% (used in premature infants) 1%	Up to 6 hours
Cyclopentolate	Parasympatholytic	0.5% (used in premature infants) 1% 2%	Up to 24 to 36 hours
Homatropine	Parasympatholytic	2% 5%	2 to 3 days
Atropine	Parasympatholytic	0.5% (special preparation only available from selected pharmacies; recommended for infants under 1 year of age) 1%, 1% ointment	1 to 2 weeks
Phenylephrine	Sympathomimetic	2.5% 10% (should never be used in children)	3 to 6 hours

Parasympatholytics make the pupil larger and temporarily paralyze the muscle that focuses the lens. As a result, they cause vision to be blurry, especially for activities where close vision is used, such as reading.

Although sympathomimetics do not cause blurring of vision like the parasympatholytics, they tend not to dilate the pupil well enough alone. As a result, some doctors choose to use both types of drops mixed in the same bottle.

Q. What are the side effects of the dilating drops in children?

A. When initially administered, the drops will likely sting, causing your child some minor discomfort. This sensation generally goes away within a few seconds. The doctor may administer an anesthetic drop before using the dilating drops to lessen or eliminate the sting.

Your child's eyes may temporarily be more sensitive to bright lights because the dilating drops expand the pupils. The duration of this effect will depend on the particular medication being used. If this reaction causes your child trouble, consider allowing him/her to wear sunglasses to minimize glare from bright lights. Many eye doctors' offices provide disposable sunglasses for patients whose eyes have been dilated.

Some mydriatics may cause a temporary whitening of the eyelids and skin around the eyes due to the constriction of small blood vessels in the skin. This effect is completely harmless and will go away as the drops wear off.

Atropine, a particular variety of mydriatic, may cause redness or flushing of the face, a warm sensation of the skin to touch, irritability, or sweating. Although these reactions are not dangerous, it does mean that a lower dose should be considered. The medication should be stopped and your child's eye doctor contacted.

In adults with *narrow angle glaucoma* (a condition that is extremely rare in children), mydriatics can cause an increase in intraocular pressure.

Other side effects are very rare. They include high blood pressure, confusion, hallucinations, and seizures. These rarely occur beyond infancy and usually only in premature babies. Eye doctors avoid these effects by using weaker concentrations in premature children. Itchy rashes can also occasionally occur.

Any eye medication may also cause side effects in the rest of the body because they are absorbed into the bloodstream. It is especially important to be aware of this with infants. As with all medicines, dilating drops should be stored out of the reach of children. Atropine, in particular, is extremely toxic and can kill if a large enough quantity is swallowed.

It is important to wash your hands thoroughly after giving these drops to prevent inadvertent dilation of your own pupils by touching your eyes.

Q. Should my child wear sunglasses after pupil dilation?
A. After dilating drops, some children are more sensitive to bright lights. Sunglasses can help to ease this discomfort if the child desires to wear them.

Q. Do the dilating drops have any other uses?
A. Some mydriatics relax the focusing muscles of the lens of the eye. This allows the eye doctor to get a more accurate measurement of the correct glasses prescription.

Making the pupil big before cataract surgery makes it easier for the surgeon to remove the cataract. In addition, keeping the pupil large is important after surgery and for patients with inflammation inside the eye (*iritis*). The use of mydriatics also prevents scar tissue (*synechiae*) from forming.

If a cataract is small, enlarging the pupil can allow the patient to see around it. Similarly, patients with out-of-position lenses (ectopia lentis) can gain clearer vision by seeing around the lens, delaying the need for surgery or sometimes even making it unnecessary.

Mydriatics tend to increase intraocular pressure in adults with narrow angle glaucoma. As a result, they can be used to help the eye to stay well-formed and recover if the eye pressure gets too low after glaucoma surgery.

One form of glaucoma (*closed angle glaucoma*) is the result of the iris and pupil sitting too far forward and blocking the drainage canals that allow fluid (aqueous humor) to flow from the eye. Dilating drops are sometimes used to treat this kind of glaucoma by restoring the normal positioning of the anatomy of the eye. This treatment is also sometimes used in children with total retinal detachment following *retinopathy of prematurity (ROP), persistent fetal vasculature cataract*, or eye tumors (*retinoblastoma*).

Dilating drops are sometimes used to treat lazy eye (*amblyopia*) by temporarily blurring the vision in a child's better (stronger) eye to force the brain to use the poorer-seeing (weaker) eye. They are also occasionally used to relax the focusing muscles of the eye in an effort to encourage a reluctant child to wear glasses.

D. YOUR CHILD'S VISIT TO THE EYE DOCTOR FOR GLAUCOMA

Q. How important is it for a child to be seen by a pediatric glaucoma specialist versus a glaucoma specialist?
A. There are many differences between caring for children and adults who have glaucoma. Where possible, you want your child to be taken care of by someone who has experience in the area of pediatric glaucoma and experience with and facilities for children. This may mean taking your child to both a pediatric ophthalmologist and a glaucoma specialist who will work together in the care of children with glaucoma.

Most adult glaucoma specialists rarely provide care for children with glaucoma. Pediatric glaucoma specialists are few and far between and, as a result, see many more children with glaucoma. There are, however, some adult glaucoma specialists who take a particular interest in pediatric glaucoma.

Q. What is a visual field test and what is its purpose?
A. A visual field test measures the quality and quantity of vision both in the middle of your child's line of sight (straight ahead) and also to all sides (*peripheral vision*). If you stare straight ahead at a target you will notice that you are able to see lots of things around you without moving your eye off the target. This is your peripheral vision. Peripheral vision is one of the first things affected in childhood glaucoma. This test also helps identify any blind spots (*scotomas*) in your child's vision.

Q. Why does the ophthalmologist measure corneal thickness?
A. Measuring central corneal thickness (CCT) has become a common part of full eye examinations for glaucoma in the last few years Studies have shown that instruments that measure eye pressure (tonometers) may overestimate intraocular pressure when the cornea is unusually thick and underestimate it when the cornea is thinner than normal. Ophthalmologists measure corneal thickness to get an idea of how accurate the readings are. CCT measurements can also be used to gauge the amount of swelling in the cornea.

Q. If my child cries hysterically when his pressure is measured, can the doctor obtain an accurate reading?
A. Pressure readings in a child who is not calm are usually inaccurate. Even if the child is just fidgety, the pressure may be artificially high. If the child is crying, the IOP measurements are extremely unreliable. This is why doctors do not force kids into doing the test. Examinations under anesthesia or sedation are often used in these situations.

Q. Can a pressure reading be higher from a child's eyes welling up with tears if he/she is upset during the exam?
A. The tears are not the problem. The presence of the tears may indicate the child was not totally relaxed when the pressure was taken. Any kind of upset, struggle, or resistance can dramatically elevate the pressure reading. The child must be calm and still for the test to be accurate.

Q. Are there any alternatives to examination under anesthesia (EUA) in toddlers with glaucoma?
A. In many cases, examining a child while he/she is awake is preferable to EUA. One disadvantage of examining a child while he/she is awake is that other important measurements, such as the length of the eye (measured by ultrasound), thickness of the cornea (pachymetry), and optic nerve photographs, are even more difficult to obtain than the eye pressure. If the child cannot remain calm and cooperative for a pressure check, he/she is even less likely to do so long enough for these other measurements to be obtained.

There are many different ways to check intraocular pressure of children who cannot sit at the slit lamp for the standard measurement. The most common include the Tono-pen®, Goldmann applanation tonometer, Icare tonometer, and air puff tonometer (pneumotonometer).

One way to entice a child's cooperation to obtain a calm pressure check without resorting to anesthetic is to have him/her come to the appointment hungry and offering a bottle or a lollipop to keep the child occupied while his/her pressure is measured. Another possible method is to measure the pressure while the child watches an age appropriate video. Eye pressure can also be measured while the child is asleep. If the child is deprived of a nap, he/she may fall asleep in time for a check in the office. Of course, there are certainly times when children will not cooperate, no matter what the parent and ophthalmologist do.

Another alternative to anesthesia is sedation. Sedatives may take quite a while to take effect, and usually do not work well for children weighing more than about 22 pounds (10 kilograms). The disadvantage is that most academic centers are subject to a number of regulations regarding sedation, making the process almost as prolonged as an examination under anesthesia.

E. YOUR CHILD'S VISIT TO THE EYE DOCTOR FOR CATARACT

Q. What is the doctor looking for?
A. When evaluating for cataract, the doctor is looking to see if the lens of the eye is clear. If it is not clear, then there is a cataract. The doctor is also looking for associated abnormalities in the eye, such as congenital abnormalities or glaucoma, that may help him/her understand why the cataract occurred and to make a plan for treatment. He/she is also seeking anything else about the eye that might limit the vision after the cataract is removed, such as retinal problems. Lastly, the doctor is attempting to determine whether there are any other eye problems that could result in poor visual development, such as amblyopia (often called "lazy eye"), or misalignment of the eyes (strabismus). With this information, he/she can better guide treatment and determine your child's visual prognosis.

Q. How can the doctor tell if my child has a cataract?
A. The eye doctor will use special equipment to look through the child's pupil to see the lens of the eye. The most important piece of equipment is called a slit lamp, which may either be a handheld device or a machine the child puts his/her chin and forehead into. The doctor examines the eye to see if light can pass clearly through the lens without any clouding.

15

Q. Can someone who is not a doctor tell if a child has a cataract?
A. The only situation in which someone can tell if your child has a cataract by simply looking at him/her is if the cataract is totally opaque and appears white, so that it is visible to the naked eye through the pupil. If the cataract is not visible to the naked eye, photographs in which the pupil of the eye would normally appear orange or red (*red reflex*) may instead show a black spot in the center of this red-orange reflex or the red reflex will be missing. Eye doctors will sometimes ask to see old photographs of a child to try to estimate when the cataract first occurred. This effect is not always possible to see in photographs taken with a digital camera, particularly if the camera used to take the picture has a red eye reduction feature.

Q. Why are drops put in the eye during the visit?
A. Two kinds of drops are usually put in the eye. The first is a numbing drop (anesthetic), which makes the other drops sting less and work better. In addition, it allows for the pressure in the eye to be measured with minimal discomfort. The second type of drop is used to dilate the pupil. The lens of the eye sits behind the pupil, and dilating the pupil allows the lens to be checked more thoroughly. Dilating the pupil also allows the doctor to see the retina and check whether or not glasses will help with vision.

Q. How often should our child be seen by the eye doctor?
A. When a cataract is initially diagnosed, the eye doctor must decide whether or not surgery is necessary. If surgery is not necessary, then the frequency of checks depends on the severity of the cataract, its impact on vision, and the age of the child. For example, a tiny cataract in a 6-year-old with 20/20 vision may only need to be followed once a year. The same size cataract in a 2-week-old baby should be followed more closely. In this situation, the infant should be seen several times in the first year of life (perhaps at 6 weeks old, 3 months old, 6 months old, and 1 year old) to ensure that the cataract is not enlarging during the critical periods in visual development.

Postoperative follow-up appointments are generally scheduled based on the length of time after surgery and whether or not complications occurred. Most patients are seen one day after surgery, a few days later, and then the following week. Thereafter, follow-up is arranged based on the progress of the child's recovery.

Q. At what age can most children have the same type of eye examination as an adult instead of examination under anesthesia?
A. Cataract examinations can almost always be done with the child awake. An anesthetic is rarely needed when checking for cataracts, even in children. The doctor may occasionally need to have the child held still, or he/she may place a small clip (*speculum*) in the eye to hold the eyelids open.

F. SUBSEQUENT (FOLLOW UP) VISITS

Q. How often should my child see the eye doctor?
A. The frequency of visits to the eye doctor depends on the specifics of your child's situation. Some circumstances require frequent examinations while others do not.

If your child has had cataract surgery, then postoperative visits may initially be scheduled as frequently as every day. The length of time between visits will likely increase based on the doctor's assessment of your child's recovery. His/her eye pressure should be checked at least once yearly. There may also be a need for additional follow-up visits to assess your child's visual development.

If your child does not have glaucoma but is at risk for developing it because of another condition, such as Sturge-Weber *syndrome* or *aniridia*, then he/she should undergo a glaucoma check twice yearly. Depending on your child, this check may be conducted with him/her under anesthesia or sedation.

If your child has active glaucoma that is well-controlled, then additional visits to the eye doctor should occur at intervals no greater than every three to four months. Visits should be no more than three months apart if your child has a glaucoma tube.

If your child has glaucoma that is active and uncontrolled, then visits may need to be more frequent. Daily visits may become necessary if the pressures are extremely high and out of control. If his/her glaucoma is active but under control, the doctor may determine that visits every week or every few weeks are warranted, depending upon the degree of activity and severity of the glaucoma.

Q. Will the doctor repeat all the tests at every follow-up visit?
A. Each doctor will have his/her own system for follow-up visits and will tailor the visit to the particular needs of your child at that time. Follow-up visits tend to be shorter than the initial consultation because the issues are generally known, so fewer tests are usually needed and the examination can be narrowed to address specific concerns. The primary purpose of a follow-up visit is to see whether your child's eye condition is under control. The type of appointment will usually involve some means of measuring the eye pressure and looking for other signs of improvement, stability, or progression of the eye issues. Whether other tests may be needed depends on a variety of factors, such as changes in your child's vision, new problems that appear to be developing, or a need to evaluate the results of a particular treatment.

G. OTHER QUESTIONS

Q. How do I help my child develop independence?
A. Encouraging independence in a child with glaucoma or a cataract is no different than for any other child. If a child has low vision, there may be unique issues which can be dealt with by consultation with appropriate low vision specialists and services.

Children with medical issues often find it helpful to understand the nature of their conditions. Even very young children are able to understand that something is wrong with their eyes and that they need to see an eye doctor regularly. You should encourage your child to talk about his/her eye problems. By doing so, he/she will eventually play a more active, independent role in his/her own care.

Knowing when to allow children to instill their own eyedrops or take other medications unsupervised is trickier, as compliance with dosages and schedules is so important, particularly for glaucoma control. If your child demonstrates responsible behavior in other aspects of life then perhaps a trial of self-administration of drops and other medications may be considered. A combined approach, where the child administers the drops or medications under supervision and is reminded of the schedule, can be the first step towards handing over the entire responsibility to him/her.

Once your child is made responsible for his/her oral medication, counting the number of pills remaining in the bottle is useful for determining if he/she is adhering to the schedule. Unfortunately, there is no equivalent process for monitoring eyedrops. If the glaucoma suddenly becomes uncontrolled shortly after your child is given the responsibility of taking his/her medications without supervision, it is possible that he/she is not using the drops or medication as intended. It may be useful to temporarily resume supervised administration. If the glaucoma comes back under control, then it may simply be that the child is not yet ready for this level of independence.

The teenage years can be particularly trying for children with chronic diseases. Teenagers often feel invincible and indestructible. It is common for children with all sorts of chronic diseases to stop taking their medications or challenge their bodies to see how little medication they can take. In addition, adolescents may not tell the truth when asked about their compliance.

These are very difficult years for parents. Open, frank discussions with your child about the nature of his/her illness, and the consequences of not taking medications, are important. Negative reinforcements, such as punishments, tend to work poorly. The goal is to have your child take responsibility for his/her own condition. Sometimes the child learns the hard way, by experiencing an exacerbation of the disease. Alternatively, if medications are not taken, a doctor may recommend surgery, which may prove to be the incentive the child needs. Some children may feel that surgery is worse than taking the medication.

Teens often object to taking their medications because the requirement identifies them as someone who has a disease or is somehow different. Altering dosing patterns can be helpful. For example, if the instructions are for the medication to be taken four times daily, ask your child's doctor to consider an alternative dosing size or schedule, such as a longer-acting variant or administering the medication three times daily (before school, after school, bedtime) that would be as effective. The effort made to limit your child's inconvenience and embarrassment over having others know about his/her medications may make him/her more willing to cooperate. This approach also has the advantage of offering some degree of parental supervision, as the medications can be given at home.

Q. How will my child adjust as he/she ages?
A. Children are surprisingly resilient and adaptive. Most children can cope with even very significant challenges much better than adults can. If a child has had a visual impairment from a very young age, he/she does not know what it means to see normally. If a young child has required multiple medications, eyeglasses, eye patching, and other interventions, then by the time he/she is a little older, he/she is probably very adept at coping with medical needs.

Children take many cues from their parents and those who are closest to them. If parents are very anxious about their children's eye conditions, chances are the children will pick up on that anxiety. Parents act as role models for their children's coping, so do your best to convey the right message to your child. This can be challenging, but if you cope well, your child is much more likely to cope and adjust successfully as he/she gets older, even when new challenges present themselves. Some families also find that professional guidance from a psychologist, family therapist or social worker can be helpful.

Q. Does television watching have any physiological impact on the eyes of infants or toddlers with glaucoma or cataracts?
A. No, watching television is not known to cause any harmful effect to the eyes of children with cataracts and/or glaucoma.

Q. Should my child wear sports goggles?

A. Eyeglasses designed for daily wear do not offer the same protection as sports goggles and other forms of protective eyewear. When sports goggles are not a practical form of eye protection, another option to consider is a protective visor or face shield. These may be more workable for certain sports, such as football or baseball.

Appropriate protective eyewear for sports is extremely important for those children who have poor vision in one eye. The idea is to protect the good eye from injury, especially during sports that involve contact, racquets, sticks, or balls. In children with two equal seeing eyes, appropriate protective eyewear may still be desirable, particularly in high-risk sports.

Some countries require all participants to wear protective eyewear for when participating in specific sports. One example of this is Canada's requirement for wearing protective eyewear while playing hockey.

Q. Does my child need to use goggles while swimming?

A. It depends on the situation. There is no need for your child to avoid swimming pools or other recreational water play opportunities because of glaucoma, cataract, or following eye surgery. If swimming goggles are used, they should be professionally fit to avoid having them put pressure on the eyeball.

Your local Public Health Department has basic policies for monitoring and maintenance that are intended to ensure safety and sanitation in public pools. Home pools may be monitored less closely, as hygienic maintenance is the responsibility of the owners. There are no special risks to most children who have had eye surgery in either setting after the initial postoperative period. The exception to this is any patient who has had trabeculectomy surgery with *mitomycin C* treatment, as the risk for infection may be higher than after other surgeries. Similarly, except for patients who have had a trabeculectomy, there are no special precautions for children swimming in the ocean following eye surgery. If your child has had trabeculectomy surgery, you should discuss when he/she may begin swimming with his/her ophthalmologist.

If your child wears contact lenses, they should be removed for swimming or he/she should wear goggles. The problem is not that the water will wash the lenses out, but that the swimming water washes out the tear film that covers the eye. Without the tear film, the contacts actually stick to the eye more tightly. Contact lens wearers should absolutely avoid having them in place when swimming in fresh water, such as lakes or ponds, due to the risk of a potentially blinding infection (*acanthamoeba*). Contact lenses can be reinserted immediately after swimming, as long as proper hygiene and cleaning have occurred.

Q. Can my child's prescription be put into sports goggles?

A. Prescription lenses can be made for most sports goggles, but this can be quite costly. It may be more economical to buy goggles that fit over your child's glasses. Stronger prescriptions are more difficult to place into sports goggles. Children who have had cataract surgery may do better wearing contact lenses under goggles that have no prescription.

Q. Why does my child stare at lights?

A. In a world of darkness, a bright light is often a great attraction. If a child has very poor vision, he/she may sometimes engage in light gazing. It is not known exactly why these children seem to be so fascinated by bright lights, but the phenomenon is well known. While this tendency seems to be more common in children who have developmental delay, not every child who stares at bright lights will be developmentally delayed. Staring at bright lights is not particularly harmful unless a child also engages in staring at the sun, which can burn the retina and lead to permanent vision loss.

Q. Why does my child dislike bright lights?
A. There are many possible reasons. Children who show an aversion to bright lights (*photophobia*) usually have something wrong with their eyes that causes the light to scatter instead of coming in as a single, focused beam.

Photophobia may occur as a result of swelling of the corneal surface, scarring of the cornea, breaks of the inner corneal layer due to congenital or *infantile glaucoma* (Haab striae) or cataract. It can also be caused by iritis, which results in an inflamed iris that can be sensitive to bright light. If the pupil is enlarged, such as after the insertion of mydriatic drops, the eye may also be offended by excess light. This reaction is similar to the effect experienced when going from a prolonged stay in a dark room immediately into a bright room. The eyes are sensitive to the new light intensity because it takes time for the pupil to constrict in order to shut out some of the light. After surgery, the eye may also be extra sensitive, especially to bright light. Some children with retinal disorders also have difficulty with bright lights.

Q. Will having glaucoma or cataract limit my child's ability to participate in sports?
A. Usually children with glaucoma or cataract are not placed under any activity restrictions beyond the recommended use of protective eyewear. Limitations or restrictions are more commonly the result of the child's vision than the cataract or glaucoma. There sometimes may be particular limitations immediately after surgery. These are often in place just during the recovery period.

Children should be allowed to try whatever sports they feel comfortable with. They will sort out their abilities. Those who grow up with poor vision in one eye and near normal vision in the other may do remarkably well at sports, and can usually hit a baseball or hockey puck as well as children with two normally sighted eyes. Even blind athletes have developed adaptations that allow them to participate in and enjoy most sports, including skiing, ice hockey, and tennis.

Q. Will my child be able to drive if he/she has glaucoma or cataract?
A. Glaucoma or cataract that has not impacted your child's vision will not prevent him/her from being able to drive. Good straight ahead and peripheral vision are necessary for safe driving in order to ensure the well-being of both the driver and others using the roads. Most states and provinces have established guidelines that address all sorts of medical conditions, including vision impairments, that could affect a person's ability to safely drive a vehicle. Some locations allow issuance of licenses with specific driving restrictions, such as allowing an individual to drive during the day but not at night. Ask your eye doctor or licensing authority about the particular laws relating to minimum vision requirements for driving in your area.

In many locations, physicians are required by law to report any patient who holds a driving license but no longer meets the criteria or visual standards for driving to the Department of Transportation (or equivalent licensing organization). Some patients may view this as being unfair, especially if they have unblemished driving records. Remember that doctors are required to do what society has deemed necessary to protect its citizens. There is almost always a system in place to appeal a doctor's decision to revoke a driver's license based on vision restrictions.

PART II: GLAUCOMA

A. GENERAL QUESTIONS

Q. What is glaucoma?
A. Glaucoma is a disorder in which pressure inside the eye is too high. This can damage various structures in the eye and lead to reduced vision or blindness.

The eye is essentially a hollow sphere that is filled with fluid. The fluid filling the front of the eye is called aqueous humor. Aqueous humor is made continuously all day, every day, by structures in the eye called the ciliary processes. These sit behind the iris and cannot be seen by an outside observer. Since fluid is continually being made, it must also be drained from the eye. This is accomplished via the drainage angle (trabecular meshwork) just underneath the outer edge of the iris. Sometimes this drain fails to allow the fluid to flow out at a sufficient rate to make necessary room for the new fluid being produced. When the fluid does not drain as quickly as it is produced, pressure builds up in the eye. This high pressure can eventually damage the optic nerve, which carries the messages of vision between the eye and the brain, and may ultimately result in vision loss.

The flow of aqueous humor to and from the eye is similar to the functioning of an ordinary sink. When the sink's drain is working properly, the water that comes from the faucet runs out through the bottom of the sink into the drain. The water does not back up into the sink. In contrast, if the drain were partially clogged, some of the fluid would still be able to escape, but some would remain in the sink, creating a small pool above the drain.

In a child younger than 5 years old, the extra pressure slowly causes the eyeball to expand (*buphthalmos*). The eye becomes longer and the cornea stretches. Without treatment, the eye could expand so far that the eye wall becomes thin enough to spontaneously rupture. Fortunately, this is an extremely rare occurrence when a patient is being treated for glaucoma. Once a child reaches the age of 4 or 5 years old, the eye is less elastic, making it much less likely that buphthalmos or rupture could occur.

Glaucoma is a very complex disease and comes in many forms. Treatment usually requires medications, sometimes several at once, and often surgical or other procedures are also needed. The goal of glaucoma treatment is to either: 1) open the drain or establish another way for fluid to get out of the eye, whether through surgery or the use of certain eyedrops, or 2) reduce the flow of fluid through the use of medication. By establishing a better balance between fluid production and drainage, the hope is that the eye pressure can be lowered to a level that does not damage the optic nerve and other ocular structures.

Unfortunately, there is no cure for glaucoma. Medications and surgery can control the disease, yet it always lurks in the background, threatening to return at any time.

Q. How rare is glaucoma? Do certain ethnic groups get it more than others?
A. The frequency of glaucoma depends on the subtype of the disease and the ethnicity of the child. Overall, it is an uncommon disease.

Congenital glaucoma is seen in between 1 and 5,000 to 22,000 newborns in North America. In the Middle East, the frequency rises to 1 in 2,500. Other authors have found that the minimal prevalence of congenital glaucoma worldwide is 2.85 per 100,000 births. A more commonly quoted figure is 1 in 12,500 live births. There is an ethnic group in Slovakia in which the rate of glaucoma is as high as 1 in 1,250.

In one study of approximately 400 patients, the relative frequency of different types of glaucoma was calculated, as shown in Table 2.

Table 2: Relative Frequency of Pediatric Glaucomas*	
Congenital or infantile glaucoma	38%
Aphakic glaucoma	20%
Sturge-Weber syndrome	10%
Anterior segment dysgenesis (e.g., Axenfeld-Rieger, Peters)	6.2%
Traumatic glaucoma	5.6%
Aniridia	4.9%
Steroid-induced glaucoma	2.6%
Juvenile open angle glaucoma (JOAG)	2.3%
Retinopathy of prematurity	2.3%
Iritis	2.3%
Persistent fetal vasculature [formerly called persistent hyperplastic primary vitreous (PHPV)]	1.3%
Neurofibromatosis†	0.7%
Coats disease ‡	0.7%
Other	8.2%

* Percentage total is more than 100% because some children in the study had more than one diagnosis

† A disorder affecting the brain, skin, and eyes. Other common elements of this condition include lightly pigmented birthmarks (e.g., café au lait spots), developmental delay, and possibly seizures, benign tumors under the skin, tumors of the optic nerves, and pigmented lesions on the iris.

‡ A condition characterized by the development of abnormal retinal blood vessels that can cause detachment of the retina and lead to glaucoma.

Q. How common is it for children with two different eye colors to develop glaucoma?
A. There are many reasons why a child might have two different colored eyes. Some are associated with glaucoma and some are not. Your child should be examined by an ophthalmologist to determine the exact diagnosis.

Q. What is ocular hypertension?
A. Some children will not have obvious active glaucoma, though their eye pressure is a bit high. This situation can be perfectly normal and never progress to full glaucoma. As an analogy, people who are exceptionally tall tend to be noticed, but do not necessarily have a disease. A doctor might do some medical tests to be sure the person's unusual height is not due to disease. Similarly, if a child has eye pressure that seems a bit high, the doctor may do some tests, or simply monitor the

child's eyes over time. Glaucoma is a progressive disease. If it is present, it will eventually show itself by causing changes in the optic nerve. The diagnosis of glaucoma would be made and treatment be indicated only if such changes developed.

Q. What is a glaucoma suspect?
A. Some children have symptoms that could be caused by glaucoma but not showing clearly elevated eye pressure. For example, a child may have some cupping of his/her optic nerve while retaining nomal eye pressure. He/she may not have glaucoma, but these other signs should prompt the eye doctor to do additional tests to ensure it is not present. These tests may include *optical coherence tomography (OCT)*, a form of ultrasound which assesses optic nerve health; visual field testing; or a measurement of the eye pressure throughout the day (*diurnal curve*) to make sure no peaks or swings in eye pressure are occurring. Even if all of these tests show normal results, the eye doctor may choose to keep following the child's condition over time to ensure no change has occurred that would indicate that glaucoma has developed.

Q. Is all glaucoma in children the same?
A. No. Children may develop glaucoma for a variety of reasons. Every type of glaucoma may affect only one eye or both eyes. The majority of cases of pediatric glaucoma fall into one of the following general categories:

- Congenital and infantile glaucoma
- *Juvenile open angle glaucoma (JOAG)*
- Glaucoma due to malformations of the eye
- Glaucoma due to *systemic* problems or syndromes
- Glaucoma due to trauma (traumatic glaucoma)
- Glaucoma due to iritis or inflammation (uveitic glaucoma)
- Glaucoma due to steroids (steroid-induced glaucoma)
- Closed angle glaucoma
- Glaucoma after pediatric cataract surgery (aphakic glaucoma)

The above list includes the major known causes of pediatric glaucoma. It should be noted that the term primary open angle glaucoma (POAG) was not used; this is a term normally used to refer to a type of glaucoma seen in adults. Another adult form of glaucoma is called *normal tension glaucoma*. In this type of glaucoma, the optic nerve is damaged as if the pressure was high even though the pressure is actually in the low normal range. There have only been two reported cases of this occurring in children.

Q. How can the doctor tell if my child has glaucoma?
A. The primary test is to measure the pressure in your child's eyes. The doctor will examine your child's eyes. He/she will also look for other signs that support a diagnosis of glaucoma, including the size of the cornea, the length of the eye, the refraction of the eye (the glasses prescription for that eye, if any), the size of the optic nerve cup, the clarity of the cornea, the presence of other abnormalities of the eye that are known to be associated with glaucoma, and the family history. The doctor will also look for signs that one or both eyes are unusually large (buphthalmos).

Q. How can I tell if my child has glaucoma?
A. If an infant or child under the age of 5 years has glaucoma, the elevated pressure inside the eye will stretch the eyeball, causing it to look bigger than normal (buphthalmos). This effect is

particularly obvious in infants. If a child has glaucoma in both eyes, it may be more difficult to detect than it would be if the eyes were different sizes.

As the eye gets bigger, especially in infants, other things might change, too. The cornea, which is normally clear, may cloud over, making it more difficult to see the pupil and the iris and causing the eye to appear bluish, gray, or as if it has a film over it. Many things may cause tearing (*epiphora*) and aversion to light (photophobia) in infants, including glaucoma.

In older children, these changes in the eye are not seen because the eye is more resistant to stretching. As a result, it becomes virtually impossible for parents to tell whether their child has glaucoma without obtaining an eye examination. Even if a child is known to have glaucoma, there are often no symptoms at all if the glaucoma is getting out of control. By the time vision loss becomes obvious, the glaucoma has usually progressed significantly.

Glaucoma usually does not cause pain, yet many parents have commented that they can tell when their children's pressures are elevated due to changes in their behavior.

Q. What is considered a good pressure reading for a child with glaucoma?
A. There is no absolute "normal" value that applies to all patients and all circumstances. In general, intraocular pressures between 10 and 20 millimeters of mercury (mm Hg) are considered "normal," but the circumstances under which the pressure is measured may affect the validity and accuracy of the measurement. Many things have to be taken into consideration. For example, a pressure in the low 20s is unacceptable in a baby with advanced congenital glaucoma, a severely damaged optic nerve, corneal *edema*, and enlarging eye size, and would certainly require surgery. The same pressure in an older child with no prior history of glaucoma, completely healthy optic nerves, corneas within the normal range of thickness, and who was perhaps a bit fidgety during measurements, may be of little concern and require nothing other than a follow-up examination. Likewise, a pressure of 9 may be entirely normal in one child but could be worrisome in another, depending on the circumstances. The only way to answer this question for your child is for you to discuss the specific factors of your child's situation with the eye doctor.

Q. Does pediatric glaucoma stabilize in adulthood?
A. There has not been much research into the long-term outcomes of children who have glaucoma. The answer to this question is a very individual one. Every case is different, but the bottom line is that your child's glaucoma will need to be monitored for the rest of his/her life.

One of the factors impacting the answer to this question is the kind of glaucoma your child has. If he/she has glaucoma as a result of treatment with steroid medications, the glaucoma is likely to go away when the steroids are stopped. It rarely persists after the steroids are discontinued unless there is another underlying disease, such as iritis, that is contributing to the glaucoma.

In children with Sturge-Weber syndrome (SWS), there are characteristically two periods when glaucoma is most likely to occur. Some children will have infantile glaucoma, requiring early surgical intervention and ongoing management. Another peak risk period for developing glaucoma starts at the age of 5 to 7 years old, and can last well into a child's teen years. During this second risk period, glaucoma may appear as an aggravation of an earlier form or develop for the first time in a child who did not have infantile glaucoma. A small number of individuals with SWS never develop glaucoma in childhood, but instead develop it in adulthood. Glaucoma rarely spontaneously resolves. All patients with SWS glaucoma, regardless of mechanism or age at onset, must be monitored for the remainder of their lives.

Children who have had cataract surgery maintain a lifelong risk for developing aphakic glaucoma and should be checked periodically. Children who have had surgery for glaucoma often need to have repeat operations, yet some do well with just a single operation.

Children whose glaucoma is a result of injury (traumatic glaucoma) may develop it immediately. As the eye heals, this kind of glaucoma may go away. One specific type of injury, angle recession, in which the drainage angle is damaged, slightly increases a child's risk for developing glaucoma later in life, even if the original injury did not immediately cause it.

Glaucoma is a disease for which there is no cure. Even if your child's glaucoma is well controlled with medications, surgery, or both, his/her eyes will need to be checked regularly to ensure the condition is not getting worse.

Many individuals' glaucoma will stay stable throughout their adulthood. In some cases, they do not require any medications after surgery; in others, minimal medication and no surgery may work. Glaucoma management is sometimes easier for adults than children. Adult patients are usually both more willing and able to comply with instructions, allowing the doctor to obtain better examination results. In addition, treatment options that require the patient to sit still, such as laser treatments, become more feasible.

Q. Why does glaucoma sometimes go away and come back again?
A. Sometimes glaucoma can be under control for months or years, making it seem as if it had disappeared. Then, suddenly, the eye pressure (IOP) starts to creep up again. In some cases, there may be a clear explanation related to other changes going on in the eye. Examples of this include the age-related increase in the abnormal blood vessels on the eye seen in children between the ages of 5 and 12 years old with Sturge-Weber syndrome and the recurrent intraocular inflammation (iritis) often seen with *juvenile rheumatoid arthritis* (*JRA*), now usually called *juvenile idiopathic arthritis* (*JIA*). The repeated inflammation causes a progressive clogging of the trabecular meshwork over time. Certain drugs may become less effective over time (*tachyphylaxis*). The growth of the eye may change the drainage pattern of fluid in the eye. The drainage angle (trabecular meshwork) of the eye may undergo progressive degeneration. In many instances, however, there is no obvious reason for the IOP increase.

Q. Does glaucoma ever go into remission?
A. A child with glaucoma whose pressure remains fairly stable with treatment is considered to have his/her glaucoma controlled rather than cured. There is currently no cure for glaucoma, so the pressure can always rise unexpectedly. There is no point at which the optic nerve becomes immune to further deterioration and damage. Only after glaucoma has caused total blindness in an eye is can it be said that there will be no further deterioration. Even then, an eye may become painful or develop other problems not related to vision.

Glaucoma due to iritis is often a secondary condition in children who have juvenile idiopathic arthritis. The iritis may disappear after several years and never reoccur, occasionally causing the glaucoma to abate. Even more rarely, an infant is born with glaucoma that spontaneously resolves itself once the eye develops more fully. Unfortunately, spontaneously resolved glaucoma is so rare that it is unwise to wait to see if it occurs rather than intervene at the first diagnosis.

Although the risk of deterioration remains, some patients may experience periods, sometimes lasting years, of "remission" during which their pressure is well controlled. Some individuals require continuous treatment with medications, but there are also those that will not need to use any medications following a successful glaucoma surgery.

Q. Should I have my child checked for any other problems now that we know he/she has glaucoma?

A. Depending on what your child's ophthalmologist sees, he/she may recommend that your child's pediatrician look for other issues. A general exam by a pediatrician is usually enough to rule out any other problems. For example, if your child has glaucoma due to Axenfeld-Rieger spectrum, then his/her teeth and belly button may be abnormal. Other forms of glaucoma are usually *isolated* to the eye only.

Q. Should a child with any ocular abnormalities have his/her pressure checked?

A. Only certain eye abnormalities cause an eye to be at risk of developing glaucoma. In particular, abnormalities of the front part of the eye (anterior segment) affecting the iris (except *coloboma*), cause the highest risk. Your child's doctor should be able to tell you if your child's eye abnormalities create a glaucoma risk.

Q. Will glaucoma cause other eye problems?

A. In addition to damage of the optic nerve and vision loss, untreated glaucoma can also cause the cornea to become cloudy. Eventually, it can become completely opaque. In infants and young children, the cornea can become so stretched and large that it actually begins to deteriorate. Certain treatments for glaucoma, particularly laser or surgical treatments, can result in a number of complications, including cataract, retinal detachment, hemorrhage inside the eye, or blindness from reasons other than the glaucoma.

Q. Will any other conditions affect the glaucoma or will the glaucoma affect other medical conditions?

A. Glaucoma itself does not appear to have an adverse influence on any other medical conditions. Likewise, other medical conditions do not seem to have a direct effect on glaucoma. Medications used to treat other conditions, such as steroids, may have an effect on the glaucoma and glaucoma medications may have an effect on other medical conditions, such as asthma.

Q. What is the angle of the eye?

A. The angle of the eye refers to the area where the fluid (aqueous humor) flows out. It is located at the junction of the cornea and iris (see Figure 2). If you think of the crystal covering of a watch as the cornea of the eye, and the face as the iris, then the arms of the watch point to the recess where the crystal and watch face are joined. Like the watch, the angle of the eye is in that recess all the way around the edge of the iris. The medical term for this area is trabecular meshwork.

Q. What is the difference between open angle and closed angle glaucoma?

A. There are a variety of different forms of closed angle glaucoma. If the iris is bowed or pushed forward, it can block the meshwork and prevent the outflow of fluid from the eye. The resulting backup of fluid causes elevated eye pressure and glaucoma.

Closed angle glaucoma is not uncommon in adults, but is rarely seen in children. When a child does develop closed angle glaucoma, it is often due to advanced retinopathy of prematurity, *persistent fetal vasculature (PFV)*, total retinal detachment, tumors inside the eye (e.g., retinoblastoma), or other, even more uncommon, disorders.

Occasionally, a child with iritis or trauma to the eye may develop scar tissue between the iris edge and the cornea in the angle of the eye (peripheral anterior synechiae) that can cause angle blockage.

Perhaps the most common form of closed angle glaucoma found in adults occurs simply because of an unusual anatomic relationship between the iris and the cornea, without any underlying eye problem (narrow angle glaucoma). This form is not seen in children, except in very unusual circumstances, as when the lens of the eye is small and very round (called microspherophakia), for example.

Any form of glaucoma in which the angle is not closed and there is nothing else wrong with the eye that would cause glaucoma is called open angle glaucoma. When open angle glaucoma occurs in an individual between the ages of 4 and 40 years, it is called juvenile open angle glaucoma (JOAG). When it occurs in an individual over the age 40, it is called primary open angle glaucoma (POAG) of adulthood.

Q. What is secondary glaucoma?
A. An eye that develops glaucoma as an isolated disease, such as congenital glaucoma, is considered to have primary glaucoma. Secondary glaucoma refers to glaucoma that develops from another problem in the eye. For example, if an eye is injured, the trabecular meshwork may be damaged. If this damage causes a reduction in the outflow of fluid, the intraocular pressure (IOP) increases and results in secondary glaucoma. Glaucoma due to intraocular inflammation (iritis) or steroid exposure are also types of secondary glaucoma.

Q. Why is childhood glaucoma sometimes misdiagnosed as some other problem?
A. Glaucoma is a rare disease in children. The initial symptoms of glaucoma in infants may mimic common eye disorders. For example, children often experience tearing. This is much more commonly caused by a blocked tear duct (*nasolacrimal duct obstruction*), than glaucoma. An ophthalmologist who does not see a lot of children in his/her practice, or another medical professional, may assume that the child has the more common disorder rather than the rarer one. Other symptoms of glaucoma, such as an enlarged eye (buphthalmos) or an aversion to bright lights (photophobia), also mimic more common disorders and can lead to misdiagnosis. Older children with glaucoma do not get the same symptoms as infants and young toddlers. Instead, they often experience no symptoms unless the pressure becomes extremely high very quickly and causes pain or the glaucoma has gone undetected for so long that visual loss is noted. There is usually no pain, and a lot of damage to the optic nerve must occur before there is a noticeable vision loss. The vision loss occurs so slowly that it is often never noticed by the child.

Q. Does high blood pressure (hypertension) have anything to do with glaucoma?
A. Although it is true that adults with adult onset glaucoma (also known as primary open angle glaucoma or POAG) have a greater likelihood of having high blood pressure than those who do not, and high blood pressure is one of the risk factors for POAG, the same is not true for children. Hypertension is quite uncommon in children. There does not appear to be any relationship between high blood pressure and childhood glaucoma.

Q. If my child has glaucoma in one eye, will he/she also develop it in the other?
A. Although some forms of glaucoma, such as primary congenital or infantile glaucoma and JOAG, occur more commonly in both eyes (bilateral), most children who develop glaucoma in both eyes will show signs of it in both eyes around the same time. Children whose glaucoma is the result of cataract surgery in one eye often get glaucoma in only that eye.

It is sometimes possible for a doctor to predict whether the other eye will get glaucoma based on abnormalities in the eye with glaucoma that may or may not be present in the other eye. For example, in a form of glaucoma called Axenfeld-Rieger spectrum, there are abnormalities of the pupil, iris, and cornea which are readily detectable and usually present in both eyes, even though the glaucoma may start in one eye and not appear until later in the other eye.

Q. If my child has glaucoma in only one eye, will the other eye be strained or harmed?
A. Having glaucoma, poor vision, or some other disease, injury, or disorder that only affects one eye does not put extra strain on the other eye or cause damage to it. The unaffected eye should remain normal unless it is already at risk for whatever caused the problem in the affected eye.

There is evidence that if one eye sees poorly, regardless of the reason, the remaining normal eye is at a greater risk of serious accidental injury. Children who have good sight in only one eye should wear glasses during normal daily activities to protect the better-seeing eye, even if that eye sees perfectly without glasses. In addition, they should also wear appropriate protective eyewear, such as sports goggles or face shields, when participating in sports. Protective glasses have lenses made out of shatter-resistant plastic (polycarbonate).

Q. What research into a cure for glaucoma is being done?
A. There are many centers around the world working toward a cure for glaucoma.

One avenue of research is gene therapy. As the genes that cause glaucoma are identified (and some are already known), researchers can begin to unravel the mystery of why glaucoma occurs. Each gene produces a product, called a protein, that has a specific function. If a gene is abnormal, then it may be possible to supply the protein in another form, fix the gene that makes it, or send in a new gene to replace the one that is not working. The treatment must be able to affect the glaucoma without having an adverse reaction in other parts of the eye or body. If the gene or repair mechanism could not be delivered as an eyedrop, it might be administered by injection or through the bloodstream. Whether these forms of gene therapy will have the ability to restore vision loss caused by glaucoma, as is already occurring in gene therapy for some retinal diseases, or just prevent further damage, is yet to be seen.

Ultimately, glaucoma damages vision by injuring the optic nerve. The process by which optic nerve cells die is a very specific, programmed form of death called apoptosis. This process is also regulated by genes. A gene therapy could be developed to manipulate the genes that lead to cell death, making it more difficult for the optic nerve cells to die. In this type of therapy, the genes that promote apoptosis would be turned off and those that protect against it would then be turned on.

Gene identification allows individuals at risk of developing glaucoma to be discovered before they get the disease. Gene therapy may help individuals who might not otherwise be aware of their risk to prevent or minimize the impact of glaucoma by encouraging them to benefit from early detection and treatment.

Research to develop new medications to help lower eye pressure is continually underway. Some of these drugs are designed to increase the eye's ability to drain the aqueous humor, while others are designed to decrease its production. Other lines of research are being pursued to find medicines that protect the optic nerve from damage and find agents that will allow regeneration of optic nerve cells killed by glaucoma. Forms of vision restoration currently being explored include optic nerve transplantation, retinal transplantation, and *bionic* forms of artificial vision.

Additional effort is being made to develop more effective ways to diagnose glaucoma earlier and treat it surgically. Some proposed testing options include better visual field testing and electrophysiology tests designed to measure the function of optic nerve cells. A number of improvements have been proposed for all forms of glaucoma surgery and are being evaluated.

Q. Can we expect a cure for glaucoma within our lifetime or within our child's lifetime?
A. The progress of science over the last decade has been astounding. Although no one can predict when a cure will come, it does appear to be safe to say that the children of today will expect better treatments, if not cures, within their lifetimes. The possibilities of research advancement are almost endless.

Q. Will stem cell research have an impact on glaucoma and other eye diseases?
A. While stem cell research will impact many different eye diseases, perhaps including glaucoma, limbal stem cells are not currently used to treat glaucoma. At this time, there are no research trials that have been initiated for which a child would be eligible.

B. WHAT CAN CAUSE GLAUCOMA?

Q. Did I do something during my pregnancy to cause my child's glaucoma?
A. This question is asked by almost every mother who has a child with glaucoma, especially if the glaucoma was present at birth (congenital glaucoma). Mothers can rest assured that nothing they did during pregnancy caused their child's glaucoma. In fact, there is almost nothing that a woman can do during her pregnancy that is known to specifically result in glaucoma. Certain drugs taken during pregnancy can result in abnormalities in a child's eye. These abnormalities tend to be multiple, resulting in many more problems other than just glaucoma. Some infections that a mother develops during pregnancy, such as rubella (also known as German measles) are also sometimes associated with glaucoma. While these infections are not the fault of the mother, immunization against them is an important part of prenatal care.

Q. Can smoking during pregnancy cause pediatric glaucoma?
A. There is no link between glaucoma and smoking during pregnancy.

Q. Can glaucoma be caused by prolonged labor?
A. No. If this were true, there would be hundreds of thousands of babies with this rare disease. Glaucoma is not caused by external force on the eye, but due to a defect in the eyeball itself.

Q. How can retinoblastoma cause glaucoma?
A. Retinoblastoma is a form of malignant eye cancer that starts in the retina cells. In some forms, cancer cells can break away from the retina and spread through the fluids of the eye. If cancer cells come through the pupil and spread in front of the iris, they can clog the drainage angle of the eye (trabecular meshwork), and make it difficult for the eye fluid (aqueous humor) to drain out normally,

resulting in glaucoma. In other cases, abnormal new blood vessel growth (neovascularization) in the iris occurs, which can also cause blockage of the trabecular meshwork.

Q. Can glaucoma be caused by contact lenses?

A. It is very rare for glaucoma to be caused by wearing contact lenses. The only way a contact lens could cause glaucoma would be if the patient had a cornea infection (*ulcer*) or severe iritis from wearing his/her lenses longer than recommended or lenses that were too tightly fit.

Q. How do dislocated lenses (ectopia lentis) cause glaucoma?

A. Ectopia lentis refers to a condition where the lens of the eye is out of position. In some cases, glaucoma occurs because the lens gets thicker and pushes the iris forward, causing angle closure (blocking of the trabecular meshwork). In others, a secondary disorder, such as Marfan syndrome, results in an underlying abnormality of the trabecular meshwork, making glaucoma more likely to occur.

In some forms of ectopia lentis, the lens can pass through the pupil and end up sitting in front of it and the iris, in the anterior chamber. This condition can result in severe acute glaucoma, because the vitreous that fills the back of the eye and is attached to the back of the lens gets "strangled" by the pupil after the lens pulls it through. This blocks the flow of aqueous humor through the pupil. The lens also irritates the iris, causing iritis, or physically blocks or injures the trabecular meshwork.

Q. How can a child with eyes that are smaller than normal get glaucoma?

A. The enlargement of the eye seen in young children with glaucoma is based on an increase in size relative to the starting size of the eye. Children who have congenital cataract often have small eyes (microphthalmia) and are actually at greater risk of developing glaucoma after cataract surgery than children with normal sized eyes. If the microphthalmic eye gets glaucoma, it may expand too rapidly, even though it may still be smaller than the size of a normal eye. It is the relative increase in size that is worrisome and indicative of glaucoma. Not all microphthalmic eyes are at risk for glaucoma.

Q. Is glaucoma due to a vitamin deficiency?

A. There is no known vitamin deficiency that causes glaucoma. At one time, there was some thought that vitamin C might play a role in treating glaucoma, but this is no longer a widely held theory.

C. WHAT CAN AFFECT MY CHILD'S GLAUCOMA?

Q. Are there any activities that might worsen my child's glaucoma?

A. Temper tantrums, excessive crying, rollercoaster rides, holding breath underwater, and strenuous activity are just a few of the activities that worry parents. Although they may temporarily raise eye pressure, the rise is so transient that it is unlikely to cause any vision damage or worsening of the glaucoma. There is some evidence that prolonged playing of wind instruments could be injurious to an eye with glaucoma. When considering limiting your child's activities, be aware that restrictions in his/her lifestyle might cause more harm than the eye problem.

Q. Can working with a computer affect my child's glaucoma?

A. Working with a computer does not harm the eyes in any way and will not cause glaucoma to worsen. People tend to blink less when looking at a computer screen. As a result of the decreased blinking, there may be a tendency for the eye surface to dry out, particularly if the eye has already been altered by surgery. Some people experience a sensation of dryness, excessive tearing, or red-eye after long periods at a computer. Any of these symptoms can be treated using over-the-counter artificial teardrops to help lubricate the surface of the eye, or avoided by making a conscious effort to blink more while using the computer. Computer use does not need to be discouraged.

Q. Will eye strain from reading for long periods bother my child's eyes or increase his/her pressure?
A. Reading is good! Prolonged periods of reading do not harm the eyes or increase eye pressure. As with extended computer use, dryness can occur. This may be treated with artificial teardrops and does not affect glaucoma.

Q. Will blowing a musical instrument temporarily increase my child's eye pressure?
A. Blowing wind instruments has been shown to cause transient rises in eye pressure. This is particularly true when playing instruments with more resistance, such as the trumpet. There is no evidence that these brief, intermittent swings in IOP increase a child's risk of glaucoma damage. If your child has advanced glaucoma, another instrument may be a better choice. Eye pressure also rises, probably to even higher levels, every time we cough or sneeze. There is no way to avoid these events, and they also do not result in additional glaucoma damage.

Q. Will weather changes affect eye pressure?
A. Weather changes do not affect eye pressure and should not have any effect on glaucoma.

Q. Can high pollution levels affect eye pressure?
A. There is no known evidence that air pollution affects eye pressure or cataract, although it can cause any eye to be irritated and red.

Q. If I am breastfeeding my child and drink coffee, will it raise his/her eye pressure?
A. There is currently no evidence that caffeine raises eye pressure in this situation.

Q. Can a sinus infection or the flu raise the pressure in the eye?
A. There is no evidence that a sinus infection or the flu can aggravate or cause glaucoma.

Q. Can traveling long distances affect glaucoma?
A. Although traveling long distances in and of itself should not affect glaucoma in any way, it is important to plan carefully for such trips. Be sure to bring enough medication to last the entire length of the trip, as medications may not be readily available at your destination. Some medications require refrigeration. Simply carrying the medication in a cooler should provide adequate temporary storage. When traveling in a car for long distances, make sure that medications are not exposed to sunlight for prolonged periods of time.

While traveling, it is also important make sure that the regular schedule of eyedrops is not disrupted. If your child is changing time zones, try to administer the medication at a consistent approximate interval. For example, if he/she is taking drops twice daily, the second dose should be taken twelve hours after the first one rather than splitting them between morning and evening. Likewise, if the medication is to be taken four times daily, it should be used every six hours when crossing time zones.

Q. Does air travel change eye pressure?

A. In general, air travel does not change eye pressure significantly because the cabin of the aircraft is pressurized in a way that closely approximates life on the ground. The only time you might be concerned is if your child has had retina surgery or another procedure that involved injection of gas into the eye. If this is the case, be sure to consult with his/her eye doctor to learn whether air travel is permitted. This type of surgery is not part of the usual treatment for children with glaucoma or cataract.

Q. Is there any food or beverage my child should avoid?

A. There are no specific dietary restrictions for individuals with glaucoma.

Q. Are there any vitamins or dietary means that will stabilize or reduce IOP?

A. There is currently no scientific evidence to support the use of any particular vitamin or dietary supplement to help with eye pressure problems. A variety of substances have been suggested in older medical literature and alternative healthcare practices, but none has been proven to have any positive effects. Some may even have harmful effects, so one should exercise caution when using such treatment.

Q. Is there any truth to the studies that suggest taking vitamin C can reduce IOP?

A. This is very old research done at a time when more people were deficient in vitamin C and the testing for its presence in the blood was very inaccurate. The doses of vitamin C that were used were often dangerously high and caused side effects. This treatment is not used or recommended today.

Q. Do tear ducts have anything to do with how the fluids in the eye drain or intraocular pressure?

A. Tear ducts have nothing to do with glaucoma. They drain tears on the surface of the eye. Glaucoma is the result of fluid inside the eyeball causing the pressure to rise. Children with glaucoma can sometimes have swelling of the cornea, which can cause them to produce excess tears in an effort to relieve the irritation. Watering or tearful eyes in glaucoma patients result from increased production of tears, not problems draining the tears through the tear ducts.

Q. Do shaky eyes (nystagmus) make the pressure higher?

A. Nystagmus can either result from a congenital abnormality in the eye muscles and/or the brain that causes the visual system to be unable to keep the eye still. It may also develop due to poor vision. Children who experience visual deprivation early in life, such as when there is a delayed diagnosis of glaucoma or cataract, may experience nystagmus because the image the child perceives is not clear enough for the brain to keep the eye still. The back and forth, up and down, or rotary shaking of the eye does not raise the IOP.

D. POSSIBLE EFFECTS OF GLAUCOMA

Q. Can my child die from glaucoma?

A. No. Glaucoma is a disorder which is confined to the eye. Although the medicines may have side effects which affect the rest of the body, and there are small risks related to use of the general anesthetics required to perform examinations or surgery, the glaucoma itself is not deadly. Some forms of glaucoma occur because of an association with certain diseases, such as Lowe syndrome, Sturge-Weber syndrome, and others. These diseases may make someone susceptible to life-threatening illnesses. Even in these cases, the glaucoma itself does not cause death.

Q. Can my child go blind from glaucoma?

A. Yes. Uncontrolled elevation of the pressure in the eye eventually kills the optic nerve, the pathway through which vision is sent from the eyeball to the brain. If the pressure is successfully controlled through medicines or surgery, as occurs in the majority of cases, then this damage can be greatly delayed, if not prevented.

Q. What is a glaucoma attack and what are the symptoms?

A. This term usually refers to acute angle closure glaucoma, where the edges of the iris come forward and block the drainage mechanism (trabecular meshwork or angle) of the eye. This form of glaucoma is extremely rare in children. An attack may cause pain, redness of the eye, an aversion to light (photophobia), and blurred vision. Your child's ophthalmologist can tell you if your child is at risk for this type of glaucoma.

Q. What is cupping of the optic nerve?

A. If glaucoma kills the nerve fibers within the optic nerve, then there are fewer of them and the central canal (optic cup) within the optic nerve enlarges. Think of a doughnut being eaten outward, starting from the hole in the middle. As there is less doughnut around the hole, the hole gets bigger.

The severity of cupping can be assessed by looking at the cup/disc ratio, which represents the percentage of the total optic nerve head surface, or optic disc, that is taken up by the cup. A cup/disc ratio of 0.5 means that the cup diameter is equal to half the diameter of the entire optic nerve head in a given dimension. This is usually measured horizontally and vertically.

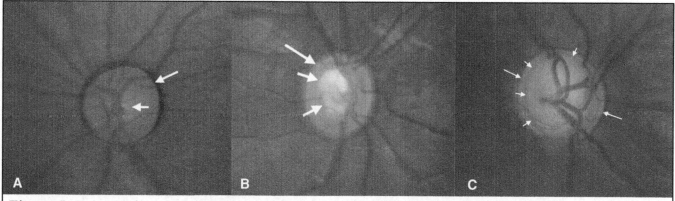

Figure 5: Progressive cupping of the optic nerve. The short arrow(s) in each image indicate the edges of the optic nerve cup, which appears as a white area in the center of the optic nerve. The edge of the optic nerve is indicated by the longer arrows. A. Small, normal cup. B. Moderately-sized cup. C. Severe cupping due to glaucoma damage.

Q. How dangerous is physiologic optic nerve cupping?

A. As long as glaucoma has been ruled out, this is a variation of normal and of no concern at all.

Q. Can cupping of the optic nerve be reversed?

A. Reversal of cupping is a phenomenon that is seen mostly in children less than 3 years old. It has occasionally been seen in older children up to approximately 10 years old, particularly if the eye pressure is lowered a large amount over a short period of time. More sophisticated methods of optic nerve analysis can sometimes still detect optic nerve damage despite an apparent reversal of cupping during a clinical exam.

Q. How can I tell if the glaucoma is getting worse or if the optic nerve is being damaged?
A. There is no way for a parent to see his/her child's optic nerve. Changes in the optic nerve due to uncontrolled glaucoma are one of the things your child's ophthalmologist will be looking for during his/her eye examinations.

In children under the age of 2 years, but sometimes up to 5 years, the glaucoma symptoms noticed previously will persist, or even become worse, if the glaucoma is uncontrolled. In children beyond the age of 5 years, these changes in the eye are not usually seen because the eye is more resistant to stretching. As a result, it becomes virtually impossible for parents to tell whether their child has glaucoma without obtaining an eye examination. By the time symptomatic vision loss occurs, the glaucoma is usually very far progressed.

Remember that your child's IOP still needs to be monitored, even if there are no changes in the appearance of the eye. This is especially true as he/she gets older because the pressure can go up quite high without any signs or symptoms.

Q. What is buphthalmos?
A. Taken literally, buphthalmos means "ox eye." The eyeball of an ox is very large and bulbous. In infants with glaucoma, the increased pressure in the eye can cause the eyeball to stretch and enlarge. The eye looks bigger and may even start to bulge forward. Buphthalmos is the term used to refer to an eye with glaucoma that has this appearance.

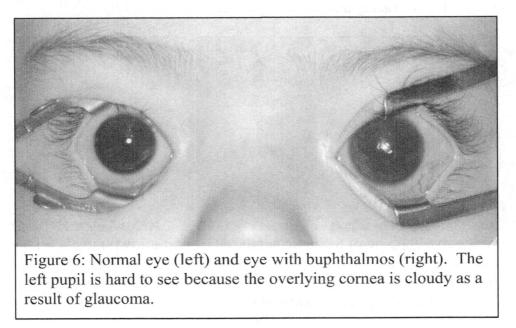

Figure 6: Normal eye (left) and eye with buphthalmos (right). The left pupil is hard to see because the overlying cornea is cloudy as a result of glaucoma.

Q. Will the glaucoma make my child's eyes bigger? Is this a good thing?
A. Excess pressure inside a young child's eye can cause it to stretch. This condition, called buphthalmos, rarely occurs after the age of 2 years, but can occur up to 5 years old. As the eye gets larger, it is actually also getting longer. This may make the eye look more prominent and the cornea and iris seem bigger. This can cause misdiagnosis, as people admire "the baby's big blue eyes," when the eyes are actually too big.

One of the goals of glaucoma treatment is to prevent the eye from enlarging. During office visits, the doctor will regularly take measurements to ensure the eye is not enlarging, indicating that the glaucoma is under control.

Q. Does difference in the size of a buphthalmic eye usually become more normal as a child grows?

A. A buphthalmic eye will never shrink to the size of a normal-sized eye, though there can be slight changes in appearance. In particular, the successful control of glaucoma can result in a slight shrinking of a buphthalmic eye in the first few years of life, and also prevent further enlargement. The relative difference between the buphthalmic eye and the normal eye will otherwise always stay the same, and both eyes will experience normal growth through childhood.

Q. Will glaucoma cause my child to have headaches?

A. Contrary to popular opinion, there are very few eye problems that are associated with headaches. Unless the eye pressure gets extremely high (in the range of 40s, 50s, or higher) very quickly, glaucoma generally does not cause pain. In situations where pain occurs, it is usually eye pain being misinterpreted as a headache. Fortunately, this kind of extreme pressure rise is not very common. When it does occur, it is usually the result of injury, iritis, dislocation of the lens through the pupil, or following eye surgery.

Q. Will glaucoma cause my child to feel dizzy?

A. Dizziness is not usually related to glaucoma, especially in children. While it is possible that a child experiencing a very severe elevation in eye pressure may feel nauseated, fatigued, and unwell, this is also unusual.

Q. Is the glaucoma causing my child pain?

A. Childhood glaucoma rarely causes pain unless the pressure is extremely high or it rises very quickly. Infants and young children with glaucoma may experience discomfort as a result of the stretching and clouding of the cornea that occur under very high eye pressure, particularly when exposed to bright light. Most children, particularly those more than 2 or 3 years old, will not notice when their pressure is elevated, making routine follow-up checks very necessary.

Q. Will my child's eyes become more fragile and need special attention?

A. In general, there is nothing about cataract or glaucoma that makes an eye more fragile. Children with very large eyes (buphthalmos) as a result of stretching from uncontrolled glaucoma may have an increased risk of eye wall rupture or retinal damage if they suffer an injury that might not have injured a smaller eye with a thicker eye wall.

The eye is also more fragile immediately after surgery, and activity restrictions may be appropriate. Children can often return to school within a few days after surgery. Your child's particular circumstances may make it appropriate for him/her to miss gym or recess for the first week or two.

Protective eyewear is a good idea for most children who participate in sports that involve racquets, balls, or physical contact, especially for those who have only one good eye. It may also be a good idea for your child to use it during the first few weeks after surgery, even if both eyes have good vision.

Q. My child suffers from severe light sensitivity even though the pressure is under control and has been for some time. Will this ever get better?

A. The answer depends on which of the many possible causes is making your child sensitive to light (photophobia). If your child had excessive stretching of the cornea due to glaucoma as an infant, microscopic cracks in the inner lining of the cornea (Haab striae) can occur. These cracks can cause light entering the eye to be deflected, resulting in light sensitivity. The way light enters the eye through a cataract can cause discomfort, making your child more sensitive to certain light conditions. Swelling (edema) of the cornea due to high pressure, seen most often in infancy, can cause light sensitivity. There are many other potential causes, including loose stitches from prior surgery, eyelashes rubbing against the cornea, and adverse reactions to eyedrops. Whether or not the photophobia can be alleviated will depend on whether the specific cause can be eliminated.

Q. Why is my child's eye white or hazy?
A. In a healthy eye, the cornea is perfectly clear and invisible to those who look at it straight on. It is only visible when it is viewed from the side. If the cornea swells with fluid (edema) as a result of the excess pressure from glaucoma, then it loses its clarity and becomes hazy. Depending on how severe the swelling is, the haziness may either be gray or white. When the haziness is densely white, it indicates that there is swelling throughout the whole thickness of the cornea (corneal stromal edema). A hazy gray cornea indicates the corneal swelling is superficial (corneal epithelial edema).

Q. Will calcium buildup on my child's cornea affect my child's sight or weaken his/her eye strength?
A. A small amount of calcium on the cornea (band keratopathy) rarely causes vision problems. This type of buildup usually occurs in an eye that has had complications as a result of chronic glaucoma or other problems, particularly if inflammation (iritis) has been a challenge. If the calcium is causing discomfort or interfering with vision, it can be removed surgically by putting a chemical on the eye that leeches it off of the surface of the cornea (*chelation*) and taken away manually. Sometimes calcium buildup that has been removed will reoccur.

Q. Will my child's coordination or balance change if his/her eye pressure rises?
A. Eye pressure is not related to coordination or balance. Some children may experience blurred vision when their eye pressure rises, but this should not affect their coordination or balance. In fact, even children with low vision usually have good coordination and balance. Any child who is experiencing new problems with coordination or balance should be examined by his/her pediatrician.

E. TYPES OF GLAUCOMA

Q. What is adult glaucoma and how is it different from pediatric glaucoma?
A. The most common form of adult glaucoma is known as primary open angle glaucoma (POAG). There is no specific age at which one can definitively say that a patient has adult glaucoma rather than juvenile glaucoma, although the cutoff is usually at 40 years old.

Juvenile and adult glaucoma are actually very similar, in that the angle is labeled as "open" and there is no other abnormality in the eye or the body that predisposes the patient to glaucoma. As in JOAG, POAG is initially without symptoms and some of the treatments are very similar. In addition, adult glaucoma does not cause the same changes in the eye (cloudiness, enlargement, tearing, and aversion to bright lights) that are seen in infantile glaucoma.

Some operations, such as *laser trabeculoplasty*, are performed on adults but not on children. There is more of an association between race, high blood pressure, and other factors and POAG that are not related to the glaucoma seen in children.

All glaucomas involve pressure in the eye that causes damage to the optic nerve. Children are not just little adults and should not be treated as such. Every child with glaucoma must be treated individually, with his/her treatment plan adjusted to suit his/her individual needs. The challenges of glaucoma treatment in children are different than those for adults. Children get different forms of glaucoma than adults and their eyes have different tissue properties. Caregivers have the added challenge of preserving vision development. Finally, children are expected to have a lifespan that will last many decades, creating an even greater imperative to save their sight.

Q. What is normal tension glaucoma?
A. Normal tension glaucoma is a form that is primarily seen in adults. The main characteristic of this type of glaucoma is that the eye pressure is normal, but the optic nerve is damaged (cupping of the optic nerve) as if the patient had high IOP. This form of glaucoma is not generally seen in children.

1. CONGENITAL AND INFANTILE GLAUCOMA

Q. What is infantile glaucoma?
A. Infantile glaucoma is glaucoma that is present at or shortly after birth. When onset is at birth it is called congenital. When the onset is after birth but during the first four years of life, it is called infantile. The terms are often used interchangeably.

Q. What is congenital glaucoma and how does it differ from infantile glaucoma?
A. Congenital glaucoma is present at birth and usually quite obvious. The affected eye (or eyes) often has a hazy or white cornea and is unusually large. Congenital glaucoma started during the pregnancy, even though it is extremely unlikely that anything the mother did or did not do during the pregnancy caused it. This form of glaucoma tends to be more severe than infantile glaucoma and is usually less responsive trabeculotomy or goniotomy. Vision outcomes are often not as good as for infantile glaucoma.

Q. Are different sized pupils a sign of infant glaucoma?
A. Twenty percent of the normal population has a small difference in pupil size (*anisocoria*) between the two eyes. Sometimes these differences are due to eye abnormalities, including maldevelopment of the pupil and iris. This condition is sometimes associated with glaucoma. If you notice a difference in your child's pupil size, he/she should see an eye doctor.

Q. If glaucoma is first diagnosed in infancy, can my child see at all?
A. Unless there are other issues, a child diagnosed with congenital or infantile glaucoma is indeed able to see. It usually takes many months, if not years, for untreated glaucoma to cause complete blindness. (In very severe cases, it can happen more quickly.) If a baby has glaucoma bad enough to cause clouding of the corneas, the child's vision is definitely blurred and treatment is needed to clear the visual message to allow normal visual development to continue.

Q. Is there anything special I should know about using medications to treat congenital or infantile glaucoma?
A. Medications are usually not the first line treatment for congenital or infantile glaucoma. Your child may be put on drops while waiting for surgery, or afterwards if surgery does not result in complete glaucoma control. Surgery is usually the first choice of treatment for this version of the disease. In children less than 1 year old, alpha-agonists should not be used.

2. JUVENILE GLAUCOMA

Q. What is juvenile glaucoma?

A. When glaucoma has its onset later in childhood, generally between the ages of 4 and 18, the term "juvenile" is used. This form of glaucoma is often referred to as juvenile open angle glaucoma (JOAG). Some doctors also define glaucoma that occurs between the ages of 18 and 40 years old as JOAG, but others prefer the term "early onset open angle glaucoma." JOAG does not cause the same changes in the eye (cloudiness, enlargement, tearing, and an aversion to bright lights) that are seen in infantile glaucoma.

JOAG often runs in families as an autosomal dominant disease. This means that each affected person has a 50% chance that each child he/she has could also develop JOAG, although the age of onset and severity may vary from person to person in the family. This difference in timing and severity is referred to as *variable expression*. A longer discussion of how JOAG and other forms of glaucoma occur in families can be found in "Part VIII: Genetics."

Q. Is there anything special I should know about using medications to treat juvenile open angle glaucoma (JOAG)?

A. The medical management of this form of glaucoma has no particular differences from treatment of adult open angle glaucoma.

Q. Is there anything special I should know about surgery for JOAG?

A. Recent studies have shown that goniotomy or trabeculotomy surgery may be useful in management of JOAG. Some surgeons prefer to perform trabeculectomy or implant glaucoma tubes when medications fail to control JOAG.

3. APHAKIC GLAUCOMA

Q. What is aphakic glaucoma?

A. Aphakic glaucoma is glaucoma that develops in an eye that has had its lens removed. Most eyes become aphakic when surgery is performed to remove the lens, usually due to a cataract or, less commonly, for the treatment of ectopia lentis. The younger the child is when cataract surgery is performed, the higher the chance of the development of glaucoma later in childhood. This development does not seem to be a complication of surgery. In fact, glaucoma can occur despite a perfect operation. Some patients may be genetically or anatomically predisposed to getting aphakic glaucoma.

Q. Is aphakic glaucoma caused by contact lenses?

A. No, aphakic glaucoma is not caused by contact lenses.

Q. Can this happen to any child who has had cataract surgery?

A. Yes. Any child who has had cataract surgery is at life-long risk for developing aphakic glaucoma. Certain types of cataracts or eyes might cause a greater risk than others.

Q. Why do children whose cataracts are removed get glaucoma?

A. Glaucoma in the aphakic eye may be either open or closed angle. The drainage angle of the eye (trabecular meshwork) is the natural outflow pathway for the fluid that circulates within the eye.

In most cases of aphakic glaucoma, the angle is open but does not seem to drain the eye's fluid effectively. As a result, the eye pressure builds up to levels which, if left untreated, could cause vision damage. It is not known whether open angle aphakic glaucoma occurs because the trabecular meshwork is congenitally abnormal or if the surgical disruption of the eye causes an injury to the angle. Other possibilities include poisoning of the meshwork by unknown chemicals liberated from inside the eye by surgery or clogging of the meshwork by the vitreous that fills the eye. Genetic factors may also play a role.

In a minority of eyes with aphakic glaucoma, the angle becomes clogged by debris or scarring after cataract surgery. If there is inflammation from surgery, then scarring can occur that blocks the meshwork (peripheral anterior synechiae). Either of these events may cause closed angle glaucoma.

Regardless of the exact mechanism or type of glaucoma, it is important that children who have cataracts removed get regular check-ups by an ophthalmologist to screen for elevations in eye pressure that may need treatment.

Q. If my child developed aphakic glaucoma, does it mean the surgeon who removed the cataracts did something wrong?
A. No. Glaucoma can occur despite a perfect operation.

Q. Would my child have developed glaucoma if the cataracts had not been removed?
A. In order to answer this question, we would have to leave cataracts in children and see what happens over time. This type of experiment would be unfair and potentially harmful to the children involved. This is unethical, so it cannot be performed.

Some children appear to get glaucoma after cataract surgery because the eye was already predisposed to it due to abnormalities in its structure. It is possible the eye would have developed glaucoma even without the cataract surgery. In very young children with dense cataracts, the removal of the cataract should occur while the infant is young. Delaying the cataract removal more than a few months means that good vision in the affected eye(s) is unlikely because the baby's brain is not receiving good vision signals from it/them.

Q. If my child developed aphakic glaucoma, does it mean it was a mistake to have the cataract surgery?
A. Your child's cataract surgery was likely done because your child needed it to allow the eye to try to develop vision. Like all interventions in medicine, the patient, family, and doctor make the decision to go ahead based on the presumption that the risks were outweighed by the potential benefits. No medical procedure is guaranteed to have a complication-free outcome. Treatment must proceed with what, on average, will be in the best interests of the child.

Q. How soon after the surgery did the glaucoma start?
A. There is usually no way to tell for sure exactly when aphakic glaucoma begins. It is important to make sure your child regularly follows up with his/her ophthalmologist to make sure that glaucoma does not develop or is treated promptly if it does develop.

Q. How often do children have glaucoma as a result of cataract surgery?
A. Not every child who has cataract surgery gets glaucoma. The rate can range from 0 to more than 30 percent. The risk depends on many factors, including the patient's eye anatomy, the type

of surgery, the type of cataract, the patient's eye size, and the patient's age at the time of surgery. The average time to development of glaucoma after cataract surgery is 5 to 8 years, but it can occur at any time.

Q. Is aphakic glaucoma usually treated with medication or with surgery?
A. Medication is usually the first line of attack for aphakic glaucoma. Many, but not all, children who have aphakic glaucoma will eventually need glaucoma surgery. The likelihood that a specific child will need surgery to treat his/her aphakic glaucoma depends on the type of cataract, the size of the eyeball, the length of time after surgery the glaucoma developed, the level of pressure elevation, the mechanism of the glaucoma, and many other factors.

Q. Is there anything special I should know about using medications to treat aphakic glaucoma?
A. The medical management of aphakic glaucoma is very similar to management of other forms of glaucoma. There is some evidence that prostaglandin analogues and pilocarpine may have a particularly good effect in treating this type of glaucoma.

Q. Are there any special considerations in the surgical treatment of aphakic glaucoma?
A. Yes. After the lens of the eye is removed, the white of the eye (sclera) is quite soft, presenting certain technical challenges for the surgeon. Special techniques may be necessary to help support the sclera during surgery. In addition, some centers no longer do trabeculectomy in aphakic eyes, partly due to the lower success rates and higher risk of infection and other complications.

An additional concern is the possibility that the vitreous may be pushed through the pupil because the lens is no longer present, particularly if the pressure gets too low after glaucoma surgery. If this occurs, the vitreous may block a trabeculectomy opening or a glaucoma tube. Special considerations need to be taken to prevent this complication.

Q. Will my child's other eye develop glaucoma?
A. Glaucoma occurs only in the eye that has had cataract surgery because that eye has had cataract surgery. The normal eye is not at increased risk for glaucoma.

Q. If one of my children developed aphakic glaucoma and another of my children also has cataract surgery, will he/she also get glaucoma?
A. It is possible, but it also may not happen. When cataracts are genetic and run in families, it is assumed that each individual who has the cataract has it because of the same genetic defect. Certain genetic defects may predispose an individual to the development of glaucoma after surgery. As a result, there is a higher chance that individuals in the same family will get glaucoma following cataract surgery if that was the experience of one family member. This is not an absolute rule, however, and there are families in which one person develops aphakic glaucoma and another does not.

Q. Can my child, who had cataract surgery and now wears contact lenses, get lens implants if he/she also has glaucoma?
A. This procedure is called secondary IOL implantation. The presence of glaucoma in a child who has had cataract surgery does not preclude the use of an intraocular lens (IOL) implant. The risks of IOL insertion become higher, as the glaucoma may be aggravated by the additional surgery. This possibility has to be considered carefully when weighing the risks and benefits of

IOL implantation in a child who had cataract surgery, is wearing a contact lens, and is doing well without an IOL.

IOLs are usually an option for most children who have had cataract surgery. Many centers choose not to implant them until a child is beyond the age of 1 or 2 years old. Even then, the risks of surgery must be carefully balanced against the benefits of implantation of an IOL. All studies done to date have shown no better visual improvement from an IOL as opposed to a contact lens.

IOL insertion may be difficult in some eyes if there is excessive scar tissue or there are inadequate residual membranes from the natural lens or cataract to support the IOL. In these cases, there are two choices: sewing the IOL into the eye or resting it on the iris (anterior chamber IOL or ACIOL). Recent research has shown that sewn-in IOLs can drift out of position, often years after the original surgery. ACIOLs can result in glaucoma or other problems. One has to carefully consider the risks and unknown long term outcomes for these procedures.

Q. Should my child's IOL be removed now that he/she has glaucoma?
A. In the vast majority of cases, removing the IOL will not take away the glaucoma. The IOL should not be removed unless the glaucoma is the result of inflammation caused by it. The IOL is unlikely to cause any aggravation of your child's glaucoma if it is not causing inflammation, nor will it interfere with glaucoma treatment.

Q. What percentage of children with IOLs develop glaucoma when there are no other eye problems?
A. IOLs have not been implanted in children long enough to know this answer exactly. The average time for onset of glaucoma after any cataract surgery appears to be about five to eight years. Other factors include type of cataract, the size of the eye, and the age of the child. The risk is highest when a child undergoes cataract surgery in the first year of life. So far, it appears that the glaucoma risk is about the same or maybe a bit lower when an IOL is implanted, especially in older children. Whether an IOL is implanted in one eye or both also does not appear to affect the likelihood of developing aphakic glaucoma.

Q. Can a child with glaucoma after unilateral cataract surgery ever develop good vision?
A. Yes, your child can have good vision in that eye, even with glaucoma. The keys to success are early intervention for the cataract, good glaucoma control with medicines and/or surgery and, most importantly, successful patching. It is even possible for your child to have 20/20 vision in that eye if all of these efforts are successful.

Q. What research is being done on aphakic glaucoma?
A. The burning question with aphakic glaucoma is, "What causes the disease?" If the cause of aphakic glaucoma were known, the condition could be better addressed. In addition to general glaucoma research, investigations continue regarding the role of factors in the vitreous that may be causing the trabecular meshwork function to fail in certain children. So far, data suggests that placing a lens implant into the eye at the time the cataract is taken out does not prevent glaucoma from developing. In the future, genetic research will also be important in aphakic glaucoma, as the gene that causes the cataract may also be involved in causing the glaucoma.

4. GLAUCOMA DUE TO EYE INJURY (TRAUMATIC GLAUCOMA)

Q. How can an injury cause glaucoma?
A. Injuries to the eye may damage the trabecular meshwork or cause an accumulation of blood within the eye. The term for an accumulation of blood in front of the iris and pupil is *hyphema*. *Vitreous hemorrhage* is the term used to describe an accumulation of blood behind the pupil and iris. In either circumstance, the blood can clog up the trabecular meshwork, preventing normal drainage of fluid from the eye and resulting in an elevated pressure. Sometimes traumatic glaucoma is transient and needs only temporary treatment with medications or surgery. Other times, the damage may be long-lasting or even permanent.

Q. Can a head injury cause or worsen glaucoma?
A. Head injuries do not cause or exacerbate glaucoma unless they involve direct blunt injury to the eye.

Q. Can an injury my child received many years ago be causing the glaucoma that recently started?
A. One specific subtype of traumatic glaucoma is called *angle recession glaucoma*. This subtype occurs as a result of direct injury to the trabecular meshwork. Angle recession glaucoma may not appear for months, or even years, after the initial injury. This form of glaucoma is actually quite rare in children. It is more commonly seen in adults.

Q. Is there anything special I should know about using medications to treat my child's glaucoma after an eye injury?
A. There are many causes of glaucoma after eye injury. Identifying the issues which may be causing the glaucoma will help to guide the treatment options. If the glaucoma is a result of inflammation due to the injury (*traumatic iritis*), then steroid treatment may be useful. If the problem is steroid-induced glaucoma, then stopping steroids may alleviate it. The mechanism of the glaucoma may also have some affect on the choice of glaucoma drug or surgery (if needed).

Q. What research is being done on traumatic glaucoma?
A. The key to treating traumatic glaucoma is to prevent its development if at all possible. If glaucoma develops because of blood inside the eye, then better treatment of hyphema may lead to the prevention of glaucoma. New drug treatments to manage hyphema and vitreous hemorrhage, and thus prevent glaucoma, are being explored. New surgical treatments for forms of traumatic glaucoma are also being investigated.

5. GLAUCOMA DUE TO INFLAMMATION IN THE EYE (UVEITIC GLAUCOMA)

Q. What are uveitis and iritis?
A. Uveitis refers to an inflammation involving the inside of the eye. If the inflammation is limited only to the front (anterior) part of the eye, mainly involving only the iris, it is sometimes called iritis or *anterior uveitis*. Iritis causes the blood vessels in the iris to become inflamed, making them leak and leading to an excess of protein and white blood cells in the fluid (aqueous humor) in front of the iris (anterior chamber).

Iritis may occur alone or in association with a systemic disease, such as juvenile idiopathic arthritis (JIA). Inflammation can also occur following surgery or trauma. It sometimes also involves the back part of the eye, including the *choroid*, and even the optic nerve and retina. Many medical professionals believe that the child's immune system is somehow responsible for most forms of uveitis, although infection can also be a cause.

The care of children with iritis usually involves a team, which includes not only the ophthalmologist, but also the pediatrician and pediatric rheumatologist. Medications to treat chronic iritis often include both eyedrops and systemic medications to dampen the immune response.

Q. What terms are used when describing uveitis and iritis?

A. The term uveitis is derived from *uvea*, which is the middle layer of the eye between the inner lining (retina) and the outer white of the eye (sclera). Uveitis can involve only the front (anterior uveitis or iritis), only the back (*posterior uveitis*), or both parts of the eye (*panuveitis*). If the area of the eye just behind the iris and in front of the retina is inflamed, this is called *pars planitis* or *intermediate uveitis*.

In addition, the actual structures of the eye that are inflamed may be described. The iris is the most forward part of the uvea. The iris actually extends underneath the sclera and continues between the sclera and the retina. Iritis refers to uveitis in which the inflammation only involves the iris. Alternatively, the term *iridocyclitis* is also sometimes used.

Choroiditis occurs when the uvea in the back half of the eye is inflamed but the iris is not. If the vitreous, which fills the eye behind the pupil and lens, is inflamed, the condition is called *vitritis*. Choroiditis and vitritis are not usually associated with glaucoma. Only iritis is known to cause glaucoma.

Iritis may also be described as granulomatous or non-granulomatous. In iritis, white blood cells form clumps, called *keratoprecipitates*. This clumping pattern can be seen by an ophthalmologist during a slit lamp examination. Keratoprecipitates appear as dots on the inside of the back of the cornea, where they settle out from the aqueous humor. When the cells form large clumps, the condition is called *granulomatous iritis*. This form is more likely to be associated with certain diseases, such as tuberculosis and *sarcoidosis*, but not always. When the clumps are smaller, the iritis is non-granulomatous. This is the more common form of the disease.

Q. What are the signs of anterior uveitis?

A. The white of the eye may become red, the pupil may be smaller than usual, and the patient may experience pain or visual blurring. Some forms of iritis, especially those occurring with JIA, are notorious for causing no symptoms until things are very serious and permanent eye damage has already occurred. If your child has JIA, he/she will need to be periodically screened by an eye doctor to detect the iritis before any symptoms develop.

Q. What causes iritis?

A. There are many causes of iritis. Unfortunately, in most cases the actual cause is unknown (*idiopathic*). When this occurs, blood tests, urine tests, and X-rays fail to reveal any cause.

The second most common cause of juvenile iritis is JIA, previously known as juvenile rheumatoid arthritis (JRA) or *juvenile chronic arthritis*. JIA is a condition in which a child has joint inflammation in addition to the iritis. The combination of JIA and iritis is most frequently seen in young girls. Generally, fewer than seven joints are involved (*oligoarthritis*) although more joints can sometimes be involved (*polyarthritis*). The child usually has a positive result from a blood test known as an *antinuclear antibody (ANA) test*. A positive result on this test indicates that the patient's immune system is attacking his/her body, causing the inflammation of the joints and eyes.

Other causes of iritis in children include tuberculosis and other infections, leukemia, sarcoidosis (an inflammation of the lungs and skin), other forms of arthritis, chicken pox (*varicella*), inflammatory bowel disease (such as ulcerative colitis and Crohn's disease), and psoriasis.

Q. How does iritis cause glaucoma?

A. When there is inflammation in the eyeball, an excess of protein and white blood cells are released into the aqueous humor. This can clog up the drain of the eye (trabecular meshwork). Alternatively, the immune process and inflammatory chemicals can attack or poison the trabecular meshwork in the same way they cause the iris to become inflamed. Glaucoma may be transient, resolving when the inflammation goes away, or long-standing, remaining even after the inflammation has resolved. Glaucoma due to iritis is sometimes called *uveitic glaucoma*.

Elevated eye pressure, whether temporary or permanent, can also be caused by the steroids often used to treat iritis. If the elevation of pressure is permanent, it is called glaucoma.

Sometimes it is not possible to determine whether the increased eye pressure in a patient with iritis is caused by the steroid treatment or the iritis itself. Unfortunately, steroids often cannot be avoided in the treatment of iritis. It is much more likely that the eye pressure will increase if the iritis is not treated than the increase being caused by steroid treatment.

Q. Do all children with iritis get glaucoma?

A. No. The risk for glaucoma depends on many factors, including the cause and severity of the iritis, the length of time that the condition persists, the number of times it occurs, and whether steroid treatment is used.

Q. If my child has iritis in both eyes but the IOP has increased in only one eye, will the IOP in the other eye also eventually increase?

A. If a child with iritis in both eyes gets elevated pressure in one eye, then the chance of getting elevated pressure in the second eye is higher. It is also possible that the IOP in the other eye will not increase. Careful surveillance is recommended.

Q. If the iritis goes away, will the elevated eye pressure also be cured?

A. Sometimes, even when the iritis is cured, elevated eye pressure may persist. This is generally due to irreversible damage that has been caused to the trabecular meshwork. In other cases, treatment of the iritis causes the cells and protein to be dispersed from the eye, causing them to flow out through the trabecular meshwork. This outflow of cells and protein can cause a sudden rise of pressure, but may reverse itself over time as the drainage improves.

Q. Is it possible for iritis to reduce elevated eye pressure?

A. When iritis is active, the production of fluid inside the eye sometimes decreases. This happens because the ciliary tissue, located directly behind the outer (*peripheral*) edge of the iris, is the tissue responsible for producing the aqueous humor in the eye. If the ciliary tissue is inflamed (iridocyclitis), then it produces less fluid. This may cause a temporary lowering of the pressure inside the eye. When the iritis is resolved and the inflammation is settled, the elevated eye pressure will likely return.

Q. Is there anything special I should know about using medications to treat elevated eye pressure in iritis?
A. In treating children with iritis who experience an eye pressure rise due to steroids, physicians are faced with a difficult dilemma. Steroids are needed to treat the iritis, yet they can also cause elevated eye pressure. It is difficult to differentiate between steroid-induced elevated eye pressure and elevated eye pressure due to iritis. It may be necessary for your child to continue using steroids to treat the iritis if other drugs that are less likely to cause elevated eye pressure do not work. When this is the case, eye pressure lowering medications are added to the steroids and, where necessary, surgery is performed.

Q. Are there any special considerations in the surgical treatment of glaucoma due to iritis?
A. Ideally, surgery should only be performed when the iritis is completely under control. Any surgery that involves entering the eye will cause inflammation. Eyes with anterior uveitis are particularly prone to postoperative inflammation.

Some physicians prefer to increase the topical and/or oral steroids that a patient is taking in order to make sure that the inflammation stays under control before, during, and after surgery. An intravenous dose of steroids is also often given during surgery. Inflammation complications, such as high pressure and scar tissue formation, are more likely to occur after glaucoma surgery in a patient with iritis. As a result, some operations may fail more easily. In particular, trabeculectomy without antimetabolites is very likely to fail in a child who has iritis.

Certain types of tube implantation may be inadvisable if your child has iritis, as the inflammation in the eye can clog the mechanism of certain types of tubes. Research has also shown that patients who have tube surgery may be more prone to erosion of the donor sclera patch graft that is used to cover the tube, making it more likely that the patch will need to be replaced at a later date.

Patients with iritis may be more prone to bleeding after surgery than other patients, particularly after goniotomy. Research has also suggested that goniotomy surgery, although perhaps the safest and least inflammatory operation for patients with iritis, may also result in a higher risk of developing pressures that are too low and having fluid accumulate in between the choroid and sclera (*suprachoroidal space*).

Lastly, procedures designed to destroy ciliary tissue within the eye, such as laser or freezing treatments, are known to cause a very inflammatory response. Unless there is no other option, these treatments should be avoided in patients with iritis.

Q. What research is being done on elevated eye pressure due to iritis?
A. Better control of iritis should ultimately lead to prevention and better control of elevated eye pressure. Many drugs have come on the market to better control iritis. In particular, these drugs are designed to modulate the body's immune response that leads to inflammation. Work has also been done on new surgical techniques (such as the use of goniotomy in iritis), and eyedrops to treat elevated eye pressure secondary to iritis.

6. STEROID-INDUCED GLAUCOMA

Q. How do steroids cause glaucoma?
A. Any steroid treatment has a chance of causing glaucoma, whether the medications are taken orally or used as drops or ointment applied to the surface of the eye. Much less commonly, steroid skin creams, intravenous *solutions*, or inhaled medications, can also cause the disease. A percentage of the population has a genetic susceptibility to steroid-induced glaucoma. We do not know exactly why they cause an elevation in eye pressure, but any child on chronic steroid treatment needs his/her IOP checked regularly.

In most cases, stopping the steroid will cause the pressure to drop, usually reverting back to normal. Unfortunately, it will sometimes remain elevated even after the steroids are discontinued. Some children must use steroids to treat a major systemic disease, such as lupus, or eye disease, such as iritis, so their use cannot be stopped to reduce eye pressure. In these cases, other medications or surgery may be necessary to control the glaucoma.

Q. Do all steroids have the potential to cause glaucoma?
A. Yes, though some kinds of steroid have a lower risk attached to them. Fluorometholone and rimexolone are examples of steroid eyedrops that have a lower risk of causing glaucoma, although they may also be less effective in fighting inflammation (which is the main purpose of steroid treatment). Drugs such as prednisolone and dexamethasone have a higher risk of causing glaucoma but a stronger ability to fight inflammation. Direct application of steroids to the eye in the form of drops or ointment is more likely to cause glaucoma than using oral, intravenous, or inhaled steroid preparations.

Q. Can inhaled steroids (i.e., puffers, nasal sprays) cause glaucoma?
A. It is not known for certain. Inhaled steroids, whether through the mouth or nose, are usually used for a short period of time, and very little reaches the eye by way of the air or the blood stream. If a child's elevated eye pressure is, in fact, only due to the use of the nasal steroid spray, then there is a good chance that it will gradually come back down once the steroid use is stopped.

Q. If my child got glaucoma from using steroid eyedrops in one eye, can the glaucoma spread to the other eye?
A. In general, glaucoma does not spread from one eye to the other. If a child is at risk for glaucoma in both eyes, and one eye gets the disease, then the remaining eye is usually at higher risk for developing it. For example, if an infant has cataract surgery in both eyes and gets glaucoma in one eye, he/she is more likely to get glaucoma in both eyes. The same is true for a glaucoma response to steroids. If an individual gets steroid-induced glaucoma in one eye, then he/she is more likely to get it in their second eye. This is especially likely if both eyes are being treated with steroids. This does not mean that the glaucoma has spread from one eye to the other, but rather that both eyes had a similarly high risk of developing the disease.

Q. Will stopping the steroids make the glaucoma go away?
A. If the glaucoma is being caused specifically by the steroids, then stopping the steroid treatment will usually make the glaucoma go away. This is not always the case if the steroids have caused irreversible damage to the trabecular meshwork.

One must be very careful about discontinuing steroid treatments. Steroids that have been used for a long time must be tapered off very slowly, as the body will have become dependent on them. The disease that is being treated by the steroids may worsen if the medication is stopped too rapidly.

Steroids are usually used to suppress and treat an underlying body or eye disorder. Without them, the eye could go blind. In cases where systemic (oral or intravenous) steroids are necessary, such as when treating lupus, stopping the treatment could even cause the person to die. Sometimes it is better to accept that the steroids are necessary and just treat the resultant glaucoma.

Q. Does steroid-induced glaucoma run in families?
A. There appears to be some genetic predisposition to having a glaucoma reaction to steroids. If this is true, then several members in a family may be likely to have the adverse reaction. There are many other factors that contribute to getting glaucoma while on steroids, so the level of risk is not identical for every individual in that family.

Q. Is there anything special I should know about using medications to treat steroid-induced glaucoma?
A. When possible, steroid-induced glaucoma can be treated by switching to another steroid with a lesser effect on eye pressure (e.g., rimexolone, loteprednol, fluorometholone) or by decreasing or eliminating the steroid use altogether. Certain non-steroid medications, such as methotrexate or *anti-TNF (tumor necrosis factor) drugs*, can be given for some forms of iritis that may reduce the need for steroids. These other drugs tend to be very expensive and usually require injections or day stays in a hospital for intravenous infusions.

If the underlying disease requires oral steroids, then the steroid is continued and the secondary glaucoma is treated accordingly. All glaucoma medications seem to be potentially useful in treating steroid-induced glaucoma.

Q. Are there any special considerations in the surgical treatment of steroid-induced glaucoma?
A. Perhaps the biggest challenge in patients suffering from steroid-induced glaucoma is the necessity of using steroids after most intraocular eye surgeries to facilitate healing and suppress postoperative inflammation. This sets up a paradox in which the medication being used to help the patient get better is also the medication that can make the patient worse. The hope is that the operation itself, which is designed to treat the underlying problem of steroid responsiveness, will keep the pressure low and allow the use of steroids postoperatively as needed.

Q. What research is being done on steroid-induced glaucoma?
A. Many investigators are working on determining the molecular causes of steroid-induced glaucoma. Some of this research involves trying to identify the genetic reason that steroid-induced glaucoma occurs.

7. NEOVASCULAR GLAUCOMA

Q. Is neovascular glaucoma a common form of the disease?

A. Neovascular glaucoma is quite uncommon in children. It is usually a reaction to chronic eye diseases, such as diabetic eye disease, many of which are seen almost exclusively in adults. Children may develop neovascular glaucoma if the retina has been detached for a long time due to conditions such as severe retinopathy of prematurity (usually associated with very premature birth), chronic iritis, or in eyes having had a tumor such as retinoblastoma.

Q. What causes neovascular glaucoma?

A. In neovascular glaucoma, tiny abnormal blood vessels grow on the surface of the iris in response to chronic inflammation or lack of oxygen to the eye. These blood vessels proliferate rapidly, and may infiltrate the trabecular meshwork or cause the iris to be pulled into and over the trabecular meshwork, causing a form of closed angle glaucoma. The vessels are quite fragile and may bleed spontaneously, which can also cause glaucoma to occur.

Q. Do the actual blood vessels or the blood in those vessels cause the problem?

A. The blood inside neovascular vessels is perfectly normal. It is the abnormal blood vessels growing in an unrestricted, unregulated fashion that causes the glaucoma.

Q. What research is being done on neovascular glaucoma?

A. New blood vessel formation (neovascularization) inside the eye is almost always secondary to another abnormality in the eye. For example, if the eye's circulation is disrupted (*central retinal artery occlusion*) or there is chronic inflammation (iritis or uveitis), then neovascularization may develop. The best way to treat neovascular glaucoma is to better treat the original eye problem or prevent it altogether. There may be ways to prevent the formation of neovascular blood vessels, such as laser treatment of the retina or injection of medications.

Once neovascular glaucoma has developed, the treatment becomes more difficult. Research has primarily focused on new surgical and pharmaceutical techniques. Gene therapy is being explored. Specific attention is being given to agents that have an effect on blood vessel growth. *Anti-VEGF (vascular endothelial growth factor) drugs*, which can be injected into the eye, show particular promise.

8. ANIRIDIA AND GLAUCOMA

Q. What is aniridia?

A. Aniridia is a congenital disorder in which the main manifestation is an absence of most or all of the iris. Although this is the most noticeable manifestation, the whole eye may be abnormal. Some of the abnormalities that can occur in a patient with aniridia include:

- Poor vision, which may or may not be correctable with glasses or contact lenses
- Strabismus (misaligned eyes)
- Glaucoma
- Cataracts
- Nystagmus (shaky eyes)
- Abnormal blood vessels in the cornea (*pannus*)
- Aversion to light (photophobia)

- Underdevelopment of the retina (macular hypoplasia)
- Underdevelopment of the optic nerve (*optic nerve hypoplasia*)
- Degeneration of the retina (*retinal dystrophy*)

Some patients develop only one or a few of the abnormalities of aniridia, while other patients develop all of them. Even within the same family, different individuals may have variable expression of the disease.

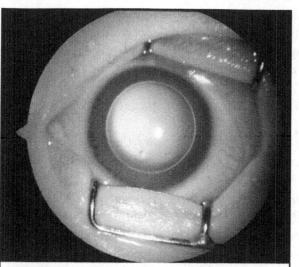

Figure 7: Eye with aniridia. Note the absence of a pupil. The central circular structure is the lens suspended in the center of the eye. The lens usually cannot be seen because of overlying iris, which is absent here. The small projections behind the edge of the cornea are the ciliary processes.

Q. What causes aniridia?

A. It appears that most cases of aniridia are caused by an abnormality in a specific gene called PAX6. The PAX6 gene is an extremely important master control gene for making the eyeball. The PAX6 gene is like an orchestra conductor. It regulates the development of many other genes that work together to make the eyeball. As a result, it is indirectly involved in the formation of many parts of the eye. This explains why there are potentially so many different abnormalities of the eye that can also occur with aniridia.

Q. What is WAGR syndrome?

A. Aniridia is sometimes also part of WAGR syndrome, which is caused when all or part of one copy of the PAX6 gene is missing (*deletion*). When this happens, neighboring genes are often missing, too. These include genes which, when missing, can result in a kidney tumor called Wilms tumor, as well as genital abnormalities and retardation. The syndrome's acronym is derived from these representative traits – **W**ilms tumor, **A**niridia, **G**enital problems, and **R**etardation.

When the first known patient in a family is diagnosed with aniridia, a *chromosome* test (*karyotype*, *microarray*, or *FISH* testing) is commonly done to see if there is a piece of *DNA* missing that might indicate WAGR syndrome. If so, kidney ultrasounds are done every three to four months to screen for kidney tumors. If these tests are not available, and the doctors cannot be sure if the chromosome problem is present, then an ultrasound will be done every six months to screen for kidney tumors. This regimen will usually last until the child is 6 to 8 years old.

Q. Do all children with aniridia get glaucoma?

A. In general, approximately 50 percent of children with aniridia develop glaucoma. All individuals with aniridia should have regular screening for glaucoma for their entire lives, since it may appear at any age. Children whose pressure cannot be measured while they are awake may require examinations under anesthesia or sedation to screen for glaucoma.

Q. If one family member with aniridia has glaucoma, will other family members with aniridia also get glaucoma?

A. Not necessarily, but it does mean that other family members are at particularly high risk of glaucoma. Everyone with aniridia should be checked regularly for glaucoma.

Q. If my child with aniridia has glaucoma in one eye, will he/she develop it in the other eye?

A. It is possible, though not certain. The eye without glaucoma is at high risk for developing it and should be monitored closely to catch it early if it does occur.

Q. Is there anything special I should know about using medications to treat glaucoma related to aniridia?

A. Infantile aniridic glaucoma should be treated like isolated congenital or infantile glaucoma. Treatment usually includes surgery. Avoiding pilocarpine might be preferable, as this drug can encourage the tiny peripheral stub of the iris to come forward into the trabecular meshwork, blocking it. Other medications commonly used to treat other forms of glaucoma can be useful in treating aniridic glaucoma.

Q. Are there any special considerations in the surgical treatment of glaucoma due to aniridia?

A. Goniotomy surgery in patients with aniridia presents unique challenges. With no iris to protect the underlying lens, the surgeon may more easily accidentally nick the lens when using instruments inside the eye. This can result in cataract. The instrument used to perform the incision in the trabecular meshwork travels directly across the whole surface of the unprotected lens. In addition, it is possible that a raised cataract on the surface of the lens (*anterior pyramidal cataract*) that is commonly seen in aniridia can block the surgeon's way to perform certain operations.

In any form of glaucoma, tube implantation or trabeculectomy may reduce the intraocular pressure too much after surgery due to over-drainage of the fluid from inside the eye. As a result, the anterior chamber of the eye can become shallow, making the lens move towards the cornea. Since a patient with aniridia has almost no iris, the lens can more easily be damaged by the tube. Additionally, the lens may touch the cornea, potentially causing damage serious enough to require urgent attention.

If a patient with aniridia has corneal problems, the surgeon's ability to see into the eye during surgery may be impaired. In addition, the cornea may be more prone to develop problems following surgery.

Q. What research is being done on aniridia-associated glaucoma?
A. Gene therapy for aniridia is being researched. Additional research in aniridic glaucoma has focused mainly on pharmaceutical and surgical techniques. Much research into transplanting the cells that cover the edge of the cornea (*limbal stem cells*), which are needed to maintain corneal health, has been conducted. Limbal stem cell transplantation may allow the surface of the eye to be repopulated with cells that no longer contain the PAX6 gene defect. Future research may involve using these same techniques for the cells inside the eye involved with the function of the trabecular meshwork.

9. GLAUCOMA SYNDROMES AND RELATED CONDITIONS

Q. What is a syndrome?
A. A syndrome is a collection of abnormalities that may affect different parts of the body and that, when present together in the same individual, form a recognizable collection of findings. Syndromes are often named after the individual who originally discovered or identified them. Many syndromes may include glaucoma as part of the overall picture.

Q. How do I know if my child has a syndrome?
A. Syndromes are very rare, though every child with glaucoma should have a full physical examination by his/her pediatrician or family physician to determine if he/she is affected by one. The overwhelming majority of children with glaucoma are perfectly healthy, with the exception of their eye problems.

Q. What causes syndromes?
A. Genetic syndromes are most often caused by defects in genes. Less commonly, they are caused by an infection during pregnancy or other influences, such as drugs ingested by the mother. Sometimes only one gene is affected. Since that gene may be used in different locations throughout the body, multiple organs can be affected at the same time. Other syndromes are the result of an abnormal chromosome and affect more than one gene. When more than one gene is affected, the effects are almost always seen in more than one organ.

A. AXENFELD-RIEGER SPECTRUM AND IRIS HYPOPLASIA

Q. What is Axenfeld-Rieger spectrum?
A. Axenfeld-Rieger spectrum is an example of a syndrome associated with glaucoma. It is primarily associated with eye problems, but other parts of the body can also be affected. Elements of Axenfeld-Rieger spectrum were originally described by two separate individuals at different times, Drs. Theodor Axenfeld and Herweh Rieger. Naming convention generally dictates that a disease, disorder, or anomaly is named for the person (or people) who first discovers or describes it. Individuals who have elements of either or both of the syndromes that Axenfeld and Rieger described are considered to have Axenfeld-Rieger spectrum.

There were originally four diagnostic categories used to describe conditions that are considered to fall into what is now called the Axenfeld-Rieger spectrum. Which descriptor was used depended on the elements the individual patient had:

- *Axenfeld anomaly*: An abnormal attachment between the edge of the iris and the edge of the cornea, appearing as a white line called *posterior embryotoxon*.
- *Axenfeld syndrome*: The presence of Axenfeld anomaly plus glaucoma.
- *Rieger anomaly*: Posterior embryotoxon with iris strands attached to the white line with other abnormalities of the eye or pupil, such as extra holes in the iris, thinning of iris, pupil offset, or pupil not round, plus glaucoma.
- *Rieger syndrome*: The presence of Rieger anomaly plus abnormalities of the teeth and/or *umbilicus*.

In recent years, it has been recognized that these four conditions have great overlap and may be the result of abnormalities in the same gene. They may be seen in various combinations even among individuals in the same family. Today, the terms Axenfeld-Rieger syndrome or Axenfeld-Rieger spectrum are more commonly used.

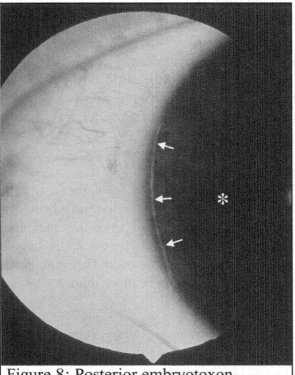

Figure 8: Posterior embryotoxon (indicated by arrows). This crescent-like white line is on the underside of the cornea. The asterisk (*) indicates the location of the iris.

Q. What is posterior embryotoxon?

A. Normally, the attachment of the outer edge of the iris to the edge of the overlying cornea is not visible during an eye examination without using special tools. In posterior embryotoxon, this attachment becomes visible because it has moved forward. In addition, there may be abnormally attached pieces of iris within the view of the examining eye doctor.

Contrary to how the term sounds, posterior embryotoxon has nothing to do with embryos or toxins. In and of itself, it does not harm the eye in any way. Instead, it is a marker for abnormal development of the trabecular meshwork and the eye's ability to drain. When an eye has posterior embryotoxon, it is at increased risk for developing glaucoma.

Q. What is iris hypoplasia?

A. *Iris hypoplasia* refers to an underdevelopment of the front layers of the iris, although the whole iris is present and the pupil is normal. The iris is thinner than usual, allowing the ophthalmologist to see the sphincter muscle that constricts the pupil, which is normally hidden in the iris. Iris hypoplasia can be seen in Axenfeld-Rieger spectrum or by itself. In either situation, it is associated with a high risk for glaucoma.

Q. Are the conditions that constitute Axenfeld-Rieger spectrum genetic?

A. Axenfeld-Rieger spectrum and iris hypoplasia are genetic disorders. At least three genes have currently been identified in which mutations can cause Axenfeld-Rieger. Both disorders are passed on in an autosomal dominant fashion, meaning that an affected individual has a 50 percent chance, with each pregnancy, of passing the trait to the child. The effects of the spectrum may be different amongst members of the same family. For example, one member of the family may have glaucoma but another may not. Any of the possible elements of this disorder may appear in different combinations in different family members.

In some instances, an affected child may have an affected parent. The child would have inherited the abnormal gene from that parent. The parent may have signs of Axenfeld-Rieger spectrum or iris hypoplasia that are so mild that he/she never realized he/she had the condition. For example, the parent may simply have posterior embryotoxon. This underscores the importance of examining parents when children are diagnosed with glaucoma.

It is also possible that neither parent carries the gene abnormality, and that the affected child is the first family member to develop the spectrum. If this occurs, then no other family members are at risk except for the children of the affected individual.

Q. Do all patients with these eye abnormalities get glaucoma?

A. No. In general, the risk of patients with Axenfeld-Rieger spectrum or iris hypoplasia developing glaucoma is estimated to be approximately 50 percent. In some families, the incidence of glaucoma is higher than in others.

Q. Why do patients with these eye abnormalities get glaucoma?

A. The commonly accepted theory is that there is some microscopic flaw in the way the trabecular meshwork is formed and functions.

Q. If my child with Axenfeld-Rieger spectrum has glaucoma in one eye, will he/she also develop it in the other eye?

A. Any individual who has Axenfeld-Rieger spectrum and gets glaucoma in one eye is certainly more likely to develop it in the other eye. All individuals with Axenfeld-Rieger spectrum should have routine, ongoing ophthalmology follow-up care that includes screening for glaucoma for their entire lives, since the glaucoma may develop at any age. Children who are not able to have their pressure measured while awake in the ophthalmologist's office may require examinations under anesthesia or sedation, perhaps twice yearly, to screen for glaucoma.

Q. Why does my child, who has Axenfeld-Rieger spectrum, have abnormalities of his/her teeth and belly button in addition to glaucoma?

A. Every cell in a person's body has the same genes, but certain genes are only used in certain cells. Since there are only about 35,000 genes available, the body often uses them in what might seem like unlikely locations to perform different functions. Each of the genes that may be abnormal in the Axenfeld-Rieger spectrum may also be used to perform other functions elsewhere in the body, particularly in the teeth and the belly button. An individual with Axenfeld-Rieger spectrum may have missing teeth, extra teeth, or abnormally shaped or placed teeth. His/her belly button (umbilicus) may also have extra skin around the edge, causing it to protrude like an elephant's trunk, or have an umbilical hernia.

Q. Is there anything special I should know about using medications to treat glaucoma in children with Axenfeld-Rieger spectrum?

A. The use of pilocarpine should probably be avoided in patients with this disorder as it can cause the edges of the iris to move forward in areas where the normal ability to drain fluid from the eye is already compromised. Other treatments, including other medications, can be used in the same manner as with other forms of glaucoma.

Q. Are there any special considerations in the surgical treatment of Axenfeld-Rieger spectrum?

A. Surgery in patients with this condition is more difficult because of the presence of strands of iris directly in front of the trabecular meshwork. When trying to perform a goniotomy, these strands block the surgeon's instruments. The surgeon must either cut the strands or maneuver between them to conduct the operation. Performing a trabeculotomy is also made more difficult, due to both the presence of the strands and the increased difficulty in passing the trabeculotomy probe into the eye. When inserting a glaucoma tube or doing trabeculectomy, the surgeon also must ensure that the strands do not block the tube or the trabeculectomy drainage hole (*sclerostomy*).

Q. What research is being done on Axenfeld-Rieger spectrum?

A. There has been much progress in understanding the genetic causes of this spectrum. Perhaps this genetic information will lead to gene therapy for the associated glaucoma, although there is no current effort to pursue this directly. New surgical techniques are also being explored.

B. STURGE-WEBER SYNDROME

Q. What is Sturge-Weber syndrome?

A. Sturge-Weber syndrome (SWS) is a congenital disorder characterized by a red birthmark, sometimes called a port wine mark (previously known as a port wine stain), that appears most commonly on the face; brain abnormalities; blood vessel abnormalities inside the eye (*choroidal hemangioma*); and/or glaucoma. Not all patients get each feature. The syndrome is named after Drs. William Allen Sturge and Frederick Parkes Weber, who recognized the combination of these elements.

Q. What causes glaucoma in children with Sturge-Weber syndrome?

A. A child with Sturge-Weber syndrome is most likely to develop glaucoma or have his/her existing glaucoma worsened during one of three periods in his/her life:

- At birth: Children with SWS may be born with congenital or infantile glaucoma. This type of glaucoma is the same as the congenital or infantile glaucoma that occurs in individuals who do not have SWS.
- Childhood to preadolescence: From approximately the ages of 4 to 12 years, there may be a new onset, aggravation, or reoccurrence of glaucoma. Just like there are abnormal blood vessels causing the port wine mark on the face, there are also abnormal microscopic blood vessels on the surface of the eye. They may not be visible externally. These blood vessels (episcleral veins) can start to enlarge (hypertrophy) over time and may become more resistant to accepting the drainage of fluid that is coming through the trabecular meshwork and Schlemm's canal from inside the eye. Normally, this fluid would then go into these vessels to be absorbed by the body. Instead, with these vessels now hypertrophied, it becomes harder for the fluid to escape the eye and IOP rises.
- Adulthood: Primary open angle glaucoma is more likely to occur in adults with SWS than those in the general population.

Q. What percentage of children with port wine marks on their faces develop glaucoma?
A. It is estimated that approximately 50 percent of patients with SWS get glaucoma. When the birthmark includes the eyelids, the risk of glaucoma increases. This is especially true when the upper eyelid is affected.

Q. If laser treatments are used to reduce the port wine mark on my child's face, will they cause glaucoma or worsen the glaucoma that already exists?
A. Laser treatments to the skin around the eye or eyelid have no effect on the eye and do not increase the chances of developing glaucoma or exacerbate glaucoma that already exists.

Q. What research has been done to develop innovative treatments for glaucoma in patients with SWS?
A. Efforts have been made to develop drugs to relax the episcleral veins so that they are less resistant to accepting the fluid draining out of the eye, causing the pressure to go down. Unfortunately, although eyedrops which are known to relax blood vessels have been tried, these eyedrops turned out to have too many side effects on the rest of the body. Research centers and drug companies are working on alternative drugs that might be able to treat the eye with fewer or more acceptable side effects. As SWS is rare, there is less financial incentive for companies to pursue these treatments because only a relatively small population of patients would actually benefit.

Q. If my child has Sturge-Weber syndrome affecting both sides of the face and brain but glaucoma is in only one eye, will he/she develop glaucoma in the other eye?
A. The risk for glaucoma in children with SWS is depends on the distribution of the port wine mark and also whether or not abnormal blood vessels are present inside the eye (choroidal hemangioma). If the birthmark involves the eyelids, especially the upper lid, the risk of glaucoma is higher. If there is a choroidal hemangioma, the risk for glaucoma is also higher. If both eyes have equal risk factors for glaucoma and one eye develops it, the other eye is more likely to develop it. If a port wine mark covers the eyelid and choroidal hemangioma is present on one side, but there is no port wine mark involving the eyelid and no choroidal hemangioma on the other side, then the risk for glaucoma in the second eye would still be low.

Q. If my child has epilepsy, will his/her seizures make the glaucoma worse?

A. The term seizure refers to abnormal, uncontrolled electrical activity in the brain that may manifest as fits or convulsions that cause body parts to shake uncontrollably. Seizures are caused by disorders of the brain, such as tumors or epilepsy. The cause of the epilepsy may be known or unexplained. Seizures do not cause glaucoma, nor does glaucoma cause them. Seizures, regardless of the cause, do not affect chronic eye pressure and do not worsen glaucoma.

Q. Will seizure surgery affect glaucoma?

A. Brain surgery for seizures has no effect on glaucoma, though it can have an effect on vision. The eye sends its vision messages to the brain through visual pathways that end up in the back areas (*occipital lobes*) of the brain. Some seizure surgery may interrupt the vision pathways and cause parts of the vision to disappear permanently. This loss of vision is called a *visual field defect*. If a patient's visual field has already been compromised due to glaucoma, additional vision loss from seizure surgery can be quite disabling.

Q. Is there anything special I should know about using medications to treat Sturge-Weber syndrome?

A. Part of the Sturge-Weber syndrome involves an overabundance of blood vessels on the membranes that cover the brain (*meninges*). Brimonidine and, to a lesser extent, apraclonidine can leak through blood vessels into the brain, causing children to become drowsy. These drugs (alpha-agonists) should be used with caution in children of any age with Sturge-Weber syndrome, particularly when the brain is involved, to avoid side effects.

Q. Are there any special considerations in the surgical treatment of Sturge-Weber glaucoma?

A. Many Sturge-Weber syndrome patients have abnormal blood vessels underneath the retina, between the retina and the sclera. This layer of the eye is called the choroid. Although the choroid is normally very vascular, in Sturge-Weber there may be excess or abnormal blood vessels (choroidal hemangioma). These blood vessels are prone to leakage or rupture if the pressure in the eye becomes too low. Special care must be taken to prevent this from happening, as the complications may lead to retinal detachment or blindness.

In addition, there can be excess blood in the drainage canal of the eye (Schlemm's canal), behind the trabecular meshwork. This excess blood may cause bleeding during goniotomy, though it can also serve as a landmark to make the Schlemm's canal more visible during trabeculotomy or goniotomy.

The surgeon may also encounter excess blood vessels on the outer surface of the eye attached to the sclera (episcleral veins). Bleeding from these vessels can be prevented or stopped by using *electric cautery* to help close the blood vessels.

Q. What research is being done on Sturge-Weber syndrome?

A. In 2013, it was discovered that a localized gene defect causes the port wine facial mark and additional blood vessels in the eye. Identification of this gene abnormality may allow for localized gene therapy. New surgical and pharmaceutical techniques are also being investigated.

F. TREATING GLAUCOMA

Q. What are the goals in treating glaucoma?
A. Glaucoma is a very complex disease and there are many forms. The goal of glaucoma treatment is to a) open the drain with surgery or medication, b) create a new drain surgically, or c) reduce the flow of fluid production with medication or surgery. By allowing a better balance between fluid production and drainage, the intent is to lower the eye pressure to a level that is no longer injurious to the optic nerve.

Q. When should one start treating glaucoma?
A. It is imperative that glaucoma be treated as soon as the diagnosis is made. Untreated glaucoma will lead to the degeneration and death of nerve fibers in the retina, depleting the optic nerve of its ability to send visual messages to the brain. Untreated glaucoma leads to blindness.

Q. How does the level of pressure impact the course of treatment?
A. In general, the range of normal intraocular pressure is considered to be 10 to 20. Some individuals have a normal pressure in the low 20s without suffering any damage to the optic nerve. This condition is called ocular hypertension. No treatment may be necessary, though continued screening may be advised. Other individuals will experience progressive optic nerve damage even with pressures less than 20. An optic nerve that is already damaged, perhaps after years of glaucoma, is more susceptible to further damage from a lower level of pressure than an optic nerve in an eye that has never had glaucoma. Therefore, each patient's level of pressure must be evaluated individually.

Q. If the pressure is treated, will the glaucoma still damage the sight?
A. Uncontrolled elevation of the pressure in the eye kills the optic nerve, which sends the messages of vision from the eye to the brain. If the intraocular pressure is successfully controlled, as occurs in the majority of cases through medications or surgery, then this damage can be greatly delayed, if not prevented.

Q. Can eye pressure be too low?
A. Yes. Sometimes after many surgeries or after an eye has had glaucoma for a long time, the eye stops making enough fluid (aqueous humor) to keep it full and of normal size. When this happens, the ophthalmologist usually tries to stimulate the eye to make fluid by taking one or more of the following actions:

- Stopping any medications, such as the usual eyedrops for glaucoma, which may be decreasing the eye's fluid production;
- Adding a steroid medication (usually eyedrops, but sometimes as an injection around the eye or a short course of oral medication) to try to decrease any inflammation around the part inside the eye that makes the fluid (ciliary body);
- Injecting a viscous material into the eye to refill it to a higher pressure in an attempt to jump-start fluid production; or
- Using an eyedrop (ibopamine) that may increase fluid production in the eye.

Other possible causes of low IOP include tears or breaks in the retina and excessive drainage of fluid after surgery. Retinal tears or breaks should be repaired, if possible. A second surgery to tie a tube shut may be helpful in cases where excessive fluid is draining.

Each case of low intraocular pressure is very different. It is very important to discuss your child's particular case with his/her doctor to decide what course of action is best. Unfortunately, if none of the above courses of action work, there is little that can be done to replace the fluid-producing capability of the eye.

Q. Would vision therapy benefit a child who has glaucoma?

A. There is no evidence that suggests vision therapy would be of benefit in controlling any variety of glaucoma. The American Academy of Pediatrics, American Academy of Ophthalmology, and the American Association of Pediatric Ophthalmology and Strabismus have issued a joint statement regarding vision therapy. It can be found on the websites of each of these organizations.

Q. At what age will my child no longer be treated by a children's hospital?

A. The answer to this question will vary by hospital, state or province, and country. Some places stop treating children at 16 years old, while others wait until 18 years old. Some physicians or hospitals have later cutoffs. When there is no eye doctor in the community familiar with treating adults who have graduated from childhood to adult glaucoma, the childhood experts may continue to treat the adult. Adults with mental retardation and glaucoma may also be under the care of pediatric glaucoma specialists because they are developmentally more like children than adults. Some children's hospitals even have special provisions to allow for developmentally delayed adults to be admitted for care.

The transition from childhood to adult care is becoming a particularly important issue. Many more children are retaining their vision and maintaining good control of their glaucoma into adulthood than did so previously. As a result, there is a growing population of adults who have a history of childhood glaucoma, and there may not be adult glaucoma specialists available with the appropriate knowledge to continue their care. Similar problems exist for the care of adults who have survived other childhood problems, such as congenital heart disease and cystic fibrosis, which were once uniformly fatal in childhood.

In places with an upper age limit for treatment, it may be advisable for your child's care to be transferred to an adult glaucoma specialist a year or two before he/she reaches the threshold age. Early transfer will allow for an overlap period during which the adult specialist can call upon the pediatric specialist if your child still needs consultation and care that the adult specialist cannot provide.

Q. Will my child's treatment vary with age or is it just dependent on his/her condition?

A. Both age and the type of glaucoma are important factors in deciding on a course of treatment. For example, in Sturge-Weber syndrome, the approach to glaucoma varies with age because the cause of the glaucoma also varies with age. The treatment must be adjusted to match the mechanism. Regardless of the cause of the glaucoma, it is also possible that a treatment that controlled your child's glaucoma when he/she was younger will become less effective as he/she gets older. As a result, different or additional medications, or even surgery, become necessary.

Psychosocial factors also play a role. In young children, every examination may require an anesthetic or sedation. As a result, several drugs may be added at a time, rather than the more standard method of altering treatment, where one drug is added at a time and the patient returns for an assessment of his/her pressure response. The degree of cooperation and tolerance of treatment are also important factors that vary with the age of the patient.

The side effects of certain drugs also vary with the age of the patient. For example, the anti-glaucoma drug brimonidine can cause severe side effects in an infant, while only causing sleepiness in an older child and no side effects at all in a teenager or adult.

Q. If other members of my family were successfully or unsuccessfully treated for glaucoma in a certain way, will my child have the same responses to the same treatment?
A. No, your child may or may not respond to that same treatment.

G. GLAUCOMA MEDICATIONS

1. GENERAL QUESTIONS ABOUT GLAUCOMA MEDICINES

Q. What drugs are commonly used to treat glaucoma?
A. There are five major classes or types of drugs (shown in Table 3, in no particular order) available to treat glaucoma by lowering IOP.

Table 3: Medications Commonly Used to Reduce Intraocular Pressure Due to Glaucoma			
Category	**Action**	**Administration Method**	**Examples**
Carbonic anhydrase inhibitor	Decreases the amount of fluid the eye makes	Oral (pill or liquid)	Acetazolamide Methazolamide
		Eyedrop	Dorzolamide Brinzolamide
Miotic	Increases the outflow of fluid through the trabecular meshwork	Eyedrop	Pilocarpine Echothiphate iodide Phospholine iodide
Alpha-agonist	Decreases the amount of fluid the eye makes, increases the outflow of fluid through the trabecular meshwork	Eyedrop	Brimonidine Apraclonidine
Beta-blocker	Decreases the amount of fluid the eye makes	Eyedrop	Timolol Levobunolol Carteolol Betaxolol
Prostaglandin analogue (acts like a prosta-glandin)	Increases the outflow of fluid through the trabecular meshwork	Eyedrop	Latanoprost Bimatoprost Travoprost Unoprostone

Q. Why do the eyedrop bottles have different colored caps?
A. In the United States and Canada, the color-coding of eyedrop bottles helps to identify the contents of the bottles. This specific color coding scheme may not be applicable in other countries.

Table 4: Color Coding of Eyedrop Bottle Caps		
Cap Color	**Medication Type**	**Examples**
Red	Mydriatic (pupil dilating)	Atropine Homatropine Scopolamine Cyclopentolate Tropicamide Phenylephrine
Green	Miotic (pupil constricting)	Pilocarpine
Purple	Alpha-agonist	Brimonidine
Yellow	Beta-blocker	Timolol Betaxolol Levobunolol
Teal or aqua	Prostaglandin analogue	Latanoprost Bimatoprost Travoprost

The colors of the caps of other types of drops are more variable. This system is useful in communications between the patient or parent and the doctor because the color of the bottle cap will often identify the type of medication without the full name being necessary. In spite of this, it is still strongly recommended that you either memorize the names of your child's medications or bring them to each doctor visit.

Q. What are preservative-free eye drops?

A. In general, eye drops are made with preservatives so that the drops can be safely stored longer and bottles can be used multiple times. Some children develop red eye, pain, or other side effects from the preservatives. By switching to a preservative-free preparation, the patient can receive the medical benefit of the drop without the side effects from the preservatives.

Preservative-free drops tend to be more expensive and come in small vials that only allow for a few doses per vial. (Technically, only one dose per vial is recommended.) If your child appears to be experiencing eye side effects from the drops, talk to his/her doctor about the possibility of using preservative-free eye drops instead. Preservative-free drops may also have an advantage in that they may be less toxic to the cornea in eyes prone to corneal problems, such as those with aniridia or corneal edema.

Q. What are generic eye drops?

A. When any medication initially comes into the market, it is manufactured by a drug company and receives a proprietary (or brand) name given by that company. After some years, the patent on a given drug expires and the drug becomes available in a generic (unbranded) form under the name of the active ingredient in the drop. For example, timolol, the generic name for a glaucoma drop, also has the brand name Timoptic®.

Generic medications tend to be less expensive than the brand-named versions. Some insurance companies will not pay for the proprietary formulation and will only cover generic medications.

One concern is whether the quality of generic drugs is the same as the proprietary forms. Studies of a variety of medications have shown that the generic medications sometimes are not as effective as the proprietary formulations. If a generic medication does not seem to be working as well as one might expect, consideration can be given to switching to a proprietary form of the same drug.

Q. Do eye medications hurt or sting?
A. Yes, most eyedrops or ointments hurt or sting at least a small amount. Some hurt or sting more than others. Ointments tend to sting less than drops. The drops designed to dilate the pupil, (such as atropine, cyclopentolate, and phenylephrine) tend to sting quite a bit. Tell your child to count to ten after the eyedrops are administered, and eventually the sting will go away.

In the office, the eye doctor may also administer a numbing eyedrop to blunt the pain of subsequent drops. These numbing eyedrops (topical anesthetics) are not prescribed for use at home because administering them too often causes damage to the cornea.

Q. Do drops always work to control glaucoma and are they always needed?
A. Some children will have glaucoma that is not controllable with medications and will instead require surgery. After most glaucoma operations, there is about a 50/50 chance that the child will be able to go without pressure controlling eyedrops for an extended period of time, though there may be eyedrops related to the healing process that are used for a short time immediately after the surgery. The pressure lowering effect of surgery currently available may not last forever, which means that the elevated eye pressure from glaucoma can return. If it does, the child will either have to start using pressure controlling medications again or receive further operations. With research progressing so rapidly, it is certainly possible that a cure will be found in the near future.

Q. How long will my child have to use eyedrops?
A. Patients with glaucoma need to keep using their eyedrops until their doctors specifically tell them to stop. Be sure to call your pharmacy for refills before the medication runs out. If there are no refills left on the prescription, call the doctor's office well in advance. This will allow time for a refill prescription to be submitted to the pharmacy. Do not wait until your next appointment with the doctor, as the medication may run out before then.

Q. Will there be a time when medications will no longer work?
A. Some drugs exhibit a phenomenon called tachyphylaxis. This means that a medication that initially worked, perhaps for weeks, months, or even years, eventually loses its effectiveness. One drug that characteristically has this problem is apraclonidine, but this phenomenon may be seen with other drugs as well. In some patients, none of the known anti-glaucoma drugs will be sufficient to control the eye pressure and prevent optic nerve damage. In these cases, surgery and other approaches must be considered.

Q. Are there any long-term side effects from drops?
A. The majority of glaucoma eyedrops do not have any known long-term side effects in children, although they may in adults. There are a few exceptions. Long-term use of pilocarpine may result in a permanently small pupil. The prostaglandin-like drugs, such as latanoprost, tend to increase the thickness and length of the eyelashes. They also occasionally cause a darkening of the skin around the eye(s) receiving the drops or, rarely, darkening of eye color, especially for hazel or light brown eyes.

Q. Why has my child's doctor prescribed steroids to treat his/her glaucoma?
A. While there is a risk of steroids causing glaucoma, they are sometimes needed to treat the condition causing it. In general, steroids suppress inflammation. If inflammation is causing the glaucoma, as in iritis, steroids or steroid equivalents are a necessary part of the treatment. Steroids are sometimes used after trauma or surgery for the same reason.

Q. If my child has two or more types of drops, how far apart should they be used?
A. It is recommended that at least five minutes elapse between eyedrops so that one drop does not wash out the other. This tends to be very impractical with children, particularly if they are using multiple medications. Some parents choose to wait one minute or less between drops. The failure to wait between eyedrops may decrease the effect of the drugs. This possibility must be weighed against the inconvenience to both the child and parent.

Q. If a child needs medications three times daily, how far apart should they be spaced?
A. Medications may be prescribed according to a strict time schedule (for example, every eight hours) or in more general terms (such as three times daily).

When the hour format is used, the doctor usually intends for the medication to be given according to that strict schedule. There are rare occasions when eyedrops are given throughout the night. The majority of the time, the child does not need to be awakened. If you have questions about which is meant, clarify it with your child's doctor.

When a drop is prescribed three times daily, it generally means it should be administered in the morning, afternoon, and evening. Four times daily would mean it should be administered near breakfast, lunch, dinner and bedtime. Twice daily would mean morning and evening. These schedules do not respect strict hourly intervals, but rather a general spacing out of the medication, so that the required number of drops is given over a relatively even period of time while the child is awake.

Q. Why must the drops be put in at regular times?
A. Each eyedrop is effective for a limited amount of time once a dose is administered. This is called the *half-life*. Eyedrops are prescribed to be taken at specific intervals based upon the known half-life for that drug. By using drops at the interval prescribed for that particular medication, a constant therapeutic level of the drug is maintained within the eye. If the drops are not administered at regular intervals, then the effectiveness drops below the appropriate level, and it becomes possible to lose control of the glaucoma.

Q. If my child is using both eye ointment and drops, does the order in which they are used matter?
A. Ointments should always be administered after drops. If the ointment is put in first, the drops will simply bounce off the ointment and not be absorbed properly.

Q. Will the eyedrops change my child's vision?
A. This depends on the drops being used. Dilating eyedrops may relax the focusing muscles of the eye, causing your child's near vision to become blurry. In the world of a young child, where fine attention to detail is less important, this effect may go unnoticed. Where an adult or teenager would obviously notice the difference, an infant or toddler would not.

Pilocarpine and other drugs in that family (green bottle tops) may also cause blurring of vision, as they induce *nearsightedness* in the eye. This blurriness can be treated with glasses.

Most other eyedrops do not blur vision. Eye ointments also cause temporary blurring of vision until the ointment dissolves onto the surface of the eye.

Q. How many drops should go into my child's eye per dose?
A. One drop per dose is all that is necessary. There is more than enough medicine in one drop to fill the area around the eye, so even if only a little goes in, it is enough. In fact, the eye can only use about 20 percent of a drop. Most of each drop will run down the cheek or go down the tear duct system into the nose.

Q. If a drop was missed at the last interval, will administering an extra drop the next time help?
A. No. The dose for all eyedrops is one drop. Using two drops is simply a waste of medication, as the extra medication will not be used by the eye. If a dose is remembered late, administer the next one as soon as possible. If it is forgotten altogether, then just administer the next scheduled dose.

Q. If my child rubs his/her eyes when I am giving the drops, should I repeat the dose?
A. No. Absorption of the eyedrop starts as soon as it touches the surface of the eye. The absorption is very rapid. If a child rubs his/her eyes, the eyedrop will remain.

Q. What should I do when my child squeezes his eyes shut so that I cannot get the drops in?
A. This is a very common situation. There are several alternative methods that can be used.

The eyeball does not have to be visible to successfully deliver eyedrops. There simply needs to be a small space between the lids through which the eyedrop will seep.

Some parents choose to put the drops in only when their children are sleeping. If the drop is one that stings, the child may stir awake momentarily. He/she will generally go right back to sleep.

Another option is to lay the child on his/her back and place the drop in the depression that forms between the eye and the side of the nose. When the child opens his/her eyes, the drop will fall onto the surface of the eye.

Figure 9 illustrates a more direct method. The adult places one thumb just below the child's eyebrow, against the bone, and the other against the bone underneath the lower eyelid. Firm pressure against the bone causes the muscles that close the eye to weaken enough for the lids to be pulled apart. By holding the bottle in one hand while using that thumb to open the eyelids, the adult can then place the drop in the eye or it can be administered by another person. When this technique is used, the eyelids will actually invert so the pink inner surface (conjunctiva) becomes visible. The eyedrops can be placed directly onto this surface and they will still be absorbed as readily as if they were placed on the eye.

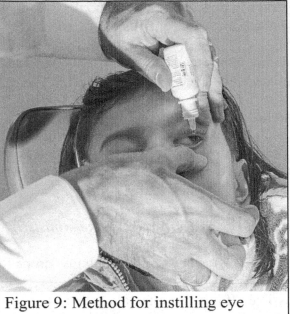

Figure 9: Method for instilling eye drops. The doctor is putting pressure on the bones above and below the eye to help pull the eyelids apart so that the drop can be instilled.

Q. How do I determine the right amount of ointment to use and how do I get it in my child's eye?
A. There is no specific dose for eye ointments. In general, a strip approximately half an inch (one centimeter) wide is considered adequate.

The ideal way to administer an ointment is for the lower lid to be pulled down so that the pink inner surface (conjunctiva) is exposed. The ointment is squeezed onto this surface. If you cannot get the lids open enough to see this surface, the ointment can be placed on the eyelashes of a closed eyelid. Some will eventually seep into the eye.

Q. How should the eyedrops or eye ointment be stored?
A. There are some eye products that should be refrigerated. In those cases, the pharmacist should provide the appropriate storage instructions when the prescription is filled. If you are unsure, ask the pharmacist for advice. Store all medications out of the reach of children and away from excess heat and direct light.

Q. How often should a new bottle of eyedrops or tube of eye ointment be obtained?
A. There is no firm rule for how often one should replace eyedrops or ointment. If there is not any written literature on the expiration date of a product, you should ask your pharmacist. Alternatively, a good rule of thumb would be to assume that the product will expire after one month if it contains a preservative to prevent contamination. Products without preservatives, such as certain contact lens solutions or preservative-free artificial tears, may not be safe to use for that long. If a drop comes in a package where single doses are in separate containers (minims), then each dosing container should be discarded after one use.

It is also wise to check medications regularly for any changes in color or the presence of foreign material. Any changes that are not expected, such as the presence of particles in a normally clear liquid, should be cause for concern and the medication should be discarded.

Q. Should the drops my child's doctor prescribed make his/her pupil bigger?
A. Mydriatic eyedrops are used sometimes to treat iritis or glaucoma. Beta-blocker anti-glaucoma drops can also cause mild pupil dilation. You should ask your child's ophthalmologist if a change in pupil size is a normal effect of the drops your child is using.

Q. Can my child wear contact lenses while using glaucoma eyedrops?
A. Silicone contact lenses and gas permeable (hard) contact lenses can be worn during eyedrop instillation. It is better to remove non-silicone soft contact lenses before administering eyedrops. They should not be reinserted until at least twenty minutes have passed after the drop has been given. Unfortunately, this may be inconvenient and time-consuming. As an alternative to removing the soft lenses, consider discussing a once- or twice-daily dosing schedule with your child's doctor. Administering the drops once or twice a day allows for them to be used in the morning before the contact lenses go in and in the evening after the contacts are removed.

Q. Can my child swim right after his/her glaucoma drops are put in?
A. Drops are absorbed almost instantly after they are inserted and will not be washed out of the eye. There is no problem swimming after the eyedrops are put in.

Q. How can I reduce the number of drops my child is taking?
A. Products exist that are combinations of two different drugs in the same bottle. If your child has been prescribed two medications that are available as combination drops, you could reduce the overall number of drops he/she has to take. For example, combination preparations are available for the combination of timolol and dorzolamide. Some insurance companies may consider these combination medications to be two medicines, and therefore charge higher co-payments.

Q. Can glaucoma drops used in one eye affect the other eye?
A. Glaucoma drops placed into one eye can cause a similar, but much weaker, response in the untreated eye. This effect is usually 10 percent or less of that seen in the eye being treated. The medication is almost always harmless to the untreated eye unless it has a very low pressure after a surgical procedure. Otherwise, there is no cause for concern about drops placed in one eye affecting the untreated eye.

Q. If my child has ectopia lentis and glaucoma, should he/she not use dilating drops at home?
A. When the pupil is dilated, the lens may more easily come forward through the pupil. Patients with ectopia lentis can have their pupils dilated under supervision in an eye doctor's office. For some patients with ectopia lentis, this can be risky and close observation is recommended. The risk of the lens coming through the pupil will differ depending on what caused the ectopia lentis and also how much the lens is out of position. Dilating drops are more likely to cause the lens to move forward through the pupil in individuals with certain disorders, such as homocystinuria (a disorder of body metabolism), or whose lens is very loose and significantly out of position.

Q. Should I tell my family doctor about the eyedrops and glaucoma if my child is ill?
A. Absolutely! Although eyedrops generally have few effects on the body, these effects may become more important when a child has other illnesses. Fortunately, most eyedrops do not have interactions with drugs given for other diseases, though there are exceptions.

Q. How can I explain why my child with glaucoma takes eyedrops to his/her sibling(s)?
A. The best way is to tell the truth in a simple, straight-forward manner. For example, you might say something like, "Your sister/brother has an eye problem called glaucoma. In glaucoma, there is too much liquid inside his/her eye. Everybody has liquid inside their eyes because their bodies make it to keep the eye healthy. Some people's eyes do not let the liquid out the way they are supposed to, so it gets stuck inside. Too much liquid inside his/her eye can hurt your brother's/sister's vision. These eyedrops help keep the amount of liquid inside his/her eye lower, so that it can live well and keep seeing. You do not need to use eyedrops because your eyes let the liquid out at the same speed that it is made."

Q. Should I use liquid or tablets for oral medication?
A. Most oral medications come in both a liquid and a tablet form. Which one is used depends on the child's ability to swallow pills or tolerate the taste of the liquid. If a child is able to use tablets, then they are a feasible alternative. Since the dosage of some medications is based on the child's weight, the calculated dose may come out to a number that is not achievable by breaking a tablet in half or into quarters. In these cases, liquid medication may be necessary. This is particularly true in very young children. If liquid medication is used, make sure to shake the bottle well before each dose.

Q. If my child cannot swallow pills, can I crush the tablet?
A. Glaucoma medicine tablets, such as acetazolamide and methazolamide, can usually be crushed and combined with food. It is recommended that a small quantity of food (approximately one tablespoon) be used to ensure that the entire amount of medication is taken. This does not apply for all medications. In particular, capsules, such as long-acting acetazolamide, should never be crushed.

Q. If my child refuses to take his/her oral medications, can they be mixed with foods or liquids? Are there any other tricks?
A. Children may object to the taste or even the smell of their oral medications. The glaucoma medication acetazolamide can be mixed in a cherry or chocolate liquid in the pharmacy. Even this may not be palatable.

The oral anti-glaucoma medications (carbonic anhydrase inhibitors) can be mixed with food or liquid. If you choose to hide an oral medication in liquid or food, it is important that you make sure the entire portion is consumed so that you are also sure the entire dose of the medication has also been consumed.

As a last resort, a liquid medication can be administered to an infant or very young child by holding the child's nose and using a dispensing syringe to squirt the dose of medication into his/her mouth. The child will have no choice but to swallow the medication so he/she can take a breath. Although this sounds cruel, it may be less harmful than putting the child through surgery, which could become necessary if medication is not taken.

Q. If my child vomits after taking the oral glaucoma medication, should I repeat the dose?
A. If your child vomits up oral glaucoma medication immediately after receiving the dose, and the amount of vomit is comparable to (or more than) the amount of medicine that was given, then it is usually safe to repeat the medication. If it appears that less than the entire dose was vomited, then repeat half the medication. After two attempts, it may not be advisable to give additional medication. This advice is specific to glaucoma medications and may not apply for other medications. Consult with your child's physician regarding instructions for other medications.

Q. How should oral medicines, such as pills or liquid suspensions, be stored?
A. General guidelines for proper storage of medicines are:

- Keep all medicine out of the reach of children.
- Store away from heat or direct light.
- Do not store capsules or tablets in the bathroom, kitchen, or other damp places. Moisture and/or heat can break down medication.
- Remove the cotton plugs from pill bottles, as they tend to draw moisture into the containers.
- Do not refrigerate medication unless you have been instructed by the pharmacist to do so.

For more specific instructions, consult with your pharmacist.

Q. Could my child go blind right away if the medicine is not used correctly?
A. Glaucoma damage from lack of medications rarely happens suddenly, unless the optic nerve is already very sick, but it is very important for your child to try to use the glaucoma medications as his/her doctor has prescribed. It is extremely unlikely that much harm will result from making a rare mistake with the schedule. On the other hand, it is quite possible that your child's eye pressure could rise higher than is safe for his/her eye if the medications are missed regularly or not administered according to the schedule that your child's doctor prescribed. It can be helpful to keep some kind of special schedule or checklist as a reminder to take the medicines properly. If you or your child have trouble keeping track of the schedule, be sure to let your child's eye doctor know. He/she may have suggestions that will be helpful.

Q. What does the expiration date on a medication mean?
A. This date refers to the time after which it is not recommended for the medication to be consumed or used because the manufacturer cannot guarantee its potency, stability, or safety after that date. Note that the medication may no longer be safe to use before the expiration date if it is not stored according to the pharmacy instructions. For example the prostaglandin-like glaucoma drugs, such as latanoprost, must be refrigerated. If they are not refrigerated, their lifespan is shortened.

Q. What does the phrase "not approved for use in children" on my child's medication mean?
A. The overwhelming majority of medications used in children, whether for the eyes or other illnesses, are "not approved for use in children." This statement simply means that research has not been done to specifically determine the medication's effects and effectiveness on children.

Drug research on children presents certain ethical challenges that are difficult to address. As a result, drug companies have largely shied away from this process. Lawmakers in the United

States have attempted to encourage drug companies to do research in children by passing legislation extending the length of company patents for those that do so. Due to this legislation, the effects of several glaucoma drops have recently been studied in children, though others have not.

Most medications are used for years on thousands of adult patients before they are prescribed to children. They are only considered safe for use in children at that point if the safety profile is acceptable in adults. In most cases, doctors will prescribe particular drugs for children after their own experience and that of their colleagues has demonstrated a certain degree of safety when used by adults. Occasionally, however, effects are noticed in children that are not experienced in adults. One example of this is sleepiness in children who take brimonidine. If you have concerns about the use of any particular drug by your child, you should discuss them with your child's doctor.

In very rare situations, a medication may be used in children when there is little history of use in adults or children. This can either be done as part of a research protocol or as "compassionate usage" with special permission by some form of oversight administration, such as an ethics committee, research committee, or hospital administration. Compassionate usage applies when the child has a life-threatening or blinding eye condition that needs immediate therapy and for which there are no other alternatives.

Q. Can children become addicted to their medications?
A. Children do not become addicted to glaucoma medications. When the ophthalmologist feels it may be safe to decrease the dosage or frequency of medications, he/she will sometimes choose to do so slowly in order to watch for any rebound effects, where eye pressure rises as the drops are discontinued.

In particular, steroid medications that have been used for more than two weeks should be tapered slowly. This is especially true for patients with iritis and patients on oral steroids. While a patient is taking oral steroids, the natural steroid hormones in the body are suppressed. These natural hormones have important functions in the maintenance of stability in the human body. If steroid medications are discontinued too rapidly, the body will not be accustomed to producing its own steroids, potentially leaving your child poorly protected against stresses such as illness or surgery. Children with iritis also may experience dramatic flare-ups of their conditions if their steroids are abruptly discontinued or tapered too rapidly.

Q. How common is it for a child to develop an allergic reaction to a glaucoma drop after being on the medication for over a year?
A. An allergy to a glaucoma drop can develop at any time after it is started, though it most frequently occurs within a few weeks to a few months after usage is begun.

An allergic reaction is generally seen as redness and itchiness in the eye being treated, sometimes including puffiness of the eyelid of that eye. Apraclonidine can cause irritation of the skin around the eye. This reaction is not uncommon for adults, though it occurs only occasionally in teenagers and almost never in younger children.

Hives are a very rare reaction to an eyedrop, and are more likely to have been caused by something else the child was exposed to. Hives are very common in children, and 95 percent of the time the environmental agent causing them is never identified.

Q. Are there any medications my child should avoid?
A. In general, there are no medications that interfere with glaucoma drops and ointments, though some eyedrops interfere with each other. One example of this is that pilocarpine and prostaglandin-like eyedrops, such as latanoprost, sometimes inhibit each other's actions.

Oral glaucoma medications, particularly carbonic anhydrase inhibitors, may interact with other systemic medications. In particular, acetazolamide should not be used in patients taking aspirin (*salicylates*), and may be dangerous in patients on seizure medications or who have problems with kidney function, electrolyte levels, and acid-base metabolism. Patients with *sickle cell disease*, heart arrhythmias, or high blood pressure should also use caution when using acetazolamide because they may experience negative side effects. Patients with allergy to sulfa medications should avoid acetazolamide and related drugs, such as methazolamide, because they may have allergic reactions to these medications as well. The possible side effects of carbonic anhydrase inhibitors are discussed in the "Carbonic Anhydrase Inhibitors" section.

Phospholine iodide, a drug rarely used in glaucoma treatment, must be discontinued at least a few days before general anesthesia, as it may cause prolongation of the effect of the muscle relaxant used for anesthesia (succinylcholine).

If your child has any underlying medical conditions or allergies, or is taking any other eye or systemic medications, notify his/her doctor.

Q. Can my child take cold and cough medications that warn against use if the user has glaucoma?
A. Many over-the-counter cough and cold preparations carry warnings on their labels instructing users not to take the medication if they have glaucoma. There are many kinds of glaucoma and only one specific form is affected by these medications: closed angle glaucoma. In this form of glaucoma, there is an abnormal anatomic relationship between the iris and the drainage angle (trabecular meshwork) of the eye. Cough and cold medications can cause further obstruction of this angle.

Fortunately, closed angle glaucoma is extraordinarily rare in children. The overwhelming majority of pediatric glaucoma patients can take these medications without any concern at all. If your child has closed angle glaucoma, your ophthalmologist may have advised you immediately about the risks of these medications. If your child has congenital glaucoma, glaucoma caused by Sturge-Weber syndrome or other syndromes, or glaucoma caused by other factors (such as steroids, injury, etc.), you can rest assured that these drugs are safe. If you have any ongoing concerns, be sure to discuss them with your child's doctor.

Q. What would happen if my child were to catch pink eye?
A. "Pink eye" is simply that: an eye in which the white is a bit pink or red in color. Pink eye is not a diagnosis. It is simply the description of the color of the eye.

When the average person refers to pink eye, he/she is generally speaking of conjunctivitis, a contagious infection of the superficial covering of the white of the eye (*conjunctiva*). The most common cause is a virus that requires no treatment, goes away on its own, and harms nothing. If other people in the house or school have it around the same time, then it is almost always simple viral conjunctivitis. It may also be associated with other mild symptoms, such as a cold with runny nose, sore throat, and fever.

Occasionally, pink eye is caused by a virus called adenovirus. This type of conjunctivitis can cause more substantial swelling of the lids and some discomfort. It is highly contagious and called epidemic keratoconjunctivitis (EKC). EKC is dreaded in eye clinics because it spreads so easily. It is more of an annoyance than a danger, although rarely the irritation to the cornea may take longer to go away than with simple viral conjunctivitis.

A less common form of pink eye is bacterial conjunctivitis. In addition to the pink color, significant amounts of pus may appear on the surface of the eye. Bacterial conjunctivitis is usually treated with antibiotic drops, though it may go away on its own, in the same manner as simple viral conjunctivitis.

Almost every child will catch some form of viral or bacterial conjunctivitis at some point in his/her life. It is important to be sure that the pink eye is not something else that may be more serious. If your child has a history of iritis, do not assume that the pink eye is an infection. It may instead be due to recurrence of the iritis.

If your child wears contact lenses, it is advisable to immediately discontinue their use until the eye is no longer red. If it takes more than 24 hours for the eye to normalize, or it is getting worse even with the contact lens out, see the eye doctor immediately. Be sure to put the contacts through their usual cleaning regimen to kill the virus or bacteria before your child uses them again. This will help prevent reinfection after the conjunctivitis is resolved.

If your child has a glaucoma tube or trabeculectomy or has had eye surgery within the past week and develops pink eye, it is important to let his/her eye surgeon know promptly, to make sure nothing more serious is going on that could also cause a pink-colored eye. When in doubt, contact the doctor.

Q. Are the medications used to treat glaucoma in congenital rubella syndrome different than those used to treat glaucoma caused in other ways?
A. Glaucoma due to congenital rubella syndrome may have several mechanisms, including inflammation, cataract surgery, and underdevelopment of the trabecular meshwork. Treatment will vary with the mechanism.

Q. What can I do if I cannot afford the medications?
A. This is a major problem in many countries throughout the world. In some countries, insurance may be available that will help cover the cost of medications. If no insurance plan is available or affordable, then you should certainly seek assistance.

The first step is to inform your child's doctor. He/she may be able to provide you with free samples obtained directly from the drug company. Some drug companies also accept direct contact from patients who need financial assistance to obtain their medications. Alternatively, your child's doctor may be aware of granting agencies, have contacts with hospital social workers or other individuals who can provide charity support, or know where to find alternate sources of funding. Your city, county, or state/province may have agencies that can assist you. Some patients have even approached their elected representatives in the government for assistance.

2. BETA-BLOCKERS

Q. What are beta-blockers?

A. Beta-blockers, also known as beta-antagonists, are drugs that lower eye pressure by reducing the production of fluid (aqueous humor) inside the eye. This fluid is produced by tissue called the *ciliary epithelium*, which coats the ciliary body. Beta-antagonists work by either affecting the blood vessels that supply the ciliary body or directly slowing down the specific cells in the ciliary body that make the fluid. There are two types of beta-antagonists: beta-1- and beta-2-blockers.

Our bodies produce chemicals, like adrenaline, that serve natural functions. They work by stimulating various cells to act in specific ways. They do so by attaching to special sites on the cell surface called receptors. Beta-2 receptors are found in the ciliary body of the eye, as well as the heart, lungs, and many other organs. Beta-1 receptors are found in the ciliary body, but not in the lungs or heart. Beta-blockers work by stopping these receptors from being able to interact with the natural body chemicals.

Betaxolol works to block mainly beta-1 receptors. As a result, lung side effects are extremely rare. Unfortunately, it is also only about 50 to 85 percent as effective as timolol or levobunolol for lowering eye pressure. Betaxolol is often used in patients who have lung diseases, such as asthma. Timolol and levobunolol are nonselective, working on both beta-1 and beta-2 receptors. Children with asthma or arrhythmia are more likely to experience side effects if timolol or levobunolol are used.

Beta-blockers are usually given twice daily, but once daily may be enough to be effective for some patients. Gel forms of timolol are also available for once-daily use. Beta-2-blockers are generally more effective in lowering eye pressure than beta-1-blockers.

Both timolol and levobunolol come in 0.25 percent and 0.5 percent strengths. The lower concentration is estimated to be about 75 percent as effective as the 0.5 percent form. This makes it more suitable for use by children under the age of 1, as the lower concentration decreases the likelihood of side effects.

Q. What are the possible side effects of beta-blockers?

A. Beta-antagonists are very effective in lowering eye pressure. They are used by many doctors as the first line of treatment against glaucoma because the success rate is high and side effects are very uncommon. The various beta-blockers are available as generic formulations, which tends to make them relatively inexpensive. Beta-blockers generally have very few side effects on the eye itself, though they may occasionally cause stinging or itching.

Timolol and levobunolol can uncommonly cause side effects in the lungs, such as wheezing or coughing, and may also cause slowing of the heart. They may also very rarely produce behavioral changes, such as restlessness or lethargy. These complications are much less common with betaxolol.

3. PROSTAGLANDIN-LIKE DRUGS

Q. What makes the prostaglandin-like drugs different from other glaucoma medications?
A. All four of the drugs in this class are chemically related to naturally occurring substances in the body called prostaglandins. There are many prostaglandins made in the human body, having a variety of different functions. In the eye, increased levels of some prostaglandins can boost the flow of fluid out of the eye, lowering eye pressure. Prostaglandin-like drugs, called prostaglandin analogues, are similar to natural prostaglandins and have this same effect on the eye. Latanoprost was the first drug in this class that was available for glaucoma treatment. It and similar drugs, such as travoprost and bimatoprost, lower the eye pressure primarily by allowing the aqueous humor to get out of the eye through an alternate route, called the *uveoscleral pathway.*

These medications are very easy to use. They only need to be taken once daily, at bedtime. Prostaglandin analogues can also be used with most of the other commonly used glaucoma medications. There is some data to suggest that it may not be wise to use them together with the miotic drugs, such as pilocarpine, because the two medications may counteract the other to some degree.

Although the use of the prostaglandin analogues often significantly reduces eye pressure in adults, many children do not seem to respond as well. Prostaglandin-like drugs seem to be most effective for lowering the eye pressure in children with juvenile open angle glaucoma. They are often not as effective in lowering pressure for children with other types of glaucoma, such as congenital or aphakic glaucoma. When they do work in children, reduction in eye pressure can be quite substantial.

Though there are only subtle differences between the different prostaglandin-like drugs, occasionally one may produce significantly better results for a particular child than the others. Prostaglandin analogues tend to be more expensive than other drugs, but they will all be available as generics (not brand named) in the not too distant future. This will reduce their cost. Latanoprost is currently available as a generic drug.

Q. How safe are the prostaglandin-like drugs?
A. In general, the prostaglandin drugs are quite safe to use. Few systemic (involving the whole body) side effects have been reported. Specific caution is recommended in patients with iritis and aphakia. Studies of the prostaglandin-like drugs in adult eyes have shown rare problems, such as an increase in inflammation and swelling in the retina and choroid in the back of the eye, in patients with these particular diagnoses. These side effects appear to be rare in children.

Prostaglandin analogues may cause cosmetic side effects. Some patients experience significant thickening and lengthening of their eyelashes and, less frequently, a slight darkening of the skin around the eye(s) being treated. Some adult patients, especially those with blue or hazel eyes, experience a browning or darkening of the iris although this seems to be less common in children. While these side effects may be cosmetically unacceptable to patients only using the drops in one eye because of the asymmetric appearance that can result, they do not appear to have any harmful effect on vision or eyes.

Prostaglandin analogues may also cause a temporary reddening of the white of the eye (conjunctival hyperemia), which also has no effect on vision. This change may be more prevalent and prominent in patients with Sturge-Weber syndrome, as they often have a preexisting prominence of blood vessels over the white of the eye.

4. ALPHA-AGONISTS

Q. What are alpha-agonists?
A. Alpha-agonists are a type of drug that stimulates receptors that control the contraction of certain involuntary muscles.

Brimonidine and apraclonidine are both alpha-agonists that are dispensed as eyedrops. The eye has many different types of cells that are involved with the various aspects of eye function. Certain cells are responsible for making the fluid that fills the eye (aqueous humor). Others are responsible for facilitating the continuous drainage of that fluid out of the eye. Blood vessels also play a role. Tiny sensors in the blood vessel walls that have special control mechanisms, called alpha receptors, govern the functioning of some cells and vessels. Brimonidine and apraclonidine are agonists, or stimulators, of these receptors. As a result, alpha-agonists lower eye pressure by both lowering the amount of fluid produced inside the eye and making it easier for fluid to drain out into the blood vessels. Brimonidine is usually given twice daily.

The standard formulation of brimonidine is generally 0.15 or 0.2 percent. A lower concentration, 0.1 percent, is also available. The 0.1 percent formulation uses a different preservative than standard brimonidine, has fewer side effects, and may be just as effective in lowering intraocular pressure. Several formulations of brimonidine are now available as generic preparations.

Apraclonidine is available as a 0.5 percent concentration. There is also a 1 percent strength that comes in small dropper packets, and is sometimes used during and after glaucoma laser procedure in adults or before and after goniotomy, particularly in children with iritis.

Q. What are the possible side effects of the alpha-agonists?
A. The different alpha-agonists may produce different side effects. Brimonidine occasionally causes eye redness, burning, or stinging. Some children may experience sleepiness after taking the eyedrops. This is particularly common in children under the age of 5 and those of any age with Sturge-Weber syndrome, especially if they have brain blood vessel abnormalities.

In infants, a single drop can cause irregular breathing (apnea), low blood pressure, low body temperature, and low heart rate. Although these symptoms will go away as the drop wears off, they can be so severe that the child must be admitted to an intensive care unit. As a result, brimonidine should not be used in infants. Although it is extremely unlikely that a child more than 3 months old will suffer these severe side effects, many pediatric glaucoma doctors feel that the drug should not be used in children under 6 months old, or perhaps even under the age of 3 years old.

Body weight, rather than age, should be the determining factor when deciding whether or not to use brimonidine. Although there is no strict cutoff, older children whose body weights are closer to those of children who are less than 3 years old, such as children with stunted growth or who are inherently smaller than the average, may also be at risk. When used in the right age groups and without side effects, brimonidine can be a very potent therapy against glaucoma.

Unlike brimonidine, apraclonidine has the advantage of not being absorbed as much into the brain tissues (also called crossing the blood/brain barrier). As a result, the sleepiness and more severe side effects sometimes seen with brimonidine appear much less frequently. The anti-glaucoma effect of apraclonidine may reduce over time (tachyphylaxis), resulting in less control of the glaucoma. This does not happen as often with brimonidine.

Use of apraclonidine and, to a lesser extent, brimonidine can result in an allergic reaction in which the eye becomes red, the eyelid swells, the skin of the lids becomes inflamed, and there may be itching, tearing, or discomfort. This reaction is much more common in adults than children and more common in teenagers than younger children.

5. MIOTICS

Q. What are miotics?
A. Miotics are medications that cause the pupil of the eye to contract. They are used in glaucoma treatment to increase the drainage rate of the aqueous humor. Miotics have a direct effect on the *ciliary muscle* inside the eye. The ciliary muscle forms a ring around the lens and causes the lens to change its shape when focusing on near or far objects. When the muscle is contracted, it also causes the trabecular meshwork to open up, allowing fluid to escape from the eye more easily and lowering the eye pressure. Pilocarpine and phospholine iodide are both miotics, but the latter is rarely used to treat glaucoma.

Pilocarpine is a plant-based drug. Natives of the Amazon found that eating the plant it comes from caused drooling, sweating, and urination. They used it as a medicine for flushing poisons from the body. European chroniclers describe its use as a medicine as early as the 17th century in Brazil. It has been used in the treatment of adult glaucoma for over 100 years, and has also been used in the treatment of childhood glaucoma for many years.

When pilocarpine is applied directly to the surface of the eye, it very rarely affects other parts of the body, such as glands or muscles. Pilocarpine comes in a droplet form of varying strengths, including 0.5, 1, 2, 4, and 6 percent. It may also be available as a longer acting gel. Starting with a 1 percent concentration and slowly increasing the strength over time may limit any unpleasant side effects.

Pilocarpine drops are usually prescribed four times a day because the drop effect is reduced after approximately four to six hours. The gel form stays in the eye longer and may be used less frequently. Compared to other glaucoma drugs, pilocarpine also has the advantage of being readily available and relatively inexpensive.

Q. What are the possible side effects of pilocarpine?
A. Pilocarpine is generally a very safe drug, though children sometimes experience uncomfortable side effects. The contraction of the ciliary muscle, which is much stronger in children than adults, can produce an aching sensation, usually felt above the eyes or in the forehead. Children may complain of headache, which often subsides after the first few days of pilocarpine use.

Pilocarpine's effect on the ciliary muscle can also keep the lens of the eye focused for near objects, blurring distance vision. Glasses can sometimes successfully correct the blurriness.

Pilocarpine also causes the pupil to be smaller. Although this can sometimes cause troubling side effects for adults, it is rarely a problem for children. Other side effects are extremely uncommon.

Pilocarpine may worsen some forms of childhood glaucoma, such as that associated with a loose, small (microspherophakia), or dislocated lens (ectopia lentis). It may be particularly effective in treating other forms of childhood glaucoma, such as in some cases of Sturge-Weber syndrome. Your child's eye doctor will help you understand what role this drug should play in treating his/her particular form of glaucoma.

6. CARBONIC ANHYDRASE INHIBITORS

Q. What are carbonic anhydrase inhibitors?
A. The body uses a special chemical (enzyme) called carbonic anhydrase to help produce the aqueous humor. Carbonic anhydrase inhibitors reduce or stop the function of this particular enzyme, reducing the amount of fluid that is made. In turn, this usually results in a reduction in eye pressure. Acetazolamide and methazolamide are oral medications in this class. Brinzolamide and dorzolamide are eyedrops. The eyedrop forms of carbonic anhydrase inhibitors are used frequently. The oral forms are usually reserved for treating glaucoma that is not completely controlled by eyedrops.

Acetazolamide and methazolamide sometimes cause significant side effects, especially in adults. As a result, they are used cautiously when prescribed for children. These drugs are prescribed according to the child's body weight, and careful attention is paid to correct dosing.

Table 5: Carbonic Anhydrase Inhibitors		
Drug	**Available forms**	**Dosing**
Acetazolamide	Liquid or pill	2 to 4 times per day
	Sustained release capsule	2 times per day
Methazolamide	Pill	2 to 3 times per day
Brinzolamide	Eyedrops	2 to 3 times per day
Dorzolamide	Eyedrops	2 to 3 times per day

When the oral medication is administered, it takes about 30 to 90 minutes for peak effect on eye pressure. Pills and liquids can be subdivided into smaller doses, making them easier for younger children to use. Unfortunately, capsules cannot be crushed or cut like tablets. As a result, they are more practical for older children. For more rapid results, acetazolamide can be given intravenously, causing the eye pressure to drop within 15 minutes.

Q. What are the possible side effects of topical carbonic anhydrase inhibitors?
A. Carbonic anhydrase inhibitors used to treat glaucoma contain a sulfa molecule. Individuals with severe allergies to sulfa should use these drugs with caution because there is a risk of allergic reactions. Otherwise, the overwhelming majority of patients who take dorzolamide have no side effects at all beyond the stinging sensation or occasional eye redness that may occur with any kind of eyedrop. Carbonic anhydrase inhibitors sometimes cause a metallic taste in the mouth, as all eyedrops are drained off the surface of the eye with an individual's tears, through a channel (nasolacrimal duct, more commonly called the tear duct). The nasolacrimal ducts empty

into the nose. Since the back of the nose is connected to the back of the mouth, liquids that drain this way can cause abnormal taste sensations. More significant side effects are very rare.

A different form of naturally produced carbonic anhydrase is also present in the cornea. There are some concerns that the carbonic anhydrase inhibitor medications used to treat glaucoma could block the function of the cornea's carbonic anhydrase enzyme and cause problems such as corneal cloudiness. As a result, some physicians believe that dorzolamide or brinzolamide should not be used in patients who already have corneal problems, such as those who have had corneal transplants. Some doctors also avoid these drops in patients with sickle cell disease or related problems with their blood hemoglobin when being used for glaucoma due to injury-induced bleeding in the eye (hyphema).

Q. What are the possible side effects of the oral carbonic anhydrase inhibitors?

A. As with the topical carbonic anhydrase inhibitors, the oral forms of these drugs contain a sulfa molecule. As a result, they should be avoided by patients with sulfa allergies. Adults and children with sickle cell disease or related problems with the hemoglobin in their blood may also react adversely to these drugs.

Adults can have serious side effects from acetazolamide and methazolamide, including a reduced number of blood cells, kidney stones, blood chemical imbalances, confusion, and depression. The main side effects experienced by children taking acetazolamide are tiredness and loss of appetite. Less commonly, children may experience diarrhea, bedwetting, more frequent urination, or tingling and numbness of hands and feet. These side effects tend to lessen with continued use. Taking the medication with food may help minimize the side effects.

Acetazolamide has safely been used in children for many years of their lives. In rare cases, a child's growth has been adversely affected. The inhibition of carbonic anhydrase can also affect the blood chemistry in the body. In particular, it may result in loss of potassium. This effect is worse in children with preexisting kidney or liver disease, or who are taking other drugs that also affect potassium levels, such as steroids, or drugs used for heart failure or hypertension. Caution and monitoring is extremely important while using carbonic anhydrase inhibitors in such children. Both acetazolamide and methazolamide are effective treatments. They have similar side effects, though these are generally milder with methazolamide.

A general principle in glaucoma therapy is to use as little medication with the least amount of risk as possible to achieve the desired eye pressure. Treatment is, therefore, almost always started with eyedrops. Oral medications are used when eyedrops alone have been unsuccessful in keeping eye pressure at the desired level. When they are called upon, however, the oral carbonic anhydrase inhibitors are very effective agents in the treatment of glaucoma.

Q. Will acetazolamide or methazolamide cause my child to wet the bed?

A. In addition to being good drugs for treating glaucoma, acetazolamide and methazolamide are also diuretics. This means that they stimulate increased production of urine. Increased frequency of urination is a common effect in children and usually has no significant medical consequences. The medication is generally given four times daily, with the last dose most commonly given before bedtime. Bedwetting (*enuresis*) that is already present may occasionally be worsened. Acetazolamide and methazolamide rarely cause new bedwetting to begin.

If bedwetting is a problem, there are a few options that you can discuss with your child's physician. The dosing pattern can be altered to three times daily by increasing each dose so that the total amount received per day remains acceptable. With this pattern, the third dose is administered at supper time, allowing time for most urination before bedtime. Another alternative is for the doctor to consider reducing the total dosage. Children are generally prescribed a total daily dose in the range of 15 to 30 milligrams per kilogram of body weight. If a child is using a high dosage within this range and experiencing bedwetting, a lower daily dose might be sufficient to control the pressure while reducing or eliminating the bedwetting.

An extended release capsule form of acetazolamide is available in some locations. It is generally taken twice daily. Unfortunately, this formulation does not come in a small enough dosage to allow its use in preadolescent children, who are most likely to have bedwetting occur.

Lastly, one might consider switching to other medications. Methazolamide has a similar effect on intraocular pressure but causes less of an effect on urination. The disadvantage of this medication is that its tablet form may be harder to break into smaller doses and a liquid form is not commonly available.

Q. Can acetazolamide or methazolamide stunt my child's growth?
A. Recent research has challenged the notion that acetazolamide causes a risk to children's growth except in those already predisposed for other reasons, but it can happen. It is not clear whether this occurs due to a decrease in appetite or chemical imbalances (*metabolic acidosis*) induced by the drug. Though the risk of this side effect appears to be low, children should have their weight and growth monitored while taking acetazolamide.

Methazolamide is not prescribed as frequently for treatment of glaucoma, so less is known about its effect on growth. Since it generally causes fewer side effects than acetazolamide, the expectation is that it would also be less likely to affect growth.

Q. Is it safe for my child to use acetazolamide liquid if I can see white stuff in the bottom of the bottle?
A. Acetazolamide is a suspension rather than a solution. This means that the medication is actually particles suspended in the liquid that appear to float around. The liquid requires quite a bit of shaking before use. Some parents use a stirring stick in the bottle to make sure that the medication is adequately dispersed. If there are particles in the bottom of the bottle, the stirring stick can be used to free them so they are once again suspended in the liquid. Even if there is no accumulation at the bottom of the bottle, shaking or stirring before use is highly recommended.

H. SURGICAL TREATMENTS FOR GLAUCOMA

Q. What surgeries are used to treat glaucoma?
A. There are several types of glaucoma surgery. The common goal of each is to reduce the eye pressure to prevent damage to the structures of the eye and worsening vision. They can be categorized as:

- *Angle surgery*: This type of surgery is performed to open the eye's natural drainage system (the angle or the trabecular meshwork) so that the fluid of the eye (aqueous humor) can leave the eye through the natural drainage route.

- *Filtration* or *drainage surgery*: This type of surgery creates a new passageway through which the fluid within the front part of the eye can drain without going through the trabecular meshwork.
- *Cycloablation* or *cyclodestruction* surgery: This type of surgery works by destroying the ciliary processes that make the fluid, decreasing the amount of fluid they produce.

Q. Which surgery is best for my child?

A. The choice of surgery is influenced by the type and severity of the glaucoma, any prior surgeries that the eye has had, how these surgeries worked, the age of the child, the personal experience and expertise of the surgeon, how healthy the child is, and how easily the child can be followed up by the surgeon. It is very important to understand that the best surgery for one child's eye at any given time may be very different from the best surgery for another child's eye, or even his/her own eye (or other eye) at a later time.

Q. Who decides which glaucoma surgery is best?

A. The decision regarding which glaucoma surgery is best for any given child's eye should be made by the family and the surgeon taking care of the child. It is important to know that there may not be just one "right" surgery for a given eye. There are often options to consider, each of which will have pros and cons. There are risks and benefits with each type of glaucoma surgery, and it is best to fully discuss these with your child's surgeon prior to making a final decision about surgery.

Q. Why would a doctor recommend surgery before using medications?

A. In pediatric glaucoma, surgery is usually only done before medical therapy in the case of isolated congenital or infantile glaucoma. In this condition, there is a mechanical obstruction to the outflow of fluid because the trabecular meshwork is incompletely formed. Medical therapy alone is unlikely to be effective in this situation. The only way to resolve the problem is to incise this area of the trabecular meshwork to allow the fluid within the eye to drain normally.

Although there has been some debate regarding the use of medical versus surgical therapy as the first line of treatment in adults, the risks and stresses of surgery tend to outweigh the potential benefits of eyedrops in most children. Some surgeons, particularly those in countries where medications may not be readily available or are too expensive, may select surgery as a more appropriate first option. Even with surgery, 50 to 60 percent of patients will still need glaucoma medications.

Q. Will surgery permanently correct the glaucoma or will it reoccur?

A. There is no surgical cure for glaucoma. Glaucoma can sometimes be controlled by surgery. Unfortunately, it can always reoccur, even after a successful surgery. In some cases, surgery may even make the glaucoma worse. One situation in which this can happen is when the surgery results in excess inflammation, driving the pressure up even higher than it was before surgery. The expected benefits of the surgery must be weighed against the risks of glaucoma damage without surgery and potential for complications from the surgery.

Q. How many operations will my child need?

A. It is impossible to predict how many operations it will take to successfully treat a child's glaucoma. It is rare for a child to require only one operation over the course of a lifetime. Most children will require more than one operation.

Q. If my child's IOP is so low that the eye appears to be shrinking, what can be done to bring the pressure back up?

A. This is a difficult situation. Sometimes, after many surgeries and after an eye has had glaucoma for a long time, it can stop making enough fluid (aqueous humor) to keep the eye full and of normal size. When this happens, the ophthalmologist usually tries to stimulate the eye to make fluid. There are a few different methods that may be attempted.

- Stopping any medications that may be decreasing the eye's fluid production, such as eyedrops or oral medication for glaucoma.
- Adding steroid medication for a time to try to decrease any inflammation around the ciliary body. Steroid medications will usually be used in the form of eyedrops, but sometimes an injection around the eye or a short course of oral medication may be a preferred option.
- Injecting a viscous material into the eye to refill it to a higher pressure in an effort to restart fluid production.
- Checking for retinal detachment, as this is a cause of low IOP that can often be repaired.
- Eyedrops that stimulate aqueous humor production may be tried, though past experiments with this process have resulted in limited success.

Each case of low pressure is very different, and it is important to discuss your child's particular case with his/her doctor(s) to decide what is best. If these courses of action do not work, unfortunately, there is little that can be done to replace the fluid producing capability of the eye. Such an eye may eventually lose all vision, shrink, and become scarred over (phthisis).

Q. Will my child still be able to wear contact lenses after glaucoma surgery?

A. Whether or not your child will still be able to wear contact lenses depends on the type of surgery and the type of contact lenses. The contours of the eye surface may have changed. There may also be concern that a contact lens might damage the surgical site. After tube surgery or trabeculectomy when mitomycin C is used, it is particularly likely that it is not advisable for contact lenses to be worn or a different fit or type of contact lens may be needed.

Q. Will the scarring from early-age surgery diminish as my child gets older?

A. There is currently no way to diminish scar tissue. Scar tissue actually has a tendency to increase with age, as tissues become tighter and thicker. New drug approaches are being researched that may reduce or prevent scar tissue formation, or even help dissolve excess scar tissue.

Q. Can my child's eye be hurt if contact lenses are used shortly after glaucoma surgery?

A. Manipulating the eye to insert a contact lens immediately after surgery can cause damage to the eye or rupture to the surgical wound. Contact lens use should generally be delayed until after healing from the surgery has been completed. Even if contact lenses can be continued, changes in their fit or size may be needed.

Some surgeries, such as trabeculectomy and implantation of glaucoma tubes, may make contact lens use either difficult or undesirable even after the eye has healed. Children who have had trabeculectomy with mitomycin treatment may experience changes in the drainage area at the surgical site that make the conjunctiva very thin. Trauma from a contact lens abutting the site can be quite dangerous and result in infection. Contact lenses may also cause damage to the surgical site for glaucoma tubes. Sometimes a larger or smaller contact can be used to allow a contact to be used after a tube so that the site of the tube is not injured by the contact lens.

I. TYPES OF GLAUCOMA SURGERY

1. GONIOTOMY

Q. What is a goniotomy?
A. Goniotomy is cutting open the drainage angle (trabecular meshwork) of the eye so that fluid can flow through this natural channel out of the eye into Schlemm's canal.

Q. How is goniotomy performed?
A. The crucial factor for successful goniotomy is to attempt to obtain a clear view of the abnormal drainage angle. In order to visualize the drainage angle, a special lens is placed on the cornea. If the cornea is too cloudy, the goniotomy will be difficult, or perhaps even impossible, to perform. It may be possible to clear the haze with short-term use of glaucoma medications or other medications that are designed specifically to clear the cornea. *Hypertonic saline* eyedrops, which have a high salt content, may be used in the operating room to further help draw fluid out of the cloudy cornea just before surgery. Another option is to scrape off the superficial layer (*epithelium*) of the cornea, as this is where the majority of the haziness generally occurs. The epithelium usually grows back within 24 hours. If the haze cannot be cleared, the surgery may also be performed using the guidance of a tiny camera, about the size of a needle, called an endoscope.

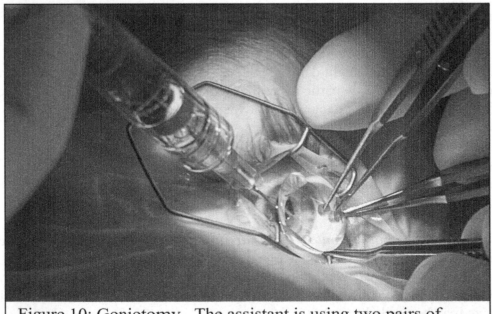

Figure 10: Goniotomy. The assistant is using two pairs of forceps to keep the eye still. The surgeon uses a pair of forceps to stabilize the lens on the eye while inserting a needle in the side of the eye to perform the procedure.

Once a good view is available, the next step is for the eye to be stabilized by the assistant using tweezers (forceps). A sharp needle or special goniotomy knife is then introduced through the cornea in front of the iris. The needle or knife is passed across the pupil and aimed at the drainage angle on the opposite side of the eye. The abnormal tissue is opened through about 120 degrees of the drainage angle. The needle or knife is then withdrawn and a patch is put on the eye. The first attempt at this operation is usually done from the side of the eye closest to the ear. If the problem is not resolved, the surgeon can return at a later date and open the rest of the angle by entering the eye on the side closest to the nose.

Q. What are the risks of the procedure?
A. There are always risks for any surgical procedure, but surgery is worthwhile if the risks are outweighed by the benefits. The surgical risks for goniotomy include complications such as:

- Failure of the procedure: If the procedure fails, the rest of the angle that was not opened the first time can sometimes be treated with goniotomy to achieve enough drainage to control the glaucoma. Alternatively, a different type of glaucoma surgery may be chosen.
- Bleeding: This occurs in approximately 50 percent of cases, but usually resolves itself in one to two days.
- Damage to the lens: The lens is located behind the pupil. The goniotomy needle or knife must pass over the pupil to perform the procedure. If the needle or knife touches the lens, the injury can result in the formation of a cataract. If a cataract forms, additional surgery to remove it may or may not be required at a later time, depending on its size. This is an unusual complication.
- Damage to the iris: Similarly, the iris can be cut. This is usually a much less significant complication than damage to the lens.
- Pupil changes: Sometimes the pupil is no longer round and centered after the procedure. It may have a teardrop shape pointing to where the surgeon entered the eye.
- Overdrainage: If the surgeon's cut is not exactly in the right place, fluid can flow beneath the trabecular meshwork into the space between the sclera and choroid (suprachoroidal space). This can cause pressure which is too low.
- Infection: It is possible for an infection to be introduced into the eye during surgery. This is a very rare complication.
- Loss of vision: Vision loss due to goniotomy very rarely occurs, but is a risk of any eye surgery.

All surgery involves the potential for complications, and every surgeon experiences them. When something goes wrong, it does not necessarily mean that the surgeon made an error. There are many factors that affect the probability that complications will occur.

Q. Will my child need drops after the operation?
A. Yes. Steroid drops are used to dampen down the body's wound healing response. When a cut is made anywhere on the body, the edges heal together. The success of the goniotomy depends on the slit made by the needle or knife remaining open. Steroids help prevent the body's healing response from sealing this opening. Your child will also be placed on antibiotic eyedrops to prevent infection.

Apraclonidine or, in older children, brimonidine is sometimes used immediately before and after surgery to prevent bleeding. Excessive bleeding is most commonly seen in children with iritis, as they tend to bleed more from goniotomy than children with other types of glaucoma.

After virtually every form of glaucoma surgery, there is an approximately 50 to 60 percent chance that the child will still need to use some glaucoma medicines to help control the glaucoma.

Q. Why would my child be prescribed atropine after one goniotomy and pilocarpine after another?
A. Medical research has yet to show us whether it is better to artificially dilate, as with atropine drops, or constrict, as with pilocarpine drops, the pupil after goniotomy, or to do neither.

The theory supporting dilation is that the dilating drops also push the iris backward, away from the area where the knife or needle has cut open the trabecular meshwork. Those who disagree worry about the iris bunching up and blocking the surgery site.

Other medical professionals believe that pupil constriction will pull the iris away from the surgical site. Opponents recognize that eyedrops which constrict the pupil also move it forward, which may inadvertently block the surgery site.

Those physicians who have not been convinced by either camp let the pupil assume its natural shape after surgery, without the influence of specific eyedrops.

Q. What is Trabectome® surgery?
A. The Trabectome® is an automated device that opens the natural drain of the eye in a manner very similar to the way goniotomy is performed. Trabectome® was popularized only recently and some believe that the added expense for use of the equipment to do the same thing that can be done more simply with a needle or a knife (goniotomy) may make it difficult to justify. The risks and postoperative medications are very much the same as in goniotomy. This procedure has not been well studied in children.

2. TRABECULOTOMY

Q. What is a trabeculotomy?
A. Trabeculotomy, like goniotomy, is an operation designed to allow fluid to flow out from the eye by opening its natural drain (trabecular meshwork). While goniotomy achieves this by opening the drain from the inside of the eye, trabeculotomy approaches the problem from outside to inside.

Trabeculotomy surgery starts by opening the covering tissues of the eye (conjunctiva, Tenon's fascia, and sclera) to reveal Schlemm's canal, which is buried in the white of the eye just beyond the iris. A small metal probe is then threaded into the canal and rotated forward into the eye, breaking through the trabecular meshwork.

An alternative method of completing a trabeculotomy involves threading a flexible stitch or a tiny, lighted, flexible probe (*illuminated microcatheter*) all the way around Schlemm's canal. The *suture* or microcatheter is then pulled to make the cut, much like a wire cheese cutter, to open the entire Schlemm's canal in a single maneuver. These procedures are referred to as 360-degree trabeculotomy, differentiating them from standard trabeculotomy, which opens approximately 120 degrees.

There are a few disadvantages to 360-degree trabeculotomy. If the probe or suture gets stuck going around Schlemm's canal, the surgeon may need to make additional incisions in the eye to move the probe forward. There also appears to be a higher incidence of bleeding inside the eye after 360-degree trabeculotomy.

Availability of instrumentation and also the surgeon's familiarity and experience with each procedure will play a role in the decision of how to proceed. Which method is best depends on a variety of factors, including the individual circumstances of the patient's condition. Regardless of the method chosen, the outer eye tissues are then sewn together once the procedure is completed.

Q. What can go wrong with a trabeculotomy?

A. There are always risks for any surgical procedure. Surgery is worthwhile if the risks are outweighed by the benefits. The surgical risks for trabeculotomy include complications such as:

- Bleeding: Bleeding inside the eye is the most common complication of trabeculotomy. It has even been said that trabeculotomy must have bleeding in order to indicate that the operation will work. Although this is not the case, bleeding is indeed very common and usually resolves on its own.
- *Cyclodialysis cleft*: Sometimes the metal instruments used in the trabeculotomy can tear the edge of the iris away from its usual origin. This results in a space between the edge of the iris and the sclera, called a cyclodialysis cleft. This is usually only a cosmetic concern, though it can occasionally cause the eye pressure to go too low or even result in retinal detachment. This is an uncommon complication.
- Pupil changes: Sometimes the pupil is no longer round and centered after the procedure. It may be shaped like a teardrop, with the point directed toward where the surgeon entered the eye.
- Damage to the cornea: If the trabeculotomy is positioned too far forward, the instrument used can strip off the layer on the back of the cornea (*Descemet's membrane*), resulting in clouding of the cornea. Fortunately, this is also quite uncommon.
- Cataract: If the lens of the eye is injured during the movement of the trabeculotomy instrument, a cataract can form. If this occurs, additional surgery to remove the cataract may or may not be required at a later time. This will depend on its size and impact on vision. Cataract formation is an uncommon complication.

As with all forms of intraocular surgery, there is always a risk of infection, loss of vision, retinal detachment, or failure of the surgery to resolve the problem. Although all of these are quite rare, approximately 50 to 60 percent of children who have trabeculotomy will still need medicines to help control their glaucoma and approximately 20 to 30 percent will need more surgery.

Keep in mind that all surgery has potential complications and every surgeon experiences them. When something goes wrong, it does not necessarily mean that the surgeon made an error.

Q. Who is most suited for trabeculotomy?

A. Like goniotomy, trabeculotomy is best for patients in whom the trabecular meshwork can be opened to restore flow of fluid from inside the eye. The surgical procedure itself involves steps that are more familiar to most surgeons than those involved in goniotomy. For this reason, some surgeons are more comfortable performing trabeculotomy than goniotomy.

Trabeculotomy is particularly useful in situations where the cornea is cloudy, making it impossible to perform goniotomy when no endoscope is available. In places where patients tend to have cloudier corneas because of delays in getting to the eye doctor, and endoscopy is generally not available, trabeculotomy is often the first choice of operation.

Q. How often do trabeculotomies fail, and is the chance of failure greater in the other eye if the surgery in the first eye fails?

A. The success rate for trabeculotomy, including patients who have surgery and still need some medications to control the glaucoma, is approximately 70 to 80 percent, depending on the research study you read. If the surgery in one eye of the same patient fails, he/she has a greater chance of it failing in the other eye, though it is possible for the surgery in the second eye to be successful.

Q. Will my child need drops after the trabeculotomy?

A. The drops used after trabeculotomy are very similar to those after goniotomy. These are described more fully in the "Goniotomy" section.

Q. What is viscocanalostomy?

A. This operation is also very similar to trabeculotomy, but has the additional step of injecting a gel-like (*viscoelastic*) substance into Schlemm's canal to dilate the passage with the intent of keeping it open to allow the fluid to exit the eye. The procedure has similar risks to trabeculotomy and similar postoperative care. The most significant difference from trabeculotomy is that the procedure can be done without entering the eyeball.

3. TRABECULECTOMY

Q. What is a trabeculectomy?

A. A trabeculectomy is a surgical procedure in which a pathway is cut from the outside of the eye to the inside to allow fluid to be drained and relieve excess pressure. This hole is called a sclerostomy. Instead of using the natural drain of the eye, as is done in trabeculectomy, a new canal is being made. This operation completely bypasses Schlemm's canal.

Just like trabeculotomy, the conjunctiva and Tenon's fascia are moved back and the sclera is penetrated. A hole is then cut into the area between the cornea and iris (anterior chamber) to allow the fluid to flow out. Unlike trabeculotomy, in this operation, the sclera is only tied down loosely, which allows the fluid to escape from underneath and then disperse underneath the conjunctiva. As the fluid flows out, a bleb is formed. The fluid is then absorbed into the bloodstream.

Q. What are blebs?

A. When someone refers to *blebs* after glaucoma surgery, he/she usually means the elevated area in the surface tissue over the white of the eye (conjunctiva) that filters the fluid (aqueous humor) out of the eye after a trabeculectomy surgery. By allowing the aqueous humor fluid to get out of the eye more easily, the bleb reduces the eye pressure and helps to prevent damage to the eye and the optic nerve.

Q. How often do blebs need revision and how successful is revision surgery?

A. Blebs from trabeculectomy surgery can cause several problems. Blebs created during the implantation of glaucoma tubes are not usually subject to these same problems.

One of the potential problems that can occur with blebs is leakage. A special medication, mitomycin (also called mitomycin C or MMC), is often applied to a child's eye during trabeculectomy surgery to keep the drainage hole from closing off due to scar tissue formation. While this treatment is very helpful to the success of the surgery, it also sometimes causes the tissue of the bleb to become thin. This thinning can cause the bleb to leak spontaneously or after minor damage to the eye.

If a leak occurs in the bleb, the eye is at significant risk of developing an infection. Bacteria can more easily enter the eye through a leaky bleb than through the normal, thicker, tissues of the eye wall. This type of infection can be very serious, requiring treatment with strong antibiotics. If the infection is not successfully treated, the patient may lose vision from that eye.

The risk of a leak developing increases over time after surgery, and is estimated to be as high as three to five percent per year. It is also possible that the age of the child at the time the bleb was created, as well as the thickness of the wall of the bleb and the possible lack of blood vessels when compared with normal tissue (*avascularity*), may affect the likelihood that a bleb will eventually develop a leak.

When a leak occurs, the bleb may need to be fixed (*revised*) through *revision surgery*. There are several ways to revise a bleb. Most solutions involve placing thicker tissue over the leaky, thin area of the bleb. As a result, sometimes the newly revised bleb will not allow fluid through it as easily as before. If the pressure rises too high, medication might be added or further glaucoma surgery might be performed. There is no scientific data available on the lifetime expectancy of a bleb after it has been revised. Most surgeons would not revise a bleb more than once or twice before closing it down and using a different type of glaucoma surgery, such as a drainage implant device.

Another problem, sometimes called *encapsulation*, occurs when the bleb is too thick. The fluid cannot leave the eye easily and the IOP will rise. Glaucoma medicines may be helpful in this situation. Alternatively, a procedure called *needling* may also be tried. This technique involves the surgeon inserting a needle into the bleb to scrape open the scar tissue inside. It is sometimes possible for older, compliant, children to have this procedure performed in the doctor's office while they are awake. The surgeon may occasionally choose to cut into the bleb to remove the scar tissue.

Q. What can go wrong with a trabeculectomy?

A. As with any operation that involves entering the eyeball, there is a risk of infection, bleeding, failure, loss of vision, or retinal detachment with trabeculectomy surgery. Trabeculectomy can also rarely result in cataract. Perhaps the most common complication is that the pressure in the eye may drop too low (*hypotony*). This extreme pressure reduction is due to an overflow of fluid through the canal created during the trabeculectomy. Sometimes hypotony will correct itself. It may also be treated by injecting the patient's own blood into the bleb to cause some scar tissue formation, partially blocking the drainage area and reducing the flow of fluid. Other methods of slowing down the fluid drainage include patching the eye or surgical revision to make the drainage area smaller.

Alternatively, sometimes the pressure will be too high after surgery, particularly if the sclerostomy becomes clogged with inflammatory debris or blood. High IOP immediately after trabeculectomy can be a temporary problem that resolves on its own. If it does not resolve itself, the surgeon can flush out the plug.

Another common complication in trabeculectomy is failure. This occurs more commonly with children than adults. Children are wonderful healers. Sometimes they simply heal the sclerostomy hole or the bleb and drainage areas under the conjunctiva so that the drainage ceases. To help prevent these complications, powerful chemicals can be applied to the eye, such as MMC or *5-fluorouracil (5-FU)*.

Q. What are mitomycin and 5-fluorouracil?
A. Mitomycin (MMC) and 5-fluorouracil (5-FU) belong to a class of drugs called antimetabolites. These drugs are primarily used in the treatment of cancer, where they are used to kill cancer cells. Likewise, they can inhibit the multiplication of *fibroblasts*, the cells that form scar tissue. This ability makes them useful in increasing the probability of successful trabeculectomy surgery. MMC and 5-FU can be applied directly to the surface of the eye during surgery. Alternatively, 5-FU can be injected around the eye immediately after surgery. Either application can be used in an effort to help retard scar tissue formation.

Q. Which is more effective?
A. In general, MMC is the stronger drug. It is usually not injected after surgery, but applied directly during surgery instead. 5-FU can also be applied during surgery, but it tends not to have as strong an effect as mitomycin. The advantage 5-FU provides is that it can also be injected after surgery.

Q. What are the side effects?
A. Both drugs are very strong, and can successfully prevent the formation of scar tissue. MMC in particular has been used quite effectively in children. One potential complication of their use, and of using MMC in particular, is that they can leave the tissues in the area of the surgery thin and susceptible to future breakdown or infection. The risk of developing this complication is cumulative over time, even after the drug is no longer being applied. This tendency can lead to serious, and potentially blinding, infections in the eye. As a result, many surgeons have shied away from using these medications in children. Unlike an 80-year-old patient with glaucoma, an 8-year-old patient has decades of expected remaining lifetime over which this cumulative risk for infection and tissue breakdown will continue to accrue.

Q. Will my child need drops after a trabeculectomy?
A. Yes. Much like after a goniotomy, steroid drops are used to fight inflammation and slow down the wound healing response mounted by the body. As a part of the healing process, the body aggressively tries to close the connection made between the anterior chamber and the tunnel (sclerostomy) draining the aqueous humor. The success of the trabeculectomy depends on this tunnel remaining open. Your child will also be placed on antibiotic eyedrops to prevent infection and pupil dilating drops. Approximately 50 to 60 percent of children will still need anti-glaucoma medication to work with the surgery to keep the eye pressure under control.

Q. What is eye massage?
A. If the aqueous humor is not flowing well through the sclerostomy, the surgeon may recommend eye massage. This is a technique that helps to push fluid out of the eye through the

sclerostomy to keep it open and flowing. This should only be done strictly according to the instructions of the surgeon.

Q. What is trabeculotomy-ectomy?
A. Some surgeons believe that combining trabeculotomy and trabeculectomy in the same operation can be useful. The surgeon uses the same surgical site to open the drainage angle (trabeculotomy) and create a new drain (trabeculectomy). This surgery has been popularized largely in India.

There is some concern that this operation may actually be no better than trabeculotomy alone and may have additional risks. It is uncommonly used in North America, unless the surgeon finds that Schlemm's canal is difficult to locate, making it impossible to complete trabeculotomy. In this situation, the surgery can be converted to a trabeculectomy without the need for a second surgery.

Q. What are non-penetrating procedures?
A. The risk of complications in surgery is increased when the surgeon has to enter, or *penetrate*, the eyeball to perform the procedure. Examples of penetrating procedures include trabeculotomy, goniotomy, trabeculectomy, and glaucoma tube surgery. A *non-penetrating procedure* allows the surgeon to avoid entering the interior of the eyeball. Incisions, similar to those done for trabeculectomy, are made in the sclera. Instead of actually creating new channels into the eye (sclerostomy), the sclera is dissected to remove tissue all the way to the last membrane that separates the outside of eye from the inside of the eye (Descemet's membrane). By doing this, the expectation is that the remaining thin membrane will allow fluid from within the eye to percolate through it instead of creating an actual hole for the fluid to drain through.

This procedure has been popularized in several countries for children, but is not used very commonly in North America. There is concern that this surgery may not be as effective in children as in adults because the Descemet's membrane of a child is thicker than that of an adult. As a result, fluid may not be able to percolate through the membrane as easily as it does in an adult. To counter this concern, the surgery may be augmented by artificial devices placed in the region of this thin area to ensure that the overlying tissues do not seal down. More research is needed.

4. SETONS/TUBES

Q. What is a seton (also known as a glaucoma tube, tube shunt or glaucoma drainage device)?
A. A *glaucoma drainage device* (also called by various other names, including *glaucoma tube, tube shunt, aqueous shunt device,* or *seton*) is a tiny tube connected to a roundish or oval plate (*reservoir*). Drainage implants are used to direct the aqueous humor within the anterior chamber to a space just outside the eye, which helps to lower the intraocular pressure. Different types of implants are made with reservoirs of different sizes and shapes. Some also have a small flow-regulator (*valve*) that separates the tube from the reservoir plate. The reservoir and the tubing are made of inert plastic (usually polymethyl methacrylate or silicone) to minimize the body's reaction to the implant.

The tube (*pars plana* or *sulcus* tube) can also be placed behind the iris instead of the anterior chamber. This position is used either because there is something about the anterior chamber which makes it difficult to put the tube there or because the tube is becoming exposed and needs to be placed further back.

Q. What is a patch graft?
A. One of the steps in tube surgery is to ensure that the tube is covered as it travels from the plate to its entry point into the eye. The natural tissues covering the eye (conjunctiva) are insufficient. Instead, the surgeon will apply a piece of cornea or sclera from an eye donated by someone who has died to cover the tube. This patch graft is tested for the AIDS virus (HIV) and hepatitis. Sometimes it will be treated to prevent its ability to transmit other infections. It is not necessary to test the donor for compatibility because the donated tissue from the donor has no blood in it. The donor patch may be visible after surgery, appearing as a white or clear square or rectangle over the tube.

Q. When is glaucoma implant surgery performed?
A. Glaucoma implant surgery is most commonly used in cases where medications or other forms of glaucoma surgery, such as goniotomy or trabeculotomy, have not been successful in controlling intraocular pressure. It is also useful for treating glaucoma in eyes that have already had cataracts removed (*aphakic glaucoma*). Some people's eyes are not suited to glaucoma implants due to the size or specific way in which the insides of their eyes are made. The decision of whether to use a glaucoma implant, and which implant is best, should be made by the family and the surgeon.

Q. What factors determine whether or not a glaucoma tube (seton) will work?
A. The success or failure of tube surgery depends on a variety of factors, including the type of shunt being used, how many prior surgeries your child has had, the level of experience of your child's surgeon, the severity of the glaucoma, whether or not complications occur, and your child's type of glaucoma, among others. Ask your child's eye doctor to address the specific factors that may be of concern for your child.

Q. What are the risks of the procedure?
A. There are always risks for any surgical procedure, but surgery is worthwhile if the risks are outweighed by the benefits. The surgical risks for tube surgery include complications such as:

- Hypotony: As with trabeculectomy, sometimes the fluid flows through the tube too quickly, causing the IOP to drop too low. Retinal detachment can be the result. Additional surgery may be required to restrict the flow through the tube or refill the eye with air, fluid, or a viscous gel (viscoelastic) to replace the fluid that flowed out too quickly.
- Tube blockage: The tube can be blocked by inflammation, blood, the iris, or vitreous (in aphakic eyes). Inflammation may be reduced and blood may be dissolved by medication. Surgery may be required to remove blockages caused by the iris or vitreous. Sometimes the tube needs to be flushed open surgically.
- Tube malposition: If the tube is placed in such a way that it touches other structures within the eye, additional complications may result. If the tube is touching the back of the cornea, it can cause corneal clouding. Chronic iritis may occur if the tube touches the iris. If the tube is touching the lens, it can cause cataract. In any of these situations, further surgery may be needed to reposition the tube.

- Tube exposure: If the patch graft covering the tube thins too much, the end of the tube may become exposed, with no covering tissue at all. This can lead to a serious, potentially blinding, infection. Your child's doctor will usually check for this at each visit. If exposure occurs, the surgeon may try to replace the patch graft. If this is not possible (usually because of scar tissue), then the tube may need to be removed and another surgery planned to control the glaucoma. Infection (*endophthalmitis*) is a very serious complication and usually requires admission to the hospital, intravenous antibiotics, sampling of the fluids inside the eye, and injection of antibiotics into the eye.

- Tube extrusion: As your child grows, the tube may become too short and literally come out of the eye. If this occurs, it may or may not be visible. Extrusion creates two problems. If the tube is completely exposed, then the risk for infection is high. If the tube is still covered by eye tissues or the patch graft, but not inside the anterior chamber, then there is no drainage of fluid and your child's glaucoma will no longer be controlled by its presence. It may be possible for the surgeon to use a tube extender to lengthen the old tube.

- Failure: There are many reasons why a tube may fail to control glaucoma. An average of 50 to 60 percent of children who have setons implanted will still need some medications to help control the glaucoma, though usually fewer than before the operation. In some cases, the tube is blocked inside the eye or the bleb over the plate becomes so scarred that fluid cannot escape from inside the tube. Patients may need surgery, another tube, or other glaucoma surgery procedures to fix these problems.

Q. If my child has glaucoma tubes, is it all right for me to massage his/her eyes to make them feel better?

A. Although eye massage is commonly used after trabeculectomy, massaging eyes in which glaucoma tubes have been implanted is probably not a very good idea. Manipulation of the eye can lead to movement of the tube. This, in turn, could cause corneal damage or even dislocation of the tube from the eye. The tube will not function properly if it or the tissues which cover it are dislodged or damaged.

Q. Is there any harm in letting a child who has a tube in one eye have his/her head upside down?

A. Although this position will transiently increase eye pressure, the short amount of time that this occurs is very unlikely to cause any significant damage. The tube itself is also not likely to be damaged or displaced.

Q. If my child receives a tube, will he/she still be able to participate in sports such as soccer or basketball?

A. Your child may not feel up to playing sports in the first week or so after surgery. There should not be any long-term activity restrictions unless there are unusual complications of the surgery or your child has other eye or medical problems that would make such restrictions necessary. You should discuss any potential activity restrictions with your child's surgeon.

Q. Will having multiple tubes in the eye prevent future procedures from being done?

A. Having more than one tube in the eye does not prevent future procedures.

Q. Is there a limit in number of glaucoma tube implant operations in one eye?
A. Most surgeons will put no more than three tube shunts in one eye before considering alternative procedures. In some cases, the surgeon may want to consider other options before implanting additional tubes if one fails. This is particularly true if the tube has eroded out of the eye. Additionally, some eyes cannot hold more than one or two tubes because of specific anatomy challenges.

Q. Is having glaucoma or tube shunt implants a contraindication for hyperbaric oxygen therapy?
A. There is no reason that having glaucoma or tube shunt implants should pose any added risk to a child undergoing hyperbaric oxygen therapy, but this circumstance has not been studied. You should discuss this therapy with your child's doctors.

Q. Is it safe for my child to swim as he/she gets older if he/she has tube shunts with valves in his/her eyes?
A. Swimming should continue to be safe as your child gets older. The tubes should not pose any additional risks, provided that the tissues over the implant reservoirs remain intact and well healed.

5. CYCLODESTRUCTIVE PROCEDURES

Q. What is cyclodestruction?
A. Cyclodestructive procedures all involve trying to kill the tissue inside the eye (ciliary processes) that is responsible for making the eye fluid (aqueous humor). By killing this tissue and decreasing the rate of fluid production, the pressure inside the eye should decrease.

Cyclodestruction can be accomplished either by using a freezing probe (*cryotherapy*) or a laser (*cyclophotodestruction*). The destructive force can be sent into the eye from the outside by touching a freezing probe or laser to the sclera. Alternatively, a laser probe can be introduced into the inside of the eye using a tiny camera (*endoscopic diode cyclophotoablation*) to actually see the tissue that is being destroyed.

Laser treatment has fewer risks than cryotherapy, but it also has less chance of killing the desired tissue inside the eye when delivered through the sclera.

Q. What is endoscopic diode cyclophotoablation treatment?
A. Use of an endoscopic diode laser allows the surgeon to place a tiny camera, not much bigger than a needle used to draw blood, into the eye. This probe contains a light beam, a video camera, and the laser. The camera and light allow the surgeon to directly visualize the ciliary tissue, and apply laser treatment while actually observing tissue destruction. Endoscopic diode treatment is the most precise, as it allows the surgeon to directly see the tissue being treated and decide exactly how much tissue to treat.

Q. Is it possible to surgically remove a portion of the ciliary body that produces fluid to reduce IOP?
A. At this time, there have been no known attempts to surgically remove a portion of the ciliary body. Such a procedure would be complicated and risky. A similar operation is done to remove tumors of the ciliary body. The complication rates are very high.

Laser treatments for glaucoma and cryotherapy that are currently in use produce a similar result with much less invasive surgery. The laser or freezing kills the ciliary body tissue in an effort to reduce the amount of fluid it produces, lowering the pressure in the eye.

Q. What can go wrong with cryotherapy and cyclophotodestruction procedures?
A. If too many of the ciliary processes are destroyed during a cryotherapy or cyclophotodestruction procedure, the untreated tissue may not produce enough fluid for the eye to sustain itself. The result can be death of the eye from shrinkage and chronically low IOP (phthisis), which can cause loss of vision in the eye. To help combat this possibility, surgeons usually do not treat all the ciliary processes at one time. Rather, only a certain percentage of the ciliary processes are eliminated and, if necessary, the treatment is then repeated at a later time to kill additional tissue.

Cryotherapy is the most powerful form of treatment in terms of IOP lowering effect and tissue destruction. It is also the most likely to be complicated by phthisis. Forms of treatment that are applied to the outside of the eye can cause inflammation, causing the eye to appear red or "angry." Bleeding and retinal detachment may also occur.

Endoscopic diode cyclophotoablation treatment is the most precise form of cyclophotodestruction. The ciliary processes can be directly viewed, allowing them to be counted and destroyed. As a result, this procedure has the lowest risk of inflammation and phthisis. As this procedure involves entering the eye, it brings with it other possible complications, such as cataract, retinal detachment, and bleeding. In rare situations, the eye pressure can even go up unexpectedly.

Although extremely uncommon, there have been a few reported cases in which a cyclodestructive procedure in one eye led to inflammation and loss of vision in the other eye.

Q. Why would the eye doctor select cyclodestruction as a treatment for my child's glaucoma?
A. Cyclodestructive procedures are often chosen after other means of surgery have failed or when it is anatomically not possible to use other glaucoma surgery options.

Q. Are there different kinds of laser treatment?
A. There are two kinds of lasers used for non-endoscopic cyclodestruction done through the sclera: *YAG* or endoscopic diode. The success rate is approximately the same with either laser. The diode laser may be gentler on the eye, causing lower levels of inflammation and postoperative pain.

Q. Why did contact laser cyclophotodestruction fail in my child?
A. One of the problems with applying a laser to the outside of the eye, especially in children, is the lack of precision as to where the laser beam goes inside the eye. Childhood glaucoma is often associated with abnormal positioning of the ciliary tissue within the eye. As a result, it is not possible to know if, or how much of, the tissue is being killed. This complication prompted the development of the endoscopic diode laser.

Q. What can go wrong with laser treatments?
A. As with cryotherapy, if too much ciliary tissue is destroyed during a laser treatment, the eye can shrink due to low pressure (phthisis) and die. Pain, swelling, and redness may also occur.

Cataract is a rare complication. The effect of laser surgery may not be seen for as long as four to six weeks. Patients often continue on their glaucoma medication until that time.

Endoscopic diode cyclophotoablation involves cutting into and entering the eyeball, which increase the risks of cataracts, retinal detachment, infection, and bleeding inside the eye. A patient who has previously had cataract surgery cannot develop cataracts from endoscopic diode surgery, as he/she has no lens, making him/her an excellent candidate for the procedure.

In some cases, the eye pressure will actually rise directly after laser treatment. This pressure spike can sometimes be successfully treated with medication.

The greatest problem with laser treatment is its high rate of failure—approximately 50 percent— with the subsequent need to repeat the treatment. This involves killing more ciliary tissue or destroying newly regenerated tissue that has spontaneously grown back, as often happens in children.

Some surgeons prefer to use laser treatment instead of implanting a second glaucoma tube if the first tube does not lower the eye pressure as far as is needed. In this case, the goal is to decrease eye fluid production sufficiently to allow the sluggish outflow through the glaucoma tube to match the rate at which the fluid is being made inside the eye.

Q. Why do adults receive laser treatments more frequently than children?

A. In primary open angle glaucoma (POAG), which mostly occurs in adults, one of the common procedures for treatment is called laser trabeculoplasty. This treatment is not used in children largely because it requires a high level of compliance on the part of the patient. The patient must sit at the slit lamp while a special lens is placed on the eye to allow the laser treatment to be performed. Most children are unable to do this until they are compliant teenagers. In addition, the mechanisms of many of the pediatric glaucomas are such that this treatment is unlikely to work. More research is needed.

Another laser treatment commonly used in adults is called *laser iridotomy*. In this procedure, the laser is used to put a tiny hole in the iris. This treatment is used for narrow angle glaucoma, a form that is extremely rare in childhood. As with laser trabeculoplasty, the patient's full compliance is required. If a young child requires an iridotomy, it may actually be easier to accomplish it by surgically placing a hole in the iris than by using a laser.

PART III: CATARACTS

A. GENERAL QUESTIONS

Q. What is a cataract?
A. The lens of the eye sits directly behind the pupil (see Figure 2). It should be completely clear. Any opacity or darkness in the lens of the eye is called a cataract, even if it is only a tiny dot or fleck (see Figure 11).

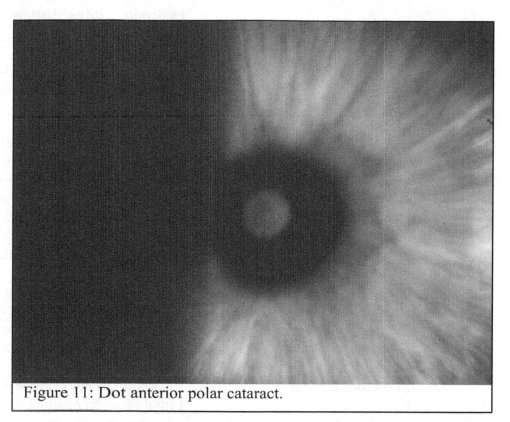

Figure 11: Dot anterior polar cataract.

Some cataracts make the entire lens opaque white (see Figure 12).

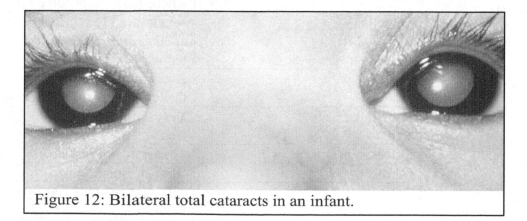

Figure 12: Bilateral total cataracts in an infant.

There are many different kinds of cataracts, some of which are listed in Table 6.

Table 6: Common Types of Cataract		
Location of cataract	**Name of cataract type**	**Description**
Front surface of lens	Anterior lenticonus	The front surface of the lens is bowed forward.
	Anterior dot polar	A tiny dot cataract on the center of the front lens surface.
	Anterior subcapsular	A cataract just under the front lens surface.
	Anterior pyramidal	A pyramid-shaped cataract extending forward from the front lens surface.
	Tractional	A cataract occurring where a portion of the iris near the pupil has incorrectly attached to the lens surface.
Back surface of lens	Persistent fetal vasculature (PFV)	The continued existence of blood vessels between the optic nerve and the back of the lens, in the hyaloid canal through the vitreous, that should have disappeared during the last trimester of pregnancy, which results in a cataract that may still contain these blood vessels.
	Posterior subcapsular	A cataract appearing just in front of the back surface of the lens.
	Posterior lenticonus	The back surface of the lens is bowed outward, towards the inside of eye.
	Posterior cortical	A cataract involving the lens in front of its rear surface.
Middle of lens	Nuclear (embryonal or fetal)	A cataract in the center of the lens.
	Sutural	A cataract in the middle of the lens where lens fibers come together.
	Lamellar	A cataract affecting only one layer of the lens, like a layer of an onion.
Edges of lens	Cortical	A cataract involving the edges of the lens rather than the center.
Throughout lens	Snowflake	Very small flecks throughout the lens.
	Pulverulent	Thousands of tiny dots of cataract.
	Cerulean	Blue globular flecks.
	Total	The entire lens is opaque and white.

An eye can have more than one type of cataract at the same time. Some cataracts blur vision, while others do not. A cataract is usually not harmful in and of itself, though it can cause a reduction in usable vision or be indicative of another health concern. A cataract usually only needs treatment when the vision is blurred.

Q. What does it mean if a newborn does not have red reflex?

A. In many photos, especially those taken with older flash cameras, the pupils of the individuals in the picture may look orange or red. This is the red reflex. The reflex is caused by light entering the eyeball and bouncing back out to the observer, reflecting the reddish-orange color of the back of the eye. The PGCFA has posted a video of this effect on its website (*http://www.pgcfa.org*).

All family doctors and pediatricians should test for the red reflex at well child visits until a child is old enough to read a chart to test vision. The doctor conducts this test by holding an instrument called a *direct ophthalmoscope* in one hand and looks through it while shining a light that creates this reflex.

If the reflex is absent, it means something is blocking the light from getting into the eye. This may be caused by a cataract or anything else that would block the light, such as a corneal scar or blood inside the eye. Another possibility is that the pupils are small, so that it is not possible for enough light to get into the eye to do the test even though the eye is otherwise entirely normal. This possibility is common in infants. It is hard for the primary care doctor to know if there is something serious or not, so any child with an absent red reflex should be seen by an eye doctor within a few days.

If the reflex looks white, it may also indicate that the patient has a cataract in that eye. Alternatively, it may also mean that there is something else white inside the eye, such as a malignant tumor (retinoblastoma). Given this concern, it is imperative that the individual be examined by an eye doctor within a few days.

Q. How common are cataracts in children?

A. The incidence rate for cataracts in children is 1 in 4,000 to 10,000, but may be higher or lower in some countries.

Q. What causes cataracts in children?

A. There are many causes of cataracts in children. What caused a particular child to develop a cataract is unknown in most cases. Most cataracts occur in otherwise perfectly healthy children.

The most common known cause is a genetic abnormality, either of the lens itself or throughout the whole body. Cataracts due to genetic abnormalities may be inherited from generation to generation but have to start somewhere. Your child may be the first affected person in the family. Cataracts can also be caused by injury, inflammation inside the eyeball (iritis), steroids taken by mouth or as eyedrops, complications of eye surgery, or non-genetic birth abnormalities, whether or not other abnormalities occur elsewhere in the body.

Q. Are cataracts contagious?

A. Cataracts are not contagious, even when they are caused by infections. However, if the cataract was caused by German measles (*congenital rubella syndrome*) or *congenital cytomegalovirus (CMV)*, then the lens still contains live virus. The virus cannot spread to others except when the lens is removed at surgery, at which time precautions are taken to prevent this from happening. Children with CMV may also have the virus in their urine, which could be a source through which infection can spread to others.

Alex V. Levin, MD, MHSc, FRCSC, with Christopher M. Fecarotta, MD

Q. How can a doctor tell the difference between a cataract acquired over time and the kind present at birth?

A. Cataracts have different shapes, sizes, locations, and even colors, all of which often allow a doctor to tell whether the cataract was acquired or congenital. The doctor may ask to see photographs taken of the child earlier in life to assist in making this determination. Sometimes, with magnification, he/she may be able to spot a cataract that was present earlier but was undetected by the parent or pediatrician. There are cases where it is never known for sure if the cataract was present at birth or acquired later in childhood. If the vision does not return to normal after surgery, we assume that the cataract was present longer, leading to the failure of full visual development during infancy and early childhood.

Q. What is the optimum time for a child with bilateral cataracts to undergo cataract surgery?

A. There have been a number of studies that have tried to relate the timing of removal of bilateral cataracts with both the expected best corrected vision and the likelihood of additional problems occurring later, most notably glaucoma. Although most experts would agree that none of these published studies is absolutely iron-clad in its evidence, taken together, there are two trends that have emerged and have influenced pediatric cataract surgeons. First, it is fairly clear that children with bilateral cataracts can develop good vision if the cataracts are removed within the first four to eight weeks after birth, rather than in the first week or two after birth. This conclusion assumes that everything else about the eyes is normal. Second, there is a tendency for glaucoma to develop more often in the eyes of children who had their cataracts removed during the first year after birth, as compared with children whose cataracts did not need to be removed for some years after birth. As a result of these findings, the current practice for most surgeons in North America is to wait until a child is approximately one month old to remove bilateral cataracts. It is hoped that the delay will decrease the likelihood that the child will later develop glaucoma while still achieving the best possible vision.

In the case of unilateral cataracts, there is a little more urgency about timing of the cataract removal. Many pediatric ophthalmic surgeons remove the cataract when the baby is just about 4 weeks old. If the baby was born a few weeks early, the surgeon may delay a little longer. This timing is chosen due to the desire to decrease the risk of glaucoma while not compromising the possibility of the child developing the best possible vision in the eye. Some surgeons prefer to remove the cataract as early as in the first two weeks of life for fear that waiting longer will cause a worse vision outcome in the affected eye. Long-term studies are still needed to determine what timing provides the best balance between maximizing vision development while decreasing the likelihood of developing glaucoma later in life.

Q. What will happen if the cataract is not removed?

A. If the cataract initially appears during the years of your child's visual development, his/her vision will be permanently damaged if the cataract is not removed in time. The most likely permanent vision problem that will develop is amblyopia.

If the cataract begins to appear after your child's visual development has ended, then its immediate removal will not result in better or worse vision than if surgery is done later. As long as normal vision development has been completed before the onset of the cataract, the cataract alone is only physically harmful to the eye if the cataract is leaking or swollen. These are very uncommon problems and usually seen only in patients with cataract due to trauma or iritis. Cataracts rarely cause long-term medical problems for the eye.

Q. What is a microphthalmic eye?

A. A microphthalmic eye is an eye that is smaller than normal when the length is measured from the front to the back. This can be measured by an ultrasound machine called an *A-scan ultrasound*. Microphthalmia is not a disease that hurts the eye, but smaller eyes tend to be underdeveloped. As a result, they may be less capable of normal vision. Microphthalmia is commonly seen in children with cataracts.

Q. What are the criteria for diagnosing an eye as microphthalmic?

A. There is no strict cutoff for defining an eye as microphthalmic. The average length of an eye depends on the age of the child.

Most of the growth of the eye occurs in the first two years of life. The average length of the eye at full-term birth is approximately 17 millimeters (about 0.7 inch). The average length at adulthood is approximately 22 millimeters (about 0.9 inch). Eyes with slightly larger or smaller lengths may also be within the normal range.

An indirect way of measuring the size of the eye is by measuring the diameter of the cornea from side to side. At full-term birth, a normal cornea measures approximately 9.5 to 10.5 millimeters (about 0.4 inch). In adulthood, the normal corneal diameter is approximately 12 millimeters (about 0.5 inch). As with general eye growth, most of the growth of the cornea takes place during the first two years of life. It is sometimes possible for the cornea to be small (*microcornea*) when the eye is of normal length and not microphthalmic.

Q. Does difference in the size of a microphthalmic eye usually become more normal as a child grows?

A. Although a microphthalmic eye will never grow to be as big as a normal-sized eye, there can be slight changes in appearance. If a microphthalmic eye gets glaucoma, it may enlarge to a more normal size during the first few years of life. This is a problem, in that the eye has glaucoma, though it does make the eye bigger. The relative difference between the microphthalmic eye and the normal eye will otherwise always stay the same, and both eyes will experience normal growth through childhood.

Q. What is persistent fetal vasculature (PFV)?

A. When the eye is developing before any baby is born, a set of blood vessels passes from the optic nerve, through the vitreous in the hyaloid canal, to the back of the developing lens. Towards the end of a pregnancy, these vessels normally dissolve. Persistent fetal vasculature occurs when these blood vessels do not dissolve. This results in a variety of eye abnormalities, the most common of which is a cataract. Persistent fetal vasculature is also associated with glaucoma, retinal detachment or scarring, and microphthalmia. It used to be known as persistent hyperplastic primary vitreous (PHPV).

Q. Is there a link between congenital cataracts and glaucoma?

A. Yes, there are several links. All children who have cataract surgery, especially in infancy, are at lifelong risk for developing glaucoma after surgery. This risk is discussed in more detail in the section on aphakic glaucoma. Some eyes with congenital cataract are also at risk for glaucoma, even if no surgery is done, because there is more wrong with the eye than just the cataract. Examples of eye and body syndromes in which this may occur include aniridia, congenital rubella syndrome, and Lowe syndrome. In each of these conditions, there is risk for both cataract and glaucoma.

Q. Why do cataracts develop in eyes that have glaucoma?
A. An eye with glaucoma may develop a cataract in any of several situations.

- If the lens is touched or damaged during glaucoma surgery, a cataract may appear at that location.
- Iritis or low intraocular pressure after glaucoma surgery can cause a cataract to form.
- Cataracts can also develop as a result of using steroids to treat the uveitic glaucoma.
- The eye may have other abnormalities in addition to glaucoma, such as aniridia, that predispose it to developing cataract.

Q. If my child has one normal eye without a cataract, will he/she develop a cataract in that eye?
A. This depends on the type of cataract and its cause. For example, if the cataract in one eye is the result of an injury, then the uninjured eye will not get a cataract. If one eye has a cataract due to steroids taken by mouth, then the other eye is at higher risk. If your child has iritis in both eyes and one eye develops a cataract, the other eye is only at risk if its iritis is out of control. If a child is born with a cataract in one eye (*congenital unilateral cataract*) that is also small (microphthalmic) and the other eye is of normal size, the normal sized eye is unlikely to develop a cataract. You should discuss the likelihood of your child developing a cataract in his/her other eye with your child's doctor.

Q. What will my child's sight be like in later childhood and adulthood?
A. It is impossible to predict what the future holds. The answer to this question primarily lies in the passing of time, compliance with treatment, and the onset of later complications. If a child has cataract surgery before his/her visual development is impaired, is fit well with contact lenses and/or glasses, complies with patching, and does not develop glaucoma, then he/she might enjoy 20/20 vision. If the cataract surgery is delayed, there is poor compliance with patching, contact lenses or glasses are not used properly, or there are complications of the cataract surgery such as glaucoma, then the vision may be significantly below normal. If your child has cataract affecting only one eye, then the other eye should always remain normal.

Q. Does my child's cataract cause his/her vision to be better at certain times of the day than others?
A. Every patient is different. As light enters the eye, it can sometimes bounce off the cataract and scatter, which can cause squinting and a strong aversion to light (photophobia). For some individuals, straight-ahead vision is quite clear until the light become too bright. Some patients have significant trouble seeing at night because lights, such as oncoming headlights, appear to have more glare or halos. Others feel more comfortable at night because, the pupil is bigger at night, allowing more vision around the cataract or because they experience less glare and discomfort from brighter illumination.

Q. Do childhood cataracts affect color vision?
A. In most cases, no. The majority of children will have normal color vision after removal of the cataract, whether bilateral or unilateral, as long as they originally had normal color vision. In some cases, children with congenital unilateral cataract that was removed after 18 months of age may have some alteration of color vision. In addition, eight percent of all boys and one percent of girls in the general population have color vision deficiencies, even without cataracts or cataract surgery. Any lack of color vision noted after cataract removal may be genetic rather than attributable to the cataract.

Q. What will my child not be able to do because of the cataract?
A. If your child enjoys good vision in at least one eye, then he/she should have few or no activity restrictions. Having a cataract operation, in and of itself, does not restrict a child from participating in any activities or endeavors except in the early weeks after surgery, while the eye is healing.

Q. Does patching to obtain good vision work on a unilateral cataract?
A. Yes, you can get good vision from patching with cataract, even if glaucoma is also present. While it may not be easy to accomplish, the keys to success are early intervention for the cataract, good glaucoma control with medicines and/or surgery, and patching, patching, patching. It is possible for a child with unilateral cataract and glaucoma to develop 20/20 vision if all of these factors are in line.

Cataract surgery may not be needed if the cataract is small. It may be possible to obtain good vision by patching the good eye and perhaps also using dilating eyedrops to enlarge the pupil to help the eye see around the cataract. If surgery to remove a unilateral cataract occurs during approximately the first eight to ten years of life, the child will almost always need to patch the good eye for some time to enhance the vision in the eye that had the surgery.

Q. Are there any other conditions associated with cataracts that my child is likely to develop?
A. Most cataracts in childhood are isolated and no other part of the body is affected. Rarely, cataracts can be part of a syndrome, or group of individual medical symptoms or dysfunctions that affect multiple body parts or processes and are commonly seen together. The presence of a syndrome may or may not be evident at the time a cataract is first diagnosed. The cataract may be the first obvious evidence of the syndrome's existence. Most of these syndromes become readily apparent during the early years of childhood. Cataracts may also occur as a result of infection (before or after birth), iritis, steroids, radiation, or other causes, all of which are usually readily apparent.

Q. Is there any research into slowing down cataract development?
A. Currently there is no known method of slowing the growth of cataracts. Much research has been conducted to find a drug that could do this, but no products have yet been successfully developed.

Q. If my child is aphakic, can he/she wear glasses instead of contact lenses?
A. An aphakic child may wear glasses when the contacts are not in. The lenses of these glasses are often quite thick, but they can still provide excellent vision. Being thicker, glasses may be more difficult to fit and wear properly, especially in infants or if only one eye is aphakic. Peripheral vision may also be reduced. A special way to make such glasses a bit more cosmetically appealing is to use lenses with a high refractive index, which are thinner.

Q. Why did my child's doctor prescribe eyeglasses to be worn over his/her contact lenses?
A. Once the natural lens is removed, your child may need extra help for seeing up close. To accomplish this, his/her ophthalmologist may prescribe a combination of contact lenses and eyeglasses to give clearer vision than contacts alone can accomplish. Contact lenses for children who have had cataract surgery are only made in certain *powers*. If the strength of contact lens that a child needs is between two of the available ready-made contact lens powers, the difference between the available contact lens power and what the child needs for clear vision can be provided by glasses.

Eyeglass lenses prescribed for aphakic children to wear over contact lenses may be any of three varieties. The first is *single vision*, which consists of one power that is used to enhance either distance or near vision. The second possible option is bifocal. Bifocal lenses contain two separate sections. The top part is for distance vision. The bottom part of the lens is used for near vision. The third possibility is *multifocal*, or *progressive*, lenses. These are sometimes called invisible bifocal lenses because they have no obvious line separating the parts of the lens that are powered for different distances.

Bifocal lenses are rarely prescribed for children under the age of 2 years. Since younger children rely much more on their near vision, the prescriptions in their glasses or contact lenses are usually *over-plussed*, which means that they are primarily focused for close-range vision. As a child grows older and becomes more interested in objects farther away, his/her contacts or glasses prescription is adjusted to give better focus at longer distances. If necessary, bifocals are then used to enhance close vision.

Some children can see both distant and near objects without bifocals. The bifocal part of a child's glasses may look different than what older people wear. Instead of a small circle of extra magnification at the bottom of the glasses closer to the nose, the reading distance portion of a child's lenses may either take the form of a larger circle or the entire bottom half of the lens (*executive bifocal*). Another name for the bifocal segment of glasses is the *add*.

Progressive lenses, a form of bifocal, provide clear vision at near, mid-range, and long distances. These lenses have the advantage of offering more viewing ranges without visible lines in the lens. This style of lens may take a while for the child to get comfortable using. They are usually prescribed for school-aged children, who have more need to see clearly at multiple distances.

Q. Why does my child's doctor want him/her to wear eyeglasses after cataract surgery even though an IOL was also implanted?
A. Children who have IOL implantation with their cataract surgery often need glasses. This necessity is especially likely for younger children because the surgeon has selected a power for the IOL that is wrong for the child's current age, but expected to be more correct for him/her at later ages. One might think of this as allowing the eye to grow into the power of the IOL. Eyes normally change shape as children get older. Rather than doing additional surgeries to keep replacing the IOL with changing powers, glasses are used to work with the IOL. By using both together, the child has the right prescription and best focus at every age.

Since an IOL cannot focus at distance and near in the same way as a natural lens, bifocal glasses may still be needed for reading vision. The glasses for children with IOLs are otherwise just like the glasses that any child would need and do not require any special manufacturing.

Q. Must my child wear glasses as well as contact lenses for close-up work?
A. Whether a child needs extra help for up close work is simply a matter of how he/she performs. Some children, almost miraculously, seem to need no extra help for near vision after cataract surgery. Their eyes somehow retain the ability to see up close even though their glasses or contact lenses are more for further distances. Other children need help to see up close. One option is for the child to have a contact lens for one eye that is focused for distance and the other set for seeing up close. Another alternative is for both of the child's contacts to be set for distance vision and he/she wears glasses for reading. These glasses may take the form of single vision reading glasses, used only when he/she wants to read or work close up, or bifocals with no prescription in the top and a near vision section in the bottom, which are worn all the time. Children who only put on glasses to read may be more likely to repeatedly lose them.

Q. Must my child's lenses have added ultraviolet (UV) protection?
A. Many doctors believe that lenses used by an aphakic child should have added ultraviolet protection. Since the lens of the eye has been removed, there is no natural filter of ultraviolet rays from the sun. Therefore, aphakic children need other means of protecting their eyes from damaging ultraviolet light. This coverage can be achieved by adding UV protection in glasses, since contact lenses do not provide this. It is less clear whether non-aphakic children need additional UV protection. Talk more about this with your child's eye doctor. Most IOLs already have UV protection so that additional UV protection in glasses may be less necessary.

Although UV protection is important, sunglasses are not practical for every child. The long-term effects of not wearing UV protection may be so small that trying to force your child to wear sunglasses just may not be worth it. If this is a concern, talk about it with your child's ophthalmologist, as there are many different opinions on this subject.

B. CATARACT SURGERY

Q. Why is surgery to remove a cataract sometimes required?
A. Cataracts do not usually harm the eyeball at all, but they may cause blurry vision. If the vision is too blurry, then the cataract needs to be removed. Some cataracts are opacities no bigger than a microscopic speck and usually have no effect on vision. Larger opacities, particularly if they are in the center of the lens, will obstruct the vision and may require surgery. In some cases the entire lens is opaque (*total cataract*). If the cataract is not affecting vision, it can potentially remain in the patient's eyeball for the remainder of his/her life without causing any harm.

Some eye doctors will talk about waiting until a cataract is ripe. A cataract is not like a piece of fruit that has to be ripe in order to be eaten. This descriptive term simply refers to the fact that some cataracts will become bigger or more opaque over time. The eye doctor does not have to wait until the cataract is ready for surgery before removing it. Rather, surgery is done when the vision is sufficiently reduced to make the potential increase in vision more worthwhile than the risks and inconvenience of surgery. In the case of children less than 10 years old, a cataract will be removed if there is a concern that it will get in the way of vision development.

Q. Why is surgery sometimes not required to treat a cataract?
A. If a cataract is not in the center of vision, or if the cataract is in the center of vision but is so small that the vision is not blurred, then cataract surgery is not needed (see Figure 11).

Small central cataracts may still put a child whose visual development is not yet complete at risk for developing amblyopia. Most children reach visual maturity between the ages of 8 and 10 years old or even a little later. Amblyopia can occur when the brain favors the eye without the cataract, using it for the majority of vision and ignoring the signals from the eye with the cataract. In that circumstance, the eye doctor may first choose to treat the child by patching the other eye to remind the brain to use the eye with the cataract to see.

Instead of surgically removing the cataract, the surgeon may prescribe dilating drops to keep the pupil bigger, effectively allowing the patient to see around the cataract. This treatment may help visual development in the affected eye. Keeping the pupil dilated allows more light to get in the eye, giving the child better vision. The dilating drop used for this purpose is designed not to blur vision like those given during your child's office eye examination. They should be applied during the day while your child is awake to keep the pupil dilated. These non-surgical treatments only work with small, visually insignificant cataracts.

There is no urgency to remove cataracts in children beyond the age of visual maturation. After that point, the existence of a cataract in one eye will not cause amblyopia because the brain does not further compound the visual loss by ignoring the eye with the cataract. As a result, the cataract could be removed years, or even decades, later with the same visual result.

If one of a child's eyes is perfectly normal and the other eye has a cataract, and he/she is beyond the age of visual development, then the cataract only needs to be removed if the blurry vision in that eye is bothering the child. Some children function perfectly well with one normal eye and are not bothered at all by having blurry vision in the other eye.

If a child younger than the age of visual maturation has a cataract that is sufficiently large and opaque to cause blurring of vision and this cannot be overcome by dilating the pupil or patching the good eye, then the cataract must be surgically removed. Otherwise, his/her vision will become permanently impaired.

Q. Can a cataract be removed with medication or a laser?
A. There is no medication or laser treatment that can remove a cataract at this time. The only way to get rid of a cataract is through surgery. Some centers have begun using a newer machine, the femtosecond laser, as part of adult cataract surgery. While surgical incisions are still required, this laser is used to help make more accurate incisions and start breaking up the hard, adult cataract to make its surgical removal easier. It is not generally used in cataract surgery for children.

A laser is sometimes used to remove scar tissue after cataract surgery. Some individuals refer to this tissue as a "second cataract," even though it is not a cataract at all. This naming may be the basis for the idea that a cataract can be removed using a laser.

Q. How urgent is it that surgery is carried out?
A. The level of urgency depends on when the cataract develops, how severely it impacts vision (for example, how large the cataract is and whether it is in the center of the vision), and the age of the child when it is diagnosed. Cataract surgery is done in children to allow them the opportunity for their vision to develop properly. The brain must get a clear visual image in order for this to occur, especially in the first four to six weeks of life, though visual development generally continues to happen through ages 9 to 11 years.

During the earliest periods, surgery is considered very urgent if a child is born with a cataract that can seriously impact his/her vision. The earlier a cataract is removed, the better the vision outcome. Many doctors prefer to wait until the patient is 4 to 6 weeks old, believing that earlier surgery may be more likely to cause complications, such as glaucoma, without a significantly better vision outcome. If surgery for a cataract present at birth is delayed beyond the age of 4 to 6 weeks, it may become more difficult for the child's brain to learn how to use the eye once the cataract is removed.

If a visually significant cataract is diagnosed after the age of 6 weeks but during the first year of life, cataract surgery is still considered fairly urgent, often requiring surgery within a few weeks or months to get the best vision outcome The later a cataract develops, the lower the level of urgency. A child diagnosed between the ages of 2 and 9 years old generally should not wait more than one to three months for surgery.

No additional harm will usually be caused by delaying surgery for a child who is beyond the age at which visual development is finished (9 to 11 years old), as long as his/her vision is sufficient to perform the activities of his/her daily life, such as participating in school and sports. This is particularly true if the child only has a cataract in one eye and the other functions well. Even if the eye with the cataract sees very poorly, there usually is no urgency at all to remove the cataract as long as the child is not bothered by having blurry vision from the affected eye. There are rare exceptions to this rule, such as situations where a cataract must be removed urgently because it is causing inflammation or glaucoma in an eye.

Q. Is cataract surgery done under general anesthetic?
A. All cataract surgery in children must be done under general anesthetic. It is possible that very mature, older teens might be able to have the operation done while they are awake, but this is quite unusual. In adults, the operation can be done while the patient is awake or under light sedation.

Q. What happens during surgery?
A. The objective of cataract surgery is to remove the lens of the eye, as the lens contains the cataract. There is no way to remove the cataract without taking the whole lens.

The child is put to sleep under general anesthesia. This usually involves administering an intravenous (IV) line, which can be time-consuming and difficult, especially in infants. Sometimes the child is first put to sleep with an anesthetic gas using a face mask. Once the child is asleep, his/her face and eye are washed with a special soap to reduce the chances of infection. Drapes are placed over his/her face so that only the eye is exposed. A speculum is used to keep the eye open during surgery.

The eyeball is not removed from the head and no incisions are made through the skin. Instead, a very small incision, usually about 3 millimeters wide, is made at the top of the eye, either in the sclera or the cornea. The surgeon looks through a microscope during surgery. If you imagine the front of the eyeball as a clock, the incision(s) are usually near the 12 o'clock position. Some surgeons make the incision at the 9 o'clock position instead.

After the eye is opened, an instrument is used to reach through the pupil and open up the lens capsule. This opening then allows the cataract and lens to be removed from the eye after they have been turned into tiny liquid pieces. Once the lens is removed, all that is left are the remnants of the lens capsule.

In very young children, the posterior lens capsule must also be opened. Otherwise, it will become cloudy and scarred, potentially obstructing vision as thoroughly as the cataract. After the posterior capsule is opened, a small amount of the vitreous is usually removed. The incision in the sclera or cornea is then closed, generally using stitches that dissolve on their own. Ointment is instilled, and a patch and shield are applied. The patient is awakened from the general anesthesia and taken to the recovery room.

If an intraocular lens (IOL) implant will be placed during the cataract surgery, then the posterior capsule may be left intact. The IOL is placed within the same capsule that held the natural lens, through the same initial incisions, although the wound may need to be enlarged slightly so the IOL can fit into the eye. In many places, there are IOLs which can be folded by the surgeon to fit through the small wound.

If the surgeon feels that the posterior capsule must be opened in a child receiving an IOL, he/she may place the IOL first and make another hole in the eye to allow for the introduction of an instrument to open up the capsule from behind it. This technique is called a *pars plana approach*, and is usually performed when it will not be possible for the capsule to be opened by a laser in the weeks after cataract surgery. Some surgeons instead choose to open the posterior capsule either before or after IOL implantation by using the same incisions that were made at the start of the surgery.

Q. Is there a method of cataract surgery that does not require stitches?
A. Surgery in which no stitches are used to close the surgical wound is used in adults but is not advised for children. Children are more active and, especially if very young, tend to cry a lot. The physical activity and emotional upset could cause the wound to open. In addition, the whole idea of this type of surgery was to allow for a smaller wound in the eye to reduce asymmetry of the eye surface, which causes *astigmatism*. It is uncommon for a child to develop significant astigmatism as a result of cataract surgery, regardless of whether stitches are used or not.

Q. How long does the surgery take?
A. On average, most cataract surgeries take less than an hour, though it may be anywhere from 30 minutes to two hours between the time your child enters the operating room and you see the surgeon after the procedure. The actual surgical time may take anywhere from 10 minutes (if an IOL is not being implanted) to an hour or more. The total time from when the child enters the operating room to when he/she awakens after the procedure depends on the amount of experience your child's surgeon has with the procedure, how long it takes to get the child under anesthesia, whether additional measurements are needed before the surgery to calculate IOL strength or check eye pressure, and how long it takes the child to wake up from anesthesia.

Q. When will my child be able to see following the surgery?
A. Assuming there are no complications, light can get into the eye as soon as the patch is removed, since there is no patch or cataract to block it. Even without an IOL or contact lens, the eye can see, though the image will be very blurry without a contact lens, an IOL, or glasses. This is a combined result of the eye no longer having a natural lens and because the eye had surgery. Some of the blurriness may go away as the inflammation or any blood inside the eye subside over the first few days following surgery. Eyes with IOLs tend to see better more quickly because the eye has a way to focus. Even with an IOL, vision is often blurry the day after surgery.

Q. What is the follow-up schedule after surgery?
A. Your child's eye will be checked the day after surgery and eyedrops will usually be started to prevent infection and inflammation. Your child will likely then be scheduled for a return checkup two to five days later, at which time the eyedrops may be adjusted.

During the first few weeks after cataract surgery, follow-up visits will be more frequent than usual so the doctor can monitor for possible complications and to ensure that the eye is healing well. After this initial period, and particularly after all eyedrops have been stopped, the focus of treatment becomes the management of visual rehabilitation through the use of glasses and/or contact lenses, if needed.

If your child is patching his/her good eye to treat amblyopia in the other eye, the frequency of follow-up visits will partly depend on how old he/she is and how much of the day is spent patched. Younger children and children who are patching for most or all of their waking hours each day (full-time patching) will require more frequent follow up visits. These may occur at intervals anywhere between every few weeks to every few months. Your child's eye doctor can help tailor the follow-up regimen to your particular child's needs.

Children who are not patching will have fewer follow-up visits. These can be spread out to as much as one visit every six to twelve months. Vigilance is required, especially with children under 5 years old, to make sure that amblyopia does not develop or, if it does, to ensure that it is treated promptly to ensure that your child retains the best possible vision.

All children who have cataract surgery are at risk for developing glaucoma. This risk is particularly high in children who have their cataract surgery in infancy, whose cataracts are a result of PFV or are in the center of the lens (nuclear cataract), who also have microphthalmia, or who have other diseases that predispose them to glaucoma (such as Lowe syndrome, iritis, or congenital rubella syndrome).

It is recommended that children who have had cataract surgery be checked for glaucoma with an eye pressure measurement at least once yearly, even if this requires an examination under sedation or anesthesia. These annual examinations are necessary to catch and treat any developing glaucoma as early as possible. In addition, at every follow-up visit, the eye doctor can look for other indicators that glaucoma may be present, such as marked changes in the contact lenses or glasses power needed, cloudiness of the cornea, decreasing vision, decreasing visual field, or changes in the optic nerve (increase in the optic nerve cup).

Q. What care is required after surgery and who gives this care?
A. Cataract surgery is generally performed as an outpatient procedure, except in children who are otherwise unwell or in very young infants. Once a child is released from the medical facility, all home care is provided by the parents or other guardians.

The most important part of postoperative care is the instillation of eyedrops. Most patients require at least two kinds of eyedrops after surgery: a steroid eyedrop, to suppress inflammation in the eye, and an antibiotic. There may also be drops to dilate the pupil. When an IOL is inserted, more steroids are often necessary to keep the eye from responding adversely to the presence of this piece of plastic in the eye. Pupil dilating drops or a steroid ointment, to be used before bedtime, may also be prescribed. Occasionally, oral steroid medication is needed to help suppress inflammation, particularly in children who have had IOL implantation. If glaucoma develops following cataract surgery, additional medications may be necessary.

Other than giving the medications, keeping the shield on the child's eye as prescribed, and attending your child's follow-up visits, no other special care is usually required. Children may attend school, although gym and boisterous activity at recess may be prohibited. Swimming is usually allowed. Children may also use the unoperated eye to watch television or read. In a perfect world, the patient leads a calm, quiet life as his/her eye heals. Unfortunately, this is a very impractical expectation for most children. Fortunately, children are very good healers and can usually engage in fairly normal activity after cataract surgery.

Q. Will further surgeries be required?
A. Any child who has cataract surgery may need additional operations, particularly if there are complications, though most children will not require further surgery. If the surgeon has chosen to leave the posterior capsule intact, then an outpatient procedure involving the use of a YAG laser may

be needed to open this membrane if it becomes cloudy. If the child is unable to sit still for this procedure, then the membrane may need to be removed surgically. Other operations may be needed to enlarge the pupil; reposition, replace, or remove an IOL; treat glaucoma; remove blood or scar tissue; or treat any infection that occurs.

Q. Should my child wear sunglasses after cataract surgery?
A. There is some data that suggests that the ultraviolet rays of the sun can cause damage to the retina, especially in aphakic children. The IOL implants used in some children have ultraviolet (UV) blocking ability. If your child has this type of IOL in both eyes, sunglasses are not necessary.

Most children will only wear sunglasses if they want to, or if they perceive a benefit from reducing the brightness of the ambient light. One has to weigh the potential benefit against the challenge of getting a child to wear sunglasses when he/she does not want to do so.

Q. Why is my child's pupil no longer perfectly round after his/her unilateral cataract surgery?
A. A pupil that is not perfectly round after cataract surgery may be a result of scar tissue, injury to the iris or pupil during surgery, or the position of an IOL. The change in shape may be more noticeable in dim light, when the pupil is naturally bigger. Your child's ophthalmologist should be able to explain why his/her pupil is irregularly shaped or different in size when compared to the other eye. An unusually shaped pupil does not usually cause any vision problem. It may not be noticeable if your child's eyes are brown.

Q. Can a YAG laser treatment after cataract surgery cause glaucoma?
A. Although the laser treatment may temporarily increase the inflammation inside the eye, contributing to a transient elevation of eye pressure, laser treatment does not generally cause long-term glaucoma.

Q. Is it true that YAG laser surgery can cause retinal detachment?
A. Although there is some truth to this for adults, the risk in children is exceedingly small and far outweighed by the benefits of improved vision.

Q. What are the possible complications of cataract surgery and how likely are they to occur?
A. The possible complications are:

- Infection: Any time an eye is open there is a risk of infection. The approximate risk is 1 in 10,000 cases for children, but it may even be lower. The risk increases for complicated surgery, re-operations, or in the presence of diseases that affect the whole body and predispose to infection.
- Bleeding: Any time an eye is open, bleeding occurs inside the eye. A small amount of bleeding is present in every case and usually does not pose a problem. The likelihood of more than microscopic bleeding occurring is not known, but it tends not to be a problem because any blood is almost completely gone by the first postoperative day.
- Retinal detachment: This is a rare complication of pediatric surgery. The exact incidence is not well-known, though it probably occurs in fewer than 1 in 30,000 to 100,000 cases.
- Loss of vision: Loss of vision would usually occur as a result of infection, bleeding, retinal detachment or other complications. The risk is therefore very low.

- Glaucoma: This is one of the greatest risks of cataract surgery. In some studies, the risk may be as high as 30 to 40 percent. Children with small eyes (microphthalmia), nuclear cataracts (cataracts involving the central core of the lens), PFV, congenital abnormalities in the structure of the front part of the eye (such as anterior segment dysgenesis, Peters anomaly, aniridia), or iritis are at the highest risk. Any child who has cataract surgery, particularly in infancy or early childhood, has a lifelong risk of developing glaucoma.

- Appearance changes: Minor abnormalities may occur that usually do not affect vision. These include a slightly droopy eyelid (ptosis) or changes in the shape or size of the pupil.

- Inflammation inside the eye (iritis): Almost every case of cataract surgery results in some form of inflammation, simply due to the operation inside the eye. Inflammation may be particularly troublesome when an IOL is implanted.

- IOL malposition (subluxation): If the IOL drifts out of position, additional surgery may be required to recenter the IOL. This occurs in less than ten percent of cases.

- Wrong IOL prescription: In order to select the correct strength of an IOL, measurements are taken of the length and shape of the eye before surgery (either with the child awake or while the child is asleep under anesthesia). Even with the use of the best available techniques, these calculations are imprecise. In addition, the correct strength of the lens may change over the course of your child's life. Surgeons try to predict this change and place an IOL which will last for your child's lifetime, but it is possible that your child will need to grow into the strength of that IOL. As a result, he/she may need to wear glasses with the IOL to get the best vision.

- Allergic reaction to medications: Any child can have a mild or severe allergic reaction to the eyedrops prescribed after surgery. This is uncommon and usually easily treatable by stopping the medication.

Q. How long after cataract surgery is my child at risk for glaucoma?
A. Any child who has had a cataract removed is at risk for glaucoma for the rest of his/her life. Glaucoma may appear within days after surgery or years later. The average time of onset is approximately eight years after surgery.

Q. How much vision could my child lose as a result of cataract surgery?
A. Complete loss of vision as a result of cataract surgery is very rare, only occurring in about 1 in 10,000 to 30,000 children or fewer. The most common cause of vision loss after cataract surgery is amblyopia. The brain will always prefer to rely on vision from a normal companion eye than from one that has had a cataract. Treatment of amblyopia is essential to a good visual outcome.

Q. What keeps the vitreous from coming forward once the lens is removed?
A. After the posterior capsule has been opened, the surgeon usually removes the front part of the vitreous filling the back of the eye to prevent its movement into the front of the eye. Doing so also helps prevent scar tissue forming in the center of vision. This procedure is called an *anterior* (or *core) vitrectomy*. Even when this is done well, the vitreous may sometimes come forward. This usually causes no problems with the health of the eye, but can occasionally result in an increased risk of glaucoma, abnormalities of the pupil shape, swelling of the retina [*cystoid macular edema (CME)*], or other complications.

Q. What replaces the lens in a child's eye?
A. Contact lenses are the most common tools used to correct vision in babies who have had cataract surgery. Babies are generally fitted with contact lenses about a week after surgery. The contacts give him/her the ability to focus. He/she will not even realize the lens is in the eye.

Glasses can also be used after cataract surgery in babies, but they are very thick and some babies will not leave them on. Most older children are likely to prefer contacts or IOLs, for cosmetic reasons, when they are more conscious of their appearances.

Q. How can my child cope seeing with just one focusing distance?
A. Your child will do fine with being able to focus at just one distance. This is how most adults over age 50 see. A bifocal segment or progressive lens in your child's glasses will allow him/her focus at intermediate and near distances. If the cataract was just in one eye, then the normal eye will take over at distances which are more challenging for the eye that had cataract surgery. Many children, especially when young, are still able to focus at variable distances even without glasses. This is called *aphakic accommodation* or *pseudophakic accommodation* and can be developed whether or not your child has an IOL.

Q. What does a baby see after cataract surgery?
A. After surgery, the objects your baby sees will appear very blurry, although sight may be better than before the surgery because an increased amount of light is entering the eye. Surgery does not usually cause a difference in an infant's behavior. Bright sunlight may cause him/her to squint until the eye becomes accustomed to the increase in light.

Q. Are there any exercises that could improve my child's vision after cataract surgery enough that he/she will no longer need glasses or contacts?
A. There are no exercises that improve developing vision. Glasses or contact lenses will allow your child to see and focus at different distances. Patching a stronger eye, if recommended by your child's doctor, is important for treating any amblyopia that has developed in a child under the age of 11.

Q. Will not wearing his/her glasses cause my baby to develop nystagmus?
A. It is very hard to get some babies to wear glasses, especially if it makes them irritable. Not wearing the glasses full-time could cause nystagmus, but it is only one of many possible causes. Examples of other reasons for nystagmus to occur include cataract surgery that was performed after the first eight weeks of life when dense cataracts had been present for more than half the child's life; something else wrong with the eye that prevents perfect vision; and coincidental infantile nystagmus, where the eye shakes because of a defect in eye muscle control. The nystagmus may have been destined to occur whether or not the glasses were worn full-time.

The presence of nystagmus is worrisome and may indicate some permanent loss of vision. That being said, there are certainly children whose nystagmus has gone away after appropriate correction with glasses or contact lenses.

Q. Will my child always need glasses or contacts after cataract surgery?
A. Your child will most likely need to wear glasses or contact lenses all of his/her life, whether or not he/she has an IOL, especially if cataracts were present in both eyes. IOLs or contact lenses do not function the same way as natural lenses, and can only provide focus at one distance. When the natural lens is removed at the time of cataract surgery, the eye loses the ability to focus. Even with

an IOL or contact lens, your child may have to wear glasses to get good close vision. He/she may also need glasses for distance vision.

It is not always possible to accurately determine the power of an IOL that a child's eye will need initially or predict what will be necessary as the eye continues to grow. The younger the child is at the time of implantation, the more difficult it is to make accurate predictions for the future. Glasses or contacts allow adjustments so that the IOL does not need to be changed. The glasses work with the IOL to achieve good focus throughout life.

Q. What is a secondary cataract and how likely is it that my child will develop one?
A. The term secondary cataract refers to the scarring of the posterior capsule that causes it to become opaque. This opacification will occur in almost all children who have cataract surgery, especially for those who have their cataract surgery in the first five years of life. In infants and some younger children, the surgeon makes a hole in the posterior capsule during surgery to prevent this from happening, but sometimes other forms of scar tissue still occur. The younger the child, the more quickly opacification of an intact capsule or formation of scar tissue is likely to occur. Whether or not genetic factors play a role is unknown. There are no known environmental factors that increase the likelihood of this occurring.

Q. Will my child's life be limited by reduced vision?
A. This is a question that must be answered individually for each patient. You should ask your child's ophthalmologist about the prognosis for his/her vision. If treated early enough, the overwhelming majority of children with cataracts who have no other eye problems enjoy excellent vision and unrestricted lives.

Q. Which sports should an aphakic child avoid to prevent further damage to his/her eyes?
A. No activity restrictions are needed except in the early postoperative period. We are unaware of any evidence that aphakic children are more at risk of retinal detachment or glaucoma as a result of sports. Appropriate protective eye wear is always recommended for children (as would be all appropriate sports gear) and this is absolutely imperative if one eye is normal and the other has poor vision. Most sports can also be played while wearing contact lenses.

Q. If my child has cataract surgery, will he/she be able to drive?
A. The mere fact that cataract surgery was performed does not restrict a person from driving. The ability to drive is based on the quality of straight-ahead vision and the degree of peripheral vision. It does not matter whether someone has had cataract surgery or any other operation on the eye. The quality of straight-ahead and peripheral vision your child enjoys later in his/her life depends on a variety of factors, including his/her age at the time of surgery, the presence or absence and degree of amblyopia, the cataract type, the time between onset of the cataract and surgery, and any complications from the surgery.

C. INTRAOCULAR LENS (IOL) IMPLANTS

Q. What is an intraocular lens (IOL)?
A. When performing cataract surgery, the surgeon removes the entire lens of the eye. The eye cannot focus properly without a lens. One option is to replace the natural lens with an artificial plastic intraocular lens (IOL). Placing an IOL in an eye during or after cataract surgery has been the standard procedure for adults for many years. Doing the same for children has become more

common over the last decade, largely as an effort to provide an alternative to the inconvenience and cost of contact lenses.

The natural lens of the eye sits within a membrane envelope called the capsule or "bag." To remove the cataract and natural lens, the surgeon makes a hole (*capsulotomy*) in the front of this bag, and then removes the lens material from within it. After this is done, the surgeon can insert the IOL into the now-empty bag. This is called in-the-bag implantation. If the bag cannot be used to hold the IOL, the IOL can be placed on top of the membrane (*sulcus implantation*). In this position, the IOL rests between the bag and the back of the iris. Sulcus implantation might be needed if the bag is loose or gets torn during surgery.

IOLs that are placed behind the iris, either in the bag or sulcus, are referred to as posterior chamber IOLs (PCIOLs). In adults, an IOL can also be placed in front of the iris, over the pupil. A special type of IOL, called an anterior chamber IOL (ACIOL), is placed during this process. This procedure is not usually recommended for children. Another type of ACIOL is fixed to the iris (*iris claw IOL*).

IOLs may be made out of a plastic called polymethyl methacrylate (PMMA), acrylic, or silicone. Silicone IOLs are rarely used in children. IOLs have a central area (optic) through which the patient views the world. Two thin, curved, flexible arms (haptics) usually help to stabilize the IOL in the membrane envelope. Certain IOL materials allow the lens to be folded as it is inserted into the eye, and then unfolded within it. This means that the incision in the eye can be smaller. Some IOLs are coated with heparin, a chemical that some medical professionals believe decreases the inflammatory response of the eye. The evidence that heparin makes a difference in the rate of eye inflammation in children is controversial.

Q. Are glasses or contact lenses used along with an IOL?

A. An IOL does not function in the same way as a natural lens. Your natural lens can focus at any distance automatically, without any effort on your part. It does not matter whether the distance is up close, as for activities such as reading, or far away. An artificial lens, like a contact lens, has its best focus at a specific distance. Often, glasses or contact lenses are needed to help see up close.

The prescription strength (power) of the IOL is calculated by taking measurements of the shape and length of the eye before surgery using keratometry and A-scan ultrasound. A compliant child can have these measurements taken while awake or they can be accomplished just before the surgery, while the child is under general anesthesia. Unfortunately, despite our best efforts, the calculations are not always perfect. In addition, it is very difficult to predict with absolute certainty what power will be required years after surgery, as the child grows and matures.

Children must often wear glasses or contact lenses to work with the IOL to get perfect vision. If IOLs are placed in both eyes, the child will more likely need glasses or contacts for reading. For distance vision, most children require only thin glasses or low-power contact lenses, though some children need fairly thick glasses until they grow into the power of their IOLs. If the power needed in the future is higher than expected, some children will always require glasses or contacts in addition to their IOLs.

Final vision outcomes in adulthood do not seem to be different when an IOL or only a contact lens is used. All studies conducted so far have shown that both methods produce the same result as a child grows up. Each lets the child see equally well, as long as there are no other complicating factors.

IOLs or contact lenses have no effect on amblyopia. A child less than approximately 7 or 8 years old will likely still need patching of his/her good eye to reverse amblyopia in the cataract eye following surgery. If the child does not patch, the vision will not improve with either contact lens or IOL.

Patients who have been using contact lenses or glasses can later choose to switch to an IOL. This can be done, even many years after the cataract removal, with a second operation to insert an IOL (secondary implantation). The IOL insertion will not improve the vision further unless contact lenses or glasses alone were unsuccessful, and provided that patching is continued, if necessary. Fewer than 10 percent of patients using contact lenses choose to undergo this second operation in later childhood, as most are happy with contacts.

When placing an IOL in a child, the hope is that it will last for his/her lifetime and never need replacement. Replacing an IOL can actually be quite difficult in children, as scar tissue can hold the IOL quite firmly in the eye.

Q. Is IOL implantation appropriate for all children?
A. Although IOL implantation is becoming increasingly popular throughout the world, professionals at many medical centers are concerned that there are additional risks to placing them in children with microphthalmia and young children, especially those under 2 years old.

Children with iritis may also be poor candidates for IOL implantation because their eyes are already prone to inflammation. Children's eyes are much more prone to having an adverse response to implantation of an IOL than those of adults. Complications would be even more likely in children who had preexisting iritis.

IOLs have been placed in infants at some facilities, though it is more difficult to ascertain the correct power of the IOL for it to last the rest of the child's life. Infants need IOLs that are very powerful, and these are sometimes not commercially available. One approach to this problem is to place two IOLs in the eye at the same time (piggyback implantation) to provide the extra power that an infant needs. At a later date, usually after a year or two, one of the IOLs is removed. This method subjects the infant to the risk of a second surgery that would otherwise not be necessary. Piggyback implantation is quite experimental and controversial.

Another theoretical advantage of IOLs is that there is constant vision correction as compared to contact lenses or glasses, which may sometimes not be worn.

Q. Which is better, intraocular lens insertion, contact lenses, or glasses?
A. It appears that visual development proceeds equally well with all three treatment options. Glasses have the disadvantage of distorting vision at the edges, which may reduce side (peripheral) vision. They may also cause more subtle variations in day-to-day vision if the lenses move back and forth across the nose. Contact lenses are expensive and may be difficult to insert or remove. IOL implantation may have additional surgical risks. For each child, an individual choice for visual rehabilitation must be made considering both family and patient factors.

One of these choices may be more appropriate than the others for a particular child. Factors to consider include cost, convenience, and suitability for that child's lifestyle. For example, if a child's parent has severe rheumatoid arthritis in his/her hands, then inserting the contact lenses may be impossible for the parent. Some children have facial structures that make the fitting of glasses very difficult. In children with corneal issues, such as those who have aniridia or have had a corneal transplant, contact lenses may be inadvisable. If a child has iritis, IOL implantation can cause excessive inflammation inside the eye.

Q. What is the youngest age at which a child can be successfully implanted with an IOL?
A. Lens implants have been used in infants as early as the first two weeks of life. Current data suggests that this practice may be associated with a higher complication rate, including a dramatically increased need for repeat surgery. So far, all published papers suggest that the vision outcome from contact lens is the same as that with lens implants.

The Infant Aphakia Treatment Trial is an important study that has been completed. Doctors from across North America participated in this research project by randomly selecting some babies to have their cataract surgery with an IOL and others without. The data about outcomes is now coming in and has consistently shown that IOL implantation in infants younger than six months of age at the time of surgery creates more complications without significant benefit to outweigh those problems.

Q. What are the advantages and disadvantages of IOL implantation?
A. Although IOLs have been placed in adults for over 40 years, regular use in children has only been popularized in the last 10 to 20 years. As a result, we do not know what will happen to an eye that has an IOL in it for a lifetime that may last more than an additional 70 years. There are no clear or certain reasons, so far, to expect any particularly major complications in the long term.

The primary advantage of IOL implantation in children who have had cataract surgery is cost and convenience. In most countries, implantation of an IOL is included in the cost of cataract surgery. In some countries, use of the newer foldable IOLs and IOLs made of more advanced materials may require additional payment. There is even less information available about results with these newer IOLs in children than the older, rigid, PMMA lenses.

Another theoretical advantage of IOLs is that they constantly correct vision. Contact lenses or glasses only correct vision when they are worn.

The potential disadvantages of IOL implantation in children are:

- Possibility of inflammation and rejection: IOL implantation can result in inflammation inside the eye (iritis) as the eye responds to the foreign material. Though it is rare for an uncontrollable rejection to occur, some children need high-dose steroid eyedrops, or even steroids by mouth, to prevent this. If the inflammation is not treated adequately, it can lead to excessive scar tissue or pigment coating on the IOL. We have learned over the years to control this inflammation well in the majority of children.
- IOL malposition (subluxation): Another possible complication is the need for additional surgery to reposition an IOL that is no longer centered in the eye. As more surgeons gain experience, this complication is less likely to occur.
- Unpredictability of IOL power: It is not always possible to accurately determine the power of lens a child will require. As a result, sometimes glasses or contact lenses are needed in addition to the IOL for the child to get the proper visual correction. Unlike contact lenses, one cannot easily replace an IOL to get a more appropriate level of power.

- Unknown very long-term safety: While IOL implantation has certainly made the lives of some parents and children easier, the risks and the benefits must be carefully considered, particularly in children under 2 years old. Much research continues to be done in this area, and success rates are increasing rapidly.

Q. Should my child have IOL surgery?

A. It is important that you have a satisfactory conversation with your child's surgeon before proceeding with IOL surgery. In particular, it is important to know if he/she is using new and innovative techniques which may not have an adequate history of success. Some centers ask patients to participate in research protocols, during which the procedure is studied carefully to assess its safety and outcome. Some of these surgical variations are still somewhat experimental in children and may have unknown long-term safety risks. Certain variations, such as piggyback implantation, sewing the IOL to fixate it inside the eye, and implantation of *tension support rings* that help a loose bag stay in place, all need further study.

The overwhelming majority of children who have IOL surgery do very well and experience excellent results. This is why most centers in the world now place IOLs almost routinely, when possible, in children over 2 years old. This has been particularly useful in countries where contact lenses or glasses may not be readily available, bringing vision to children who would otherwise be left blind due to untreated cataracts.

Q. Are contacts equivalent to having implants?

A. The vision with contacts, glasses, or implants is the same. Some children with bilateral contacts do not wear bifocals because they have one contact for far viewing and one for near. This is called *monovision* and is much easier to accomplish with contacts than glasses.

Q. Which type of intraocular lens is better, the soft type or the hard type?

A. There are two categories of lens implants which can be placed into an eye after removal of a cataract—rigid and foldable.

Rigid IOLs are made of a plastic polymer, usually PMMA, that is already in its final shape when implanted. This type of IOL was used in children for many years. Rigid lenses are very stable in terms of their shape and size, and the plastic material can remain inside an eye for decades without causing any problems. The only disadvantage of rigid lenses is that the incision in the eye needs to be the same size as the widest part of the IOL—about 6 to 7 millimeters.

Foldable IOLs are made of a flexible plastic-like material. Soft lenses made of acrylic are now the most common type of IOL implanted into children's eyes. They can be folded in half, or even rolled into a tube shape, allowing them to be squeezed into the eye through a smaller incision (usually about 3 to 4 millimeters).

Q. What are multifocal IOLs?

A. A multifocal IOL is designed to give the patient the ability to see both at a distance and up close without additional glasses. These are rarely used in children because the needed prescription varies too much as the child grows. In addition, these IOLs require perfectly central placement behind the pupil, which can be difficult to achieve in children.

Q. What are "specialty" IOLs?
A. This term was coined to describe IOLs that have features that allow for more exacting qualities, including filtering of particular wavelengths of light, multifocal focusing, and/or the correction of astigmatism (*toric IOLs*). They are often more expensive than traditional lenses because insurance may not cover the full cost. These lenses are rarely used in children

Q. How do I decide what IOL is best for my child?
A. There are many factors to be considered, including availability, eye anatomy, eye size, the age of your child, and the surgeon's preferences. Your child's ophthalmologist and you should discuss the pros and cons of the various lens types.

Q. Can a child, who is now 12 and had cataract surgery very soon after birth but no IOLs implanted at that time, have IOLs placed now?
A. Yes, implants are now possible, but this would require surgery. The only reason to put a child through an operation, with the associated risks and inconveniences, would be if he/she is having difficulty with his/her contact lenses or glasses. Putting an implant in now (secondary implantation) may raise some surgical challenges due to accumulated scar tissue in the eye that determine what options are available (or not) to complete the procedure.

Q. I had cataract surgery as a child and IOLs were not placed at the time. Would it be useful to have them implanted now, or is it considered cosmetic surgery at this point?
A. It is never too late to put in an implant, but any amblyopia that set in during childhood is not reversible now. This means that whatever your vision is in contact lenses or glasses before surgery will be your best possible vision after IOL surgery. Some eyes are not able to safely or easily have lens implant surgery after cataract removal for anatomic reasons. Your ophthalmologist can help determine if your eye could safely receive a lens implant.

If you wear glasses, then the surgery would be considered largely for the purpose of improving your appearance and perhaps, removing the inconvenience and cost of glasses, and improving the quality of your vision, especially your peripheral vision. You could achieve the same vision result with contact lenses or glasses. If you cannot wear contact lenses and wear glasses but cannot stand them, secondary IOL implantation may be the right thing for you.

Going from contact lenses to implants does not change your appearance or vision, so it would only be done for convenience, long-term cost savings, or because there is some medical reason you can no longer wear contacts.

Q. If my child has an IOL placed after cataract surgery, will it expand as his/her eye grows?
A. An implant does not change over time, but your child's prescription for glasses may. In this situation, the implant is not taken out and replaced. Instead, glasses or contact lenses are prescribed to work with the implant to get the correct total prescription and focus.

Although it is true that the eye grows over time, most of this occurs in the first two years of life. If the implant changes position in the eye over time, then additional surgery may be needed. Routine replacement of the implant due to growth is not a normal practice.

Implants are designed to last a lifetime, but we have only been putting them in children with some regularity since about 1990. Some of the newer implants have been in use for much shorter periods.

Consequently, we do not have the 90-year follow up that reflects the age to which your child will likely live. Implants have been used in adults for decades without long-term harm.

PART IV: SURGERY

A. GENERAL QUESTIONS

Q. What questions should I ask the doctor before scheduling surgery?
A. What questions you choose to ask are up to you. Here are some suggestions that may help you:

- Where do we go on the day of surgery?
- What time do we arrive at the medical site for the surgery?
- Who will we see at each stage of the day of surgery?
- Who is responsible for my child's care at each stage of the day of surgery?
- How many times has the surgeon done this operation in children?
- What can my child have to eat or drink before surgery and when do they have to stop eating and drinking?
- Will a breast pump be available for use on the day of surgery?
- If I'm staying overnight with my child, do I need to bring my own bedding, food, drinks, etc.?
- What will happen the day after the surgery?

Q. Why must my child stop eating and drinking so long before surgery?
A. The instructions not to feed a child before surgery ensure that his/her stomach will be empty while he/she is under anesthesia. If you do not follow these instructions, your child's operation, test, or treatment will be delayed or cancelled.

It is very important that there be nothing in your child's stomach when he/she is anesthetized. During anesthesia or sedation, it is possible for food or liquid to come back up the tube between the throat and the stomach (*esophagus*) towards the mouth (commonly known as *reflux*), as it sometimes can do when one is lying on his/her back or unconscious. If this occurs while your child is anesthetized, the food or liquid could accidentally get into his/her lungs (*aspiration*). This does not happen to someone who is awake because the body has natural mechanisms that protect from this. When someone is under anesthesia, these protections are not active.

Remember that lollipops, candy, chewing gum, and popsicles, even if sucked and not chewed or swallowed, are all considered food and may not be eaten within the windows below. Just the act of chewing stimulates excess stomach fluid.

Q. How long before surgery must my child stop eating and drinking?
A. Please note that these instructions may vary slightly between hospitals or surgical centers. They are intended as guidelines only. Check with your child's surgeon for specific instructions.

In general, make sure your child stops eating solid food at least eight hours before receiving anesthetic. For example, if your child is scheduled for surgery at 8 a.m., do not give him/her anything to eat or drink after midnight. Older children should not consume food or liquids after midnight, even if the surgery is later in the morning or early afternoon.

Younger children and infants may only have clear liquids during the period of three to eight hours before the anesthetic is administered. For example, if your child is scheduled for surgery at noon, stop giving clear liquids at 9 a.m. Clear liquids are those liquids you can see through and include water, clear or colored gelatin without fruit, ginger ale, clear juice that contains no pulp, children's electrolyte replacement beverages, sports drinks, and other similar clear drinks. Ask your child's doctor whether your child can have clear fluids during this timeframe at the hospital where he/she is having surgery. Do not give your child milk during this period. Older children may be required to stop consuming clear liquids earlier.

Your child, regardless of age, cannot have anything to eat or drink from three hours before the anesthetic until after he/she wakes up. For example, if your child is having surgery at 3 p.m., he/she cannot have anything to eat or drink after noon. The surgeon may make an exception to allow a sip of water for the purpose of taking a required medication that must be taken within this time window.

If your child is breastfeeding, stop giving him/her breast milk four hours before the anesthetic is administered. For example, if your child is getting the anesthetic at 2 p.m., stop breastfeeding at 10 a.m.

Many parents fear that their children will become dehydrated or starve during these periods where intake is not allowed, especially if surgery is delayed. During anesthesia, a small tube is inserted into a vein (*intravenous line*) to give the child sugar water. This keeps him/her well hydrated and receiving nutrition to make up for not being allowed to eat or drink before surgery. If it is medically necessary for your child to receive hydration or nutrition, special precautions can be taken to ensure that he/she is not deprived In such cases it may be recommended that the child be admitted the night before surgery, and perhaps even remain in the hospital overnight after surgery.

Q. How can I help my child be less nervous about his/her treatment?
A. To help your child feel less nervous about whatever treatment he/she will undergo, explain what will happen in simple words that he/she will understand. If your child knows what to expect before coming to the hospital, he/she will be better able to deal with the operation, test, or treatment. Children who are not told the details of what will happen tend to let their imaginations run wild and may become more fearful. Just before the surgery, your child may receive a premedication from the *anesthesiologist* that will help to relax him/her before entering the operating room.

Q. When should I call my child's doctor if I am concerned about my child's health before surgery?
A. To reduce the chance of any problems, your child needs to be as healthy as possible before receiving an anesthetic. If your child has any of the following problems the day before or on the day of the operation, test, or treatment, call his/her doctor to find out whether the procedure can still be conducted:

- fever
- wheezing
- cough
- very runny nose
- feeling unwell

If your child has any of these symptoms, the doctor may determine that it is safer to postpone the procedure.

Q. What if my child has pain after the operation, test, or treatment?
A. If your child has pain after the procedure, he/she will be given medicine to reduce or alleviate it. This is done before your child wakes up from the general anesthetic. He/she can continue taking pain medication after going home, but the type of medicine should be discussed with the surgeon or discharging nurse before your child leaves the medical facility. Some pain medicines, such as aspirin or ibuprofen, may increase the chance of bleeding and should be avoided.

Q. What is informed consent?
A. Informed consent is a legal phrase meaning permission obtained after appropriate information about the risks of an activity is presented to the decision maker.

Every surgeon is required to obtain permission from the patient or his/her substitute decision maker, who acts as the patient's advocate, before performing surgery. When the patient is a child, the child's legal guardian (usually the parent) is responsible for giving this permission, often referred to as consent.

Before making the decision, the decision-maker must understand the nature and purpose of the surgery; what is expected to happen before, during, and after surgery; the risks, including both severe risks that occur uncommonly and minor risks that occur commonly; and expected outcomes. The explanation should include what any "reasonable" patient would want to know about surgery. The discussion should also address other options, such as alternative forms of surgery, other medical treatments, and the risks of not having surgery. The surgeon should indicate who is doing the surgery, how long it will take, and how soon it should be performed. Sometimes physicians in academic health sciences centers are operating with trainees. Parents are entitled to know who will be present and what the division of labor will be during the course of the operation.

Informed consent can only come from a competent decision-maker. If the surgeon feels that the legal guardian is too emotionally distraught, or otherwise not exhibiting the full capacity needed to make an informed decision about the child's care, alternate arrangements for permission need to be sought. As an example, if a legal guardian is under the influence of alcohol, the surgeon may judge him/her unable to make such important decisions.

Q. Can I refuse to allow my child to have surgery?
A. A parent or legal guardian may feel that the decision of the eye doctor is not in his/her child's best interests. This applies to both medications and surgery. You should never be afraid to ask another eye doctor for a second opinion. It is the duty of every doctor to help a patient desiring a second opinion find a capable provider who can fulfill that role.

Doctors are not always right. Likewise, parents sometimes make bad decisions. The doctor is obligated to protect the best interests of the child, who may not be mature enough to make a truly informed decision about his/her own care. If the doctor feels the parent or guardian is not acting in the best interests of the child, then he/she must take action. If a parent's or guardian's decision to refuse treatment runs clearly against the standard of care and the physician feels that the child will likely suffer as a result of this decision, then he/she has the option of notifying Social Services or the judicial system to obtain a court order reversing the decision. Fortunately, this is a rare circumstance, which can usually be avoided by ongoing dialogue and teamwork between the family and the doctor.

Infants and young children do not have the maturity to understand medical decisions and may react negatively out of fear. When this occurs, doctors sometimes must use forceful methods, such as safely restraining the child or carrying a crying child into the operating room, to facilitate compliance from the child. Doctors prefer to avoid such actions as much as parents dislike them.

There are some situations in which a child may be able to refuse treatment. If a child is able to make his/her own informed consent decisions, he/she may be considered a "mature minor" whose decisions have equivalent weight to those of the parent. It is also very hard to force a grown child or teenager to do something. An angry, refusing teenager cannot simply be sedated and carried into an operating room.

Preoperative medications, such as the sedative midazolam, can be given to the child in the preoperative area so he/she becomes sleepy and less resistant to coming into the operating room. These medicines reduce anxiety. Pediatric anesthesiologists, nurses, and eye doctors are well versed in calming children down and making the process of surgery as easy as possible.

Q. What role does the child have in deciding whether or not to have surgery?

A. The rules defining a child's role in decision-making will vary depending on the country, state, or province. For example, there is no legal age for giving consent in Ontario, Canada. If the surgeon feels that a child fully understands everything about the surgery, then the child can give his/her own consent. When children are somewhere in between the level of maturity when they understand everything presented and that at which they understand very little, they can give their signed *assent*, which indicates their agreement to go ahead despite the lack of full understanding of the circumstances and potential consequences. Assent should be sought whenever possible.

Q. Should I tell my child about the surgery?

A. In general, children should be active participants in their own care. In most situations, full disclosure to the child by the surgeon and the parent prevents the scenario in which a child is left knowing something is going on but imagining what that might be. Children tend to imagine things that are almost always bigger or worse than the truth, and often beyond the wildest imaginings of a parent. The truth is usually comforting when compared to their fantasies and fears.

Q. How does the doctor decide whether or not to do surgery?

A. In general, surgery is considered for pediatric glaucoma only after medical treatment has failed. In some cases, such as in children with congenital or infantile glaucoma, surgery may be the appropriate first line of treatment. In other cases, where all other medical options have been exhausted, the surgeon must weigh the risks of surgery against the potential benefits. If the risks of surgery are outweighed by the benefits, then the surgeon will choose to proceed. Factors that influence the type of surgery chosen include the type of glaucoma your child has, what surgical procedures have been done before to alleviate the condition, the level of acceptable risk for a particular eye, patient preference, and the surgeon's experience.

Q. What happens on the day of surgery?

A. The general process is similar in most facilities in the United States and Canada, though specific practices may vary from hospital to hospital and doctor to doctor. You will be told how long before surgery your child must stop eating and drinking. After checking in at the hospital, your child will be taken to a preoperative area where he/she will be checked to make sure there are no health concerns. He/she will be given eyedrops to dilate the pupil. Your child will then be taken to the room in which the surgery takes place (operating room) by a nurse and you will move to the waiting room. In some facilities, you may be allowed to accompany your child into the operating room.

Surgery is often scheduled for an hour or more to include time for putting the child under anesthesia, preparing him/her for surgery, doing the surgery, and waking the child from anesthesia, but it may be completed sooner. The doctor or his/her representative will come to see you or call you immediately after surgery. You or your child's other parent will go to the recovery room when your child awakens or shortly thereafter. Your child will usually be able to leave the hospital within a few hours after surgery.

Q. Can the doctor operate on both eyes at the same time?

A. One of the most dreaded complications of almost any kind of eye surgery is infection inside the eyeball (endophthalmitis). Endophthalmitis often results in loss of most or all vision in the affected eye. When this infection occurs, it is presumed that bacteria were transmitted from the operating room or equipment into the eyeball. Every attempt is made to ensure that the operating room is a sterile environment. Surgeons scrub their hands and arms with soap for several minutes before surgery; heat, gas, or chemical disinfectants are used to kill germs on equipment; specially prepared sterile drapes are used over tables and the patient; and rooms are cleaned thoroughly between patients. Despite all our efforts, not every single bacterium can be eliminated.

It is generally assumed that endophthalmitis comes from bacteria that were in the operating room on the day of surgery. This means that surgery on two eyes on that same day puts both at risk for this dangerous complication. Getting this infection in both eyes would be particularly terrible and has the potential to be extremely visually disabling.

Even though endophthalmitis is an extremely rare complication, the risk of it occurring in both eyes after simultaneous surgery is greater than the risk of complications from undergoing general anesthetic twice. In modern times, general anesthesia is extremely safe. Severe complications, such as death or brain damage, are extraordinarily rare. In a healthy child, it is generally safer to operate on each eye separately on different days, even if those days are consecutive, than to operate on both eyes during the same operation. If the child has an underlying medical condition that increases his/her risk of complications from general anesthesia, then the risk of infection from simultaneous surgery may be less than the risk of two separate exposures to general anesthetic. In this situation, bilateral simultaneous eye surgery can be considered.

Despite these factors, some surgeons perform simultaneous bilateral surgery even in the absence of medical risk factors for anesthesia.

Q. Does the doctor remove the eyeball to do the surgery?

A. Although this is a common myth, in reality the eyeball is never removed to perform any kind of surgery other than *enucleation*. Enucleation is the permanent removal of the eyeball. This procedure is done for blind and painful eyes that cannot be treated in any other way.

Q. Who will perform the surgery?

A. Residents and fellows are trainees working under the supervision of the attending physician, (sometimes called consultant staff). Part of the training of a resident or fellow necessarily requires him/her to learn how to do the surgical procedures. In fact, every attending physician received his/her training this way.

Surgical experience is provided in a very graded, supervised fashion, in which the trainees are allowed to perform very small parts of procedures before progressing, over years, to the whole procedure. When residents begin their training, they may simply observe, or possibly help hold tissues aside (*retract*) during literally hundreds of procedures before performing a surgical action. The first surgical actions they perform may simply involve opening or closing the incision while the attending physician performs the main part of the surgery. Gradually, the resident will be allowed to perform parts of the operation, and will eventually do the whole operation under supervision. Having already completed a residency, fellows may be allowed to progress more rapidly, but pediatric glaucoma or cataract procedures are rarely done by residents. During the fellowship, the fellow is considered a beginner and starts fresh with these procedures, step by step, during his/her fellowship.

Attending staff may vary their level of supervision based on several factors. The main parameters they consider are the skill and responsibility of the trainee. If the trainee does not have adequate skill and responsibility to proceed with the further steps of surgery, then he/she will not be allowed to do so. Most surgeon/teachers are standing with their trainees during each procedure and are able to take over at any time should they feel things are becoming too difficult or complicated for the trainee. In some centers, the attending surgeon may not be in the room for the surgery if he/she feels that the trainee is advanced enough and has sufficient skill and responsibility to operate alone.

This method of training is known as *graded responsibility*. It has been shown to be very effective, as well as safe for patients. Several research studies have shown that outcomes of surgery in virtually every specialty are the same whether or not the attending staff or a trainee does the surgery under the supervision of attending staff. Patients must keep in mind that academic health science centers, sometimes called teaching hospitals, boast excellent outcome records largely because of their stimulating educational environments, which keep attending staff on their toes. Such centers assure that the patients have excellent supervised medical and surgical care.

It is certainly understandable that patients may have some discomfort with this approach. Patients can ask their surgeons to do the surgery, and some surgeons will honor this request. Other surgeons may feel strongly about their teaching roles, and require that trainees be involved. In these cases, physicians may elect to help the patient find another care provider who is willing to operate without trainees.

Patients also benefit from the participation of trainees. The patient is contributing to the education of the next generation of physicians by allowing their participation in his/her treatment. Trainees often have more interest in particular patients and spend more time with them. This conduct is often both comforting and reassuring. Likewise, trainees facilitate the staff person's ability to attend to other work, which contributes to the patient's care. Some of the most famous surgeons would not have achieved as much without the assistance of their trainees. This success is a testimony to the symbiotic relationship between attending staff, trainees, and patients.

Q. Where will I wait while my child gets surgery?

A. Most operating theaters throughout the world have a preoperative waiting room where children and their caretakers gather before the child is taken into the actual operating room. After the child is taken into surgery, parents are usually escorted to a waiting room until the surgery is over. After the surgery, the surgeon or his/her designate will come out to inform the caretakers that the surgery has been completed and provide any additional relevant information.

Q. How long will my child be hospitalized for cataract or glaucoma surgery?
A. Cataract and glaucoma surgery are now generally outpatient operations, in which the child comes in, has surgery, and goes home, all in the same day. In some hospitals, babies may have to stay overnight to make sure that they tolerate the general anesthetic. Different hospitals may have different rules about exactly what is the minimum age when a baby can be discharged on the day of surgery without being admitted overnight. Children with other medical problems may also need to stay overnight. An overnight stay is rarely needed just because of the eye condition.

Q. How do I involve my child's siblings in his/her recovery from surgery?
A. The period of surgery may be difficult for siblings, particularly since the child being operated upon requires more attention. When possible, siblings can be given some responsibility in caring for the child who had surgery. This method may help to increase the siblings' self-esteem, and also increase their empathy for the patient. Other approaches include having one parent spend special time with the sibling, or allowing the sibling to visit with a favorite relative or friend during the patient's recovery.

Sometimes a young sibling is especially interested in seeing what has happened to his/her brother/sister. He/she may even try to remove the patch or shield to see what is going on underneath. Careful supervision of young children is necessary during recovery, both for the safety of the patient and the understanding of the sibling. Children have big imaginations, which sometimes lead to bizarre ideas about surgery. Frank, open conversations are usually the best way to educate children—both patients and siblings—about the realities of surgery and its impact on the family.

Q. Will my child lose any vision due to the surgery? If so, how much?
A. There is a risk of vision loss any time surgery is performed inside an eye. Vision loss can occur due to corneal problems, cataract, bleeding, infection, retinal detachment, or optic nerve damage. In patients with advanced glaucoma who may have already had significant injury to their optic nerves from the glaucoma, surgery can result in a sudden blindness. This is sometimes referred to as *snuff*.

Surgeons weigh the risks versus the benefits before proceeding with any operation. Surgery is only appropriate when the risk of vision loss from surgery is less than the risk of vision loss from the disease.

Q. Is my child's surgery being done on an outpatient basis just to save money?
A. Although there are certainly economic factors that enter into a hospital's ability to keep patients overnight, no surgery should be performed on an outpatient basis if it is unsafe to do so. Years ago, patients who had cataract surgery were admitted for a week or more, their heads held still by sandbags on either side. Modern technology has made this surgery much safer, enough so that patients can be in and out on the same day. The same is true for most pediatric eye surgery.

Another factor to be considered is the possibility that a patient who needs to be admitted, such as a car accident victim, might be turned away because an individual who could have been adequately served as an outpatient was occupying an inpatient bed. Pediatric eye surgery seldom requires an overnight admission, and patients heal, and feel, better at home. Additionally, there are many patients in hospitals who have serious infections. It is not unusual for patients to actually catch an infection while they are in a hospital.

There are situations when a child will be required to stay in hospital overnight. Some localities and hospitals have regulations that children under a certain age, usually young infants or babies born prematurely, must stay for one night of observation after anesthesia. This is because infants may experience irregular breathing patterns after anesthesia. Children with medical disorders that require extra monitoring, such as seizures, diabetes, or heart disease, may also be asked to stay in hospital overnight. If a child needs intravenous antibiotics after surgery, such as after an injury in which the eyeball is cut open by a stick, then this must be delivered as an inpatient. If a child must stay overnight, most hospitals allow at least one parent to stay in the room with him/her.

Q. What is peripheral iridectomy?
A. Peripheral iridectomy is a surgical procedure in which a hole is cut in the edge of the iris to allow fluid to drain into the front part of the eye.

In rare instances, the fluid that is made in a child's eye gets trapped behind the iris and cannot get through the pupil at the front of the eye to drain. As the fluid continues to be produced, the iris is pushed forward (*iris bombé*) to the extent that it begins to block the drainage angle and trabecular meshwork, causing a form of closed angle glaucoma. This complication most commonly occurs in patients with iritis when scar tissue (*posterior synechiae*) forms between the edge of the pupil and the lens. This scar seals the two together, trapping the fluid behind the iris. Other causes of fluid buildup include ectopia lentis, when a loose lens moves forward and blocks the ability of the fluid to flow from behind the iris through the pupil, and conditions where the lens is pushed forward by something from behind, such as a tumor inside the eye or retinal detachment.

The only way to treat iris bombé is to offer the fluid an alternative route to get to the front of the eye so that the iris is no longer pushed forward. Cutting the posterior synechiae or removing the lens of the eye may be one approach. Peripheral iridectomy also allows the fluid to come forward. The iris will then settle back, exposing the angle of the eye and allowing the fluid to drain out comfortably, relieving the glaucoma. In older children, the hole can be placed in the iris using a laser. This is not possible in children who have trouble remaining stationary and keeping their eyes still.

During cataract and glaucoma surgery, particularly during trabeculectomy surgery, the surgeon may put in a preventative peripheral iridectomy. If a patient with iritis undergoes cataract surgery, putting in a preventative peripheral iridectomy may decrease his/her risk of developing angle closure glaucoma after the surgery, but it may also increase the risk of bleeding inside the eye or aggravate the iritis. In trabeculectomy surgery, the peripheral iridectomy is put in to prevent the edge of the iris from flowing out the eye through the new drainage hole (sclerostomy), which could clog the hole and lead to failure of the operation.

B. ANESTHESIA AND SEDATION

Q. What is the difference between sedation and general anesthesia?
A. These terms are often confusing, since both conditions are associated with forms of sleep induced by medication.

Sedation is a medically controlled state of decreased consciousness. There are two types of sedation: conscious sedation and deep sedation.

In conscious sedation, the patient is able to maintain the protective reflexes of coughing and gagging. He/she is also able to maintain breathing independently and continuously and respond appropriately to physical or verbal commands. It is a state of extreme relaxation.

Deep sedation is a form of general anesthetic. The patient is unconscious and not easily aroused. He/she requires medical support to ensure that he/she continues breathing smoothly, usually with some type of device, such as a tube in the mouth or a mask on the face.

An example of sedation is when an adult takes a sleeping pill at home to provoke sleep at night. This is a state of very light sedation. Sedation in the hospital is a medically controlled state of decreased consciousness that allows the patient to maintain normal automatic functions, such as breathing and swallowing, and to retain appropriate responses to physical stimulation, such as pain responses.

A general anesthetic is a mix of medicines that puts your child into a deep sleep. You may also hear it referred to as sleep medicine. While in this deep sleep, your child will not feel any pain during the surgery.

General anesthesia is a form of deep sedation, and is the type most often used in children. Anesthesia is medically controlled unconsciousness from which a patient cannot be aroused. Your child cannot wake up while under anesthesia. This condition is associated with loss of the ability to breathe without help, swallow secretions normally present in the throat, and respond to physical stimulation. These effects generally go away once the anesthesia has worn off. During anesthesia, the child must receive the help of an anesthesiologist, who uses machines, breathing tubes, and medications to control the child's body, allow good breathing, and monitor the child's health.

Sedation or general anesthesia for any surgical procedures must be administered by qualified personnel who possess the knowledge and the skill necessary to provide proper care. Furthermore, all patients receiving sedation or general anesthesia must be treated in an area where monitoring machines are available to check the heart rate, blood pressure, and breathing.

Q. Can my child die from general anesthesia?
A. Death is a risk of general anesthesia, though it is extremely rare, especially if the anesthesiologist has been trained to administer anesthesia to children of all ages. Based on recent surveys, the estimated risk of anesthesia-related death is between 7 in 100,000 and 6 in 1,000,000 uses. There is a greater chance that your child will die in your car on the way to the hospital than from anesthesia.

The most important factor is that the anesthesiologist must be familiar with how the drugs being used work specifically in children and what side effects are likely to occur during and after their administration. The doctor must also know how to resolve complications that may occur, such as breathing problems induced by the medication.

Certain risks may be higher for children with particular conditions. If a child has asthma, narrow air passages (*laryngomalacia*), or a cold, he/she may have more problems breathing after surgery. Children with seizures may have a temporary increase in the frequency of their seizures.

Q. Does my child have to be put to sleep using general anesthesia for surgery?
A. Surgery for glaucoma requires microscopic attention to fine detail. The patient must be absolutely still. Although adults can undergo some of their glaucoma surgery while they are awake,

general anesthesia is almost always required for children undergoing surgical procedures. If a child cannot be examined while awake, sedation may be used instead of full anesthesia if no surgery is being performed.

Q. Who gives my child the anesthetic?
A. The doctor that gives your child the general anesthetic is called an anesthesiologist or anesthetist, depending on which country you are in. In some countries, the term anesthetist describes the doctor. In other countries, it refers to a nurse anesthetist, a nursing professional who is specially trained to assist an anesthesiologist in administering general anesthesia. During your child's operation, test, or treatment, the anesthesiologist or anesthetist will check your child's breathing, heartbeat, temperature, and blood pressure.

Q. How will the anesthesiologist give my child the anesthetic?
A. There are two ways in which the anesthesiologist may initially administer the anesthetic. He/she may give your child the anesthetic intravenously. Alternatively, he/she may use a face mask to administer a gas or inhalation anesthetic. Both are usually used together in some way. The variation is in which is administered first. The initial selection depends on the child, the operation, and the anesthesiologist.

Q. Can I choose the anesthesiologist who will put my child to sleep?
A. This depends on the policy of the particular hospital or medical facility. If you have a preference for a certain doctor, do not hesitate to speak up and ask whether or not your request can be fulfilled. Keep in mind that anesthesiologists often work shifts, as they have to sometimes be present at night for emergencies. They also cover multiple parts of many hospitals and may not be available on the day or at the time your child's procedure is scheduled.

Q. What should I do if I have questions about the anesthesia?
A. On the day of your child's operation, test, or treatment, your child's anesthesiologist will meet with you to answer your questions and talk about your concerns before surgery. You can also call your surgeon or the medical facility's anesthesia department to ask questions or express any special concerns you may have.

Q. Why does my child need to be sedated even though he/she is not having surgery?
A. There are a number of reasons why your child might be sedated. Some children cannot be examined awake because they cannot sit still for the necessary length of time; cannot keep their eyes still; or will not allow specific measurements, such as eye pressure readings, that are essential to monitor their eyes.

There is no specific age at which sedation might be required. Some children are able to be examined while awake at relatively early ages, while others require sedation even at later ages.

The goals of sedation in the pediatric patient are to:

- guard the patient's safety and welfare;
- minimize physical discomfort or pain;
- minimize negative psychological responses to treatment by softening or eliminating the memory of the procedure;
- control behavior that can disrupt the examination or affect the validity of the tests; and

- return the patient to a state in which safe discharge, as determined by recognized criteria, is possible.

Q. What is the procedure for sedation?

A. Prior to sedation, a health evaluation that includes a physical examination and a check of breathing status is conducted, an informed consent agreement for the procedure is obtained, and food and liquid intake are checked. There are strict rules for when the patient must stop eating or drinking prior to the procedure. Having food or liquid in the stomach is dangerous, as it can come up during sedation or anesthesia and enter the lungs. This can cause severe breathing problems, infection, or even death.

The nurse or anesthesiologist providing the sedation will ask a number of questions which will help to determine whether sedation is appropriate and the depth of sedation that might be required for the planned procedure. You should expect to be asked several questions, including some related to any breathing problems your child may have, such as a recent cold, cough, and/or fever. You will also be asked again about the last time your child ate or drank anything, since the use of sedation when a patient has consumed food or liquid too recently is hazardous. The presence of allergies or any other medical conditions, whether specific to the child or within the family, may also influence the final decision to use sedation.

Once the decision to provide sedation is made, the procedure will be similar to general anesthesia. The room where the patient will be will include similar equipment, such as blood pressure, heart rate, and temperature monitors. Oxygen levels will be closely watched using a small wire taped to the finger or toe. Most often, an intravenous catheter is inserted to give medicine. This is usually placed on the back of the hand, but may sometimes be placed in the crook of the elbow or on the foot instead. The doctor may occasionally elect to begin the sedation by administering the first medication by mouth (*premedication*).

After the procedure, your child will be brought to a room for surveillance until the recovery from the effect of the medication is complete and he/she has regained full consciousness. In some cases, your child's sedation may take place in the same room where he/she will also wake up and be observed until discharge. In some institutions, you may be allowed to be with the child throughout the entire sedation and procedure. In others, you may be required to wait until your child is awake before you will be allowed to enter the recovery area.

Chloral hydrate sedation is usually the best choice for accomplishing a sedation examination. This option is available in some outpatient clinics. The medicine is a liquid that the child drinks. Some children resist and may even spit or vomit the medicine out. The child must be carefully and continuously monitored for several hours after receiving the medication. This supervision is necessary to ensure that any of the rarely experienced complications, such as unsafe breathing or swallowing difficulties, may be addressed and resolved immediately.

Chloral hydrate sedation is only effective in putting children up to a certain weight to sleep. The exact maximum weight depends on the dosage allowed at the institution where the sedation is being given. Some hospitals allow higher dosages than others. All children will eventually grow to a weight where chloral hydrate will no longer work in getting them to sleep. Another challenge is that approximately 10 percent of children who receive chloral hydrate become hyperactive instead of sedated. If a child has grown beyond the maximum weight or has this unusual reaction to the chloral hydrate and cannot be examined while awake, he/she will require general anesthesia for the examination.

Q. How is the sedation medication administered?

A. Sedation must be administered in a facility that has the appropriate equipment and expert personnel who can manage any emergency situation that may arise. The type of setting depends on the type of sedation. Certain medications, such as chloral hydrate, are given by mouth and may be delivered in a clinic setting under the supervision of a nurse, where oxygen levels and heart rate are appropriately monitored. Outside of the operating room, sedation is administered only to healthy patients and those with very mild systemic diseases that are not active.

Q. Why might sedation be chosen over anesthesia, or vice versa?

A. There are several factors guiding the anesthesiologist to choose sedation over general anesthesia or vice versa. The age of the patient will influence the decision, the younger receiving mostly general anesthesia rather than sedation for safety purposes. Medical conditions (such as heart problems, breathing difficulties, severe obesity, etc.) will also contribute to the decision. The surgical procedure to be performed will have a direct impact on the final decision. For instance, an eye examination under anesthesia could be achieved in a 3-year-old child under sedation, whereas the same patient undergoing cataract surgery will need general anesthesia.

Q. Can I be with my child when he/she goes to sleep under sedation or anesthesia?

A. This depends on the hospital's or medical facility's policy. Some facilities allow one or both parents to accompany the child into the operating room until he/she is asleep under general anesthesia. Others allow parents to watch the entire surgery or view it on video. Ask your surgeon or anesthesiologist about the policy of the hospital where your child is having the examination or procedure performed. Keep in mind that each facility creates a policy that works best for its environment. Ultimately, the decision of the surgeon and anesthesiologist on an individual case should be respected.

Parents or caregivers are usually allowed to be with the patient until he/she is taken into the area for sedation. They may sometimes be allowed to remain until the child goes to sleep, and to be present when he/she awakens. In some facilities, the parents may even be allowed to stay throughout a sedation procedure, though not for a procedure involving general anesthesia. Some parents like to be with their children as they fall asleep, but others are uncomfortable. Some children do better with parents being there, while others become more resistant to the medical team's care. Some parents may not enjoy watching if their child vomits the medicine given for sedation or resists the medication and procedures necessary to get them sleeping.

Q. What aftereffects of sedation or anesthesia should I be looking for once my child wakes up?

A. The potential side effects following the administration of sedation will depend on the depth of sedation, the medication used, and the procedures performed. All three factors will have a direct influence on the way your child reacts to the sedation.

General anesthesia is more often associated with side effects than sedation due to the complexity and types of medication used. The potential side effects depend on the medication used and the surgical procedure performed. The most frequent side effect is vomiting. Nausea and vomiting are amplified by motion, which may complicate the trip home. Your child may also feel discomfort or pain that is a result of the procedure and are not related to the anesthesia.

Your child will not be allowed to leave the hospital until he/she has regained complete consciousness, though he/she may remain drowsy for some time

Other complications from sedation or anesthesia are rare, but do occasionally occur. These problems may include breathing too fast (*hyperventilation*); short stoppages of breathing (*apnea*); inability to breathe because the throat is closed off (*obstructed airway*), usually due to spasm of the vocal cords (*laryngospasm*); or problems with blood pressure or heart rate.

Your child will not feel any pain or discomfort from the sedation or anesthesia, though there may be some from the actual procedure. He/she will likely also not remember what occurred while he/she was asleep.

Q. What is an EUA?
A. EUA is an abbreviation for Examination Under Anesthesia. This term refers to a situation where a patient is placed under general anesthesia for an examination.

Q. Why is EUA chosen over sedation or vice versa?
A. The most common reasons for choosing sedation versus EUA are convenience, availability, and preference. Some parents enjoy being with their sleeping children during the entire examination if that option is available. Other parents prefer not to see their children while they are sleeping or being examined.

An EUA might be preferred as a matter of convenience, lack of availability of a lesser sedation level, and the child's reaction to the medication used for sedation. In many hospitals, a doctor can conduct tests on several patients under anesthesia in the operating room. An outpatient clinic may not have the needed equipment and resources to be able to accommodate as many cases under sedation. This limits the number of appointments a facility has available for sedation examinations.

Children with increased medical risks, such as those with asthma or heart problems also usually undergo EUA, as the presence of an anesthesiologist during the examination is advisable. He/she has the necessary skill to handle potential complications in these higher-risk individuals.

C. WHAT TO EXPECT AFTER SURGERY

Q. How do children react to surgery?
A. The procedure is usually far more stressful for the parents than it is for the child. Often, the child shows no symptoms of having had surgery by the next day.

Your child may sleep more than usual after surgery. He/she will be wearing an eye patch, which will remain on until the following day. During the night, some children try to take the patch off. It is important to keep the patch on so he/she does not rub the eye. If needed, acetaminophen may be used to keep your child comfortable overnight.

Older children and teenagers have a variety of responses that vary from acting as if nothing happened to complaining and requiring more attention and care. There is no "right" way to respond to the procedure. Parents must adjust their responses to provide the child with the care and support he/she needs. The main things to look out for on the first night are excessive pain not controlled by acetaminophen or recurrent vomiting, either of which should lead you to call the surgeon.

Q. Where will my child go after his/her operation, test, or treatment?
A. After the procedure, your child will go to the recovery room, sometimes called the *postanesthetic care unit* (*PACU*). Specially trained nurses will watch your child. These nurses will check your child's breathing, heartbeat, temperature, and blood pressure regularly. You will be called to be with your child as soon as he/she wakes up.

Q. What will my child look like in the recovery room?
A. Each child has a unique response to general anesthetic. Some children enjoy a long sleep, while others wake up quickly and may even be irritable or crying. Vomiting is a rare occurrence.

Your child will have a patch and a shield over the eye that was operated on. The patch may be slightly wet or bloody. He/she may also still have an IV line in his/her hand or foot. This is used to provide fluids while he/she is sleeping, which is particularly important after the period of not eating that was required before surgery. A clip with a red light may be attached to one finger or toe. This is called a pulse oximeter, and measures the amount of oxygen in the blood. It is unlikely that your child will need an oxygen mask or any other significant equipment.

Q. When will I be able to see, hold, and feed my child after surgery?
A. Although the policies differ from hospital to hospital, most facilities allow a parent to enter the recovery room as soon as his/her child is awake. In some cases, parents are allowed to join their children before they awaken. In a busy hospital setting, it may be necessary for the nursing staff to wait until the activity in the unit has quieted before visitors are allowed.

Once you enter the recovery area, you will probably be able to hold your child right away. In many cases, this is actually preferred, as it helps to keep the child calm.

The nurses will give you instructions on when you can feed your child. In most hospitals, this is allowed as soon as the child is awake. You may be encouraged to start with something light, such as apple juice or sugar water, particularly if your child is a young infant. Breastfeeding babies are usually allowed to be fed immediately upon waking.

Q. Will I be in the same room with my child as he/she recovers?
A. Different hospitals have different policies. In most pediatric hospitals in North America, one or both parents are invited into the recovery room to comfort the child once he/she is awake and stable.

Breastfeeding mothers, parents of young or particularly frightened children, and parents of children whose only seeing eye has been patched as a result of the surgery may be allowed to visit the recovery room earlier. These exceptions are made in compassionate response to the special nature of the child's situation.

There may be a temporary delay in allowing parents to come in if there is a high level of activity in the recovery room. Some children will also sleep longer than usual after surgery and not require the immediate attention of their parents.

Q. What is a postsurgery briefing?
A. After surgery, you should expect the surgeon to speak to you about how the procedure went. Some surgeons will ask a trainee or other designated representative to share this information with you. This conversation may occur immediately after surgery or, if the surgeon is busy with other

cases, by phone or at a more convenient time later in the day. This session is designed to give you information about the procedure, results, and postoperative care.

Q. What should I know about taking my child home after surgery?
A. Most children tolerate surgery very well and will be back to normal the same evening or on the day after surgery. Your child can eat after surgery if he/she feels up to it, but it is best to proceed slowly. Start with light foods, such as clear liquids, soup, rice, crackers, and toast for older children, and sugar water or clear apple juice for infants. Breast feeding can start as soon as your child is awake.

All children are different and may react differently to surgery, anesthesia, or sedation. Some will have nausea, vomiting, or sleepiness after surgery. The nature and severity of your child's reactions will also depend on the type of surgery performed. Recovery from an EUA or sedation is likely to be fairly rapid with no discomfort. Glaucoma tube implantation surgery has a longer recovery time and your child may be uncomfortable during this period.

Some discomfort, blurry vision, redness, and blood-tinged tears are normal after eye surgery, but if your child has severe pain or fever, or you have any worries about how he/she is doing after surgery, you should call his/her ophthalmologist for further guidance. Acetaminophen is usually the recommended medication for relief of your child's discomfort or irritability. Aspirin and other over-the-counter pain medications should be avoided, as they may increase the risk of bleeding.

Some children sleep a lot after surgery. This is of no concern, especially during the first 24 hours. It is possible that your child will not open the unoperated eye until he/she has fully recovered from the aftereffects of surgery and is comfortable. Whether your child chooses to sleep or be wide awake, the key to his/her recovery from the effects of surgery is drinking adequate amounts of fluids and relief of discomfort. You can tell if your child is getting enough fluids by seeing that he/she urinates at least once.

Each ophthalmologist has different instructions for care of the operated eye after each procedure. Some surgeries require an eye patch to be worn until the next day, while others do not. Some doctors will have you put drops in the eye the evening after surgery. Others will wait until the next day, or not require drops at all the day of surgery. It is best to make sure you understand your child's postoperative instructions before you leave the hospital, and ask his/her recovery room nurse or ophthalmologist if you have any questions.

Q. How much pain will my child have after surgery?
A. Remarkably, eye surgery rarely causes much pain. Most discomfort can be reduced or eliminated by over-the-counter acetaminophen. Pain that is not comforted by this should be reported to the surgeon. Aspirin, ibuprofen, and other drugs in the same class as ibuprofen, are often discouraged after surgery, as they may contribute to bleeding.

Sometimes children will complain that it feels as though there is something between the eye and the eyelid. This is usually simply a stitch (suture), and the sensation associated with it will gradually go away.

Q. What should I do if my child is vomiting after surgery?
A. If your child is vomiting, then allow him/her to consume only clear liquids. Anti-vomiting medication may be taken if it has been prescribed by his/her doctor. Upset stomach and vomiting

can be quite frightening for your child, and can also cause *dehydration*. Frequently give him/her small amounts of clear liquids. As his/her stomach starts to calm, try giving your child small amounts of bland food, such as crackers or toast, to help the stomach to settle. If you are concerned, or if your child is vomiting large amounts for a long time, call his/her doctor or go to an emergency care facility near your area.

Q. How long before the bandages come off?

A. The patch and shield usually stay on until the first postoperative appointment, which generally occurs the day after surgery. At that time, although the patch is removed, the surgeon may decide to reapply the shield after the examination. The shield protects the eye, keeping it from being accidentally bumped while awake or during sleep. The surgeon may request that the shield be used for as long as one to two weeks after surgery.

Q. When do the immediate postsurgery follow-up visits occur?

A. This depends on the type of surgery. The child will usually be seen one day after any operation in which the eye is opened (intraocular surgery), such as cataract removal, glaucoma surgery, or corneal transplant. After this first visit, he/she will usually be scheduled for an additional visit two to five days later to rule out infection and assess his/her progress. Some operations, such as trabeculectomy and implantation of glaucoma tubes, may require more frequent follow-up, perhaps as often as every day, until the eye is settled and the drainage out of the eye is determined to be occurring at an acceptable rate. If all is well, the next visits may be one week later and then gradually spaced out over time.

Q. What happens in the first postsurgery follow-up visits?

A. The main goals of the immediate postsurgery follow-up visits are to assess your child for discomfort, look for complications, assess inflammation inside the eye in response to surgery, check for adequate wound healing, ensure that no vision has been lost as a result of surgery, and evaluate the success of the surgery. Each postoperative examination is very similar to a routine eye examination, although it will often be much shorter, as the exam needs to address the patient's specific needs on that day. If the child is uncomfortable or the lids are swollen, the duration of the exam may also be limited by the child's ability to participate.

Q: How often will the follow-up visits be after my child has stabilized?

A. The follow-up schedule for patients who have cataract surgery is determined by how well the eye is healing, the amount of inflammation in the eye, and the readiness for glasses or contact lenses. Once all is stable and the child is off of the postoperative eyedrops, then additional follow-up visits may be as infrequent as once or twice yearly, provided there are no concerns about amblyopia and vision development that may require patching and more frequent monitoring.

Follow-up after glaucoma surgery is tailored individually for each child and depends on how well his/her glaucoma is controlled. Even with the best control, children are usually seen no less frequently than every three to four months. If a child has just had surgery, has started new medications, or is experiencing problems obtaining good control of the glaucoma, then more frequent follow-up visits may be necessary. The initial effects of some glaucoma drugs can be assessed within days. Others require a longer period of time before their full effect can be assessed. Your child's eye doctor can help you plan the proper follow-up regimen for your child.

Q. What restrictions will there be to my child's activities after surgery?
A. Different surgeons have different recommendations for activity levels after surgery and may advise activity restrictions for different periods. Most children feel groggy for a day or so after surgery. It is best for them to stay at home during this period. Once your child is feeling comfortable, he/she may return to school. Children often rebound quite quickly, so this may occur as early as the day after surgery. If your child has had glaucoma surgery, he/she may require up to about one week of recovery time before returning to school. If the child requires eyedrops or other medication during school hours, then you must ensure that the school is prepared to give these medications. Most doctors recommend that children not participate in contact sports or rough physical activity for at least the first week after surgery. As the surgeon observes the eye healing, inflammation settling, and the absence of complications, then the amount and level of activity can be increased.

It can be very difficult to restrict activity, especially in young children. In most cases, no special efforts need to be made to prevent a child crying. An exception to this general rule may occur when the child has undergone goniotomy, trabeculotomy, trabeculectomy, or tube implantation. In these cases, it is often requested that the child be kept as happy and calm as possible to minimize the chance of bleeding within the eye that could occur with straining or crying. Of course, keeping a child from crying can be extremely difficult and may be unreasonable to expect.

The surgeon may advise that the child initially wear a shield, both while awake and sleeping, to protect the eye from accidental injury or rubbing. Eyeglasses can be used instead of a shield while your child is awake. Bathing or showering is usually deferred until the eye patch is off.

Children are generally back to their normal lifestyles within, at most, a week or two after the majority of surgeries. If a child only had an examination under anesthesia or sedation, he/she is usually back to normal later that same day.

Q. Why does my child appear to have an extra pupil since his/her surgery?
A. The appearance of your child's pupil may change after glaucoma or cataract surgery. It may become irregular in shape or may not dilate or constrict as well as it did before. These changes are simply due to the trauma of surgery inside the eye and may resolve over time. Even if they are permanent, they usually do not affect vision and do not mean that anything bad or worrisome has happened.

As a part of some surgical operations, such as trabeculectomy, a small piece of tissue is removed at the edge of the iris, in the area of the glaucoma surgery. This is done to prevent the iris tissue from plugging the drainage site. The shape of this hole is usually oval or triangular. Since the pupil is simply a hole in the center of the iris, this surgical hole will appear to be black, just like the pupil. If the surgery was done on the upper part of the eye, this extra hole is usually hidden by the upper part of the eyelid.

Occasionally an extra hole in the iris can occur as a complication of surgery. An example of how this might occur is if the iris is torn or cut inadvertently. This also usually has no visual effect or worrisome outcome.

Q. Why is there an area on the white part of my child's eye that looks like a blister?
A. There are four reasons why a blister-like area may appear on your child's eye over the sclera after surgery.

- Medications, such as antibiotics or steroids, are often injected underneath the conjunctiva covering the sclera at the end of surgery. This causes the conjunctiva to bulge forward, forming a blister-like elevation over the surface of the sclera. This usually resolves in the first day or two after surgery. If a long-acting steroid is used, there may also be some white particles visible underneath the swelling.
- Bleeding around the eye can sometimes cause the conjunctiva to elevate, giving the appearance of a blister.
- Surgery is a kind of trauma, or injury. When a part of the body is injured, the tissues swell. Surgical trauma to the eye can result in the swelling of the conjuctiva for the same reason.
- If swelling of the conjunctiva is associated with an itchy sensation and persists long after surgery, your child may be experiencing an allergic reaction. This is called chemosis. It does not affect vision, but may be uncomfortable or itchy. Treatments may include using artificial tears or other eyedrops, discontinuing other eyedrops, or giving the child oral anti-allergy medicine.

Q. Is it acceptable for my child to rub his/her eyes after surgery?
A. Eye rubbing is generally very much discouraged, particularly when the surgery involves an incision into the eye. Eye protection in the form of a patch, shield, or eyeglasses, may be recommended for use for the period shortly after surgery. Encourage your child to gently pat the eye with a tissue, rather than rub, if he/she feels compelled to do something to relieve tearing, itchiness, or pain after surgery.

D. CORNEAL TRANSPLANTATION

Q. Why do opacities of the cornea occur?
A. The cornea is the structure at the very front of the eye, in front of the pupil. Its main function is to focus the light that enters the eye. When it is working properly you often do not notice it, because it is crystal clear and you can see directly through it. If the cornea becomes cloudy, it does not work properly and you will not be able to see well. The effect is like trying to look through a window that is fogged.

If fluid or scar tissue builds up in the cornea, it becomes cloudy. On the inner surface of the cornea is the *endothelium*. It has cells that continuously pump fluid out of the cornea to keep it clear. If this pump does not work properly, the fluid will build up and cause the cornea to become cloudy.

Children with glaucoma may develop cloudiness of the cornea for two reasons. First, high pressure from the glaucoma may damage the endothelial cells, allowing fluid to accumulate in the *stroma*. Second, children with glaucoma may have other eye abnormalities in addition to the glaucoma, including opacities of the cornea (e.g., Peters anomaly, sclerocornea). Additionally, a traumatic injury to the cornea can leave a corneal scar that obscures vision from that eye.

Q. What is corneal transplantation?
A. In children who have glaucoma and cloudy corneas, successful glaucoma surgery may result in clearing of the cornea. Sometimes the pressure may decrease, but the cornea still remains cloudy. For these patients and those who have corneal cloudiness for another reason, corneal transplantation may provide a new, clear cornea (see Figure 13).

In this surgery, the center portion of the patient's cornea is removed and replaced by a cornea from a donor. The donor cornea will come from someone who has died and generously donated his/her eyes. In the United States and most Canadian provinces, people may place an organ donor notice on their driver's licenses. This notice indicates that the individual wishes his/her organs to be used for transplantation if he/she dies. The donor cornea is tested for AIDS and hepatitis, and usually treated to prevent the transmission of infection. In some countries, corneal donation is less common, so patients may have more difficulty receiving corneal transplant surgery.

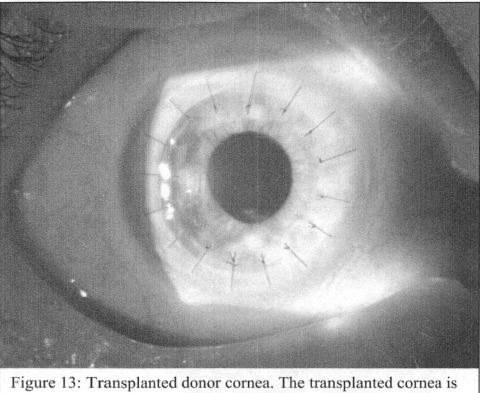

Figure 13: Transplanted donor cornea. The transplanted cornea is in the clear central cornea over the pupil with sutures (stitches) around the edges. The surrounding host cornea remains cloudy because it was not replaced. The sutures will be removed at a later date. (Photo courtesy of Dr. Christopher Rapuano, Wills Eye Hospital, Philadelphia, PA)

Corneal transplantation is more challenging in children than adults for two reasons. First, a child's eye is less rigid than an adult's. This makes it more difficult to sew the new cornea in place. Second, and more important, is the risk of rejection. Each person has a unique immune system that activates when something foreign enters the body. If an organ is transplanted from one individual to another, the recipient's immune system may think that the transplanted organ does not belong in the body and will try to reject it. Children usually have very robust immune systems, making it more likely that their bodies will reject transplanted tissue. As a result, they need to take eyedrops (usually steroids) to suppress their immune systems for an extended period after their transplants.

If your child needs a corneal transplant, be sure to select a surgeon who is familiar with the procedure and comfortable with performing it in young children. Your child will need to be followed carefully by the doctor for a long time after the transplant. Corneal transplants require a lot of work by all involved, including the patient, the family, and the doctors. This great effort is worth it when your child's eye remains clear and he/she is able to see better than before.

There are newer "partial" corneal transplant surgeries being developed and used in adults. These are not commonly performed in children. In selected cases, these procedures may have a role in helping children with corneal opacities. Examples of these procedures include *Descemet stripping endothelial keratoplasty (DSEK)* and *anterior lamellar keratoplasty (ALK)*. In DSEK surgery, the innermost portion of the cornea, containing the endothelial cells, is removed and replaced. In ALK surgery, only the front-most portion of the cornea is removed and replaced. Most of these partial transplant techniques are not suitable for children with severe corneal opacities.

Q. What is Peters anomaly and what does it have to do with cloudy corneas?
A. Peters anomaly (also known as Peters sequence) is an abnormality in the way the cornea and lens of the eye form (see Figure 14). During the formation of the eye, the lens actually develops as an ingrowth of the overlying cornea that later moves into the eyeball. If the separation of the lens and cornea does not take place properly, the child has Peters anomaly. Children with Peters anomaly usually have cloudy corneas and may require corneal transplantation. Children with Peters anomaly may also have cataract, glaucoma, or both.

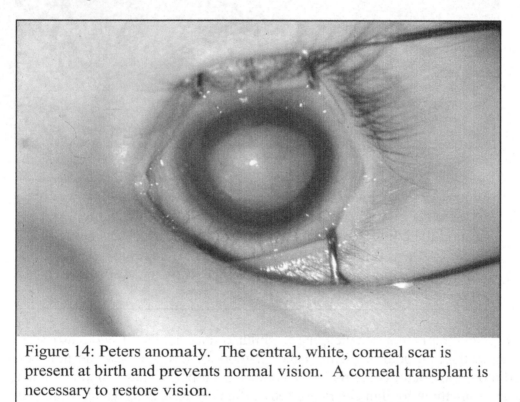

Figure 14: Peters anomaly. The central, white, corneal scar is present at birth and prevents normal vision. A corneal transplant is necessary to restore vision.

E. ENUCLEATION AND EVISCERATION

Q. Will my child's eye have to be removed?
A. Removal of the eyeball (enucleation) is the last resort in the management of glaucoma. Eye doctors try very hard not to perform enucleation for two reasons. First, in young children, a growing eyeball is necessary to stimulate the surrounding bone and skin tissues to grow properly, thus

avoiding facial deformity. Second, even the best prosthetic eye moves less smoothly than a natural eye, often making it less cosmetically acceptable than a natural eye.

Unfortunately, when the eye is blind and painful, comfort sometimes cannot be achieved unless the eyeball is removed. If the glaucoma in a blind eye is uncontrolled to such an extent that the eye is expanding and its wall is thinning, enucleation may need to be performed to prevent the eye from rupturing or becoming extremely abnormal in appearance.

Enucleation is generally only performed on completely blind eyes. There must be a compelling reason, such as pain that cannot be treated with medications, for a sighted eye to be removed.

Q. After the eyeball is removed, what is put in its place?
A. To fill up the volume previously taken by the eyeball, a small *implant* is placed into the surrounding tissue that held the original eyeball. Once the tissues heal, an ocularist paints an artificial shell or cap that matches the other eye (*ocular prosthetic*). This shell, which once might have been made from glass or metal, is now generally made of a plastic called polymethyl methacrylate (PMMA). It goes over the remaining tissues, supported by the implant, to render a matching appearance to the patient's other eye. Today, an individual with an ocular prosthetic does not have a glass eye.

Implants come in several shapes and are made from a variety of materials. You and your child's surgeon should discuss the various options, each of which may impact your child's appearance, growth, and eye movement.

Unfortunately, after removal of the eye and placement of an implant, your child will still have no vision at all from the eye. The technology does not yet exist to create and implant artificial eyeballs that see or perform eyeball transplants from another person.

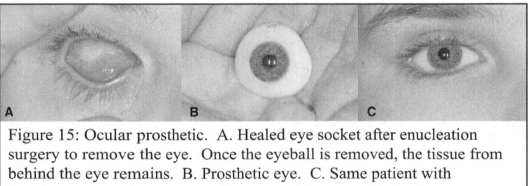

Figure 15: Ocular prosthetic. A. Healed eye socket after enucleation surgery to remove the eye. Once the eyeball is removed, the tissue from behind the eye remains. B. Prosthetic eye. C. Same patient with prosthetic eye in place, providing an excellent cosmetic result. (Photo courtesy of Dr. Carol Shields, Wills Eye Hospital, Philadelphia, PA)

Q. What can go wrong with enucleation surgery?
A. Enucleation involves cutting the optic nerve, which contains the major blood vessels to the eye. As a result, bleeding is generally the biggest complication, although this can be controlled during surgery. There can sometimes be problems fitting the prosthetic shell. It is also possible that your child will have problems with infection or irritation in the remaining socket tissue, though infection is an uncommon complication of enucleation. Surgery may be needed to reposition the implant if it becomes exposed or moves out of position.

Q. What is evisceration?

A. *Evisceration* is an alternative to enucleation. In this procedure, the whole eyeball is not removed. Rather, the white of the eye (sclera) is left behind. The implant is put inside the remaining "cup" of sclera and then tissues (conjunctiva) are sewed over, as in enucleation. The prosthetic shell is then placed over these tissues just like in enucleation. The advantage of evisceration is that leaving the sclera means the eye muscles are still attached naturally. This often gives the prosthetic eye more movement. One technique that gives extremely good movement is to connect the prosthetic shell to the implant by drilling a hole into the implant and fashioning a peg on the back of the prosthesis that connects into the hole. This procedure is not often recommended for children.

Q. What can go wrong with evisceration?

A. There may be some bleeding, but since evisceration does not involve cutting the optic nerve and its blood vessels, it is less likely that bleeding problems will occur than in enucleation. Other potential problems include the possibility that the body will reject the implant or the tissue overlying the implant could break down. The risks related to the prosthetic shell are the same as for enucleation, although the eye often moves better.

Q. Are there alternatives to enucleation or evisceration?

A. If the eye is not painful, then it can certainly stay in place. As long as the cosmetic appearance is deemed acceptable, then no additional action needs to be taken to make it look more normal. If the eye is smaller than usual, particularly if it is a lot smaller than average, then an artificial shell painted to look like your child's remaining natural eye can be fitted over it to improve its appearance. The small eyeball remains in place but is hidden by the shell. This has the added benefit of encouraging surrounding tissue growth and avoiding the need for surgery.

PART V: GLASSES AND CONTACT LENSES

A. GENERAL QUESTIONS

Q. *What questions should I ask the doctor?*
A. What questions you choose to ask are up to you. Here are some suggestions that may help you.

- Where do we go to get the glasses or contact lenses (if needed)?
- Who will pay for glasses, contact lenses, patches, and medications?
- What does my insurance cover?
- How much will glasses, contact lenses, patches, and/or medications cost?

Q. *Will my child need glasses or contact lenses?*
A. It is impossible to predict whether a child with normal vision will need glasses later in life. If a parent wears strong glasses or contacts, then there is a higher chance that the child will eventually need them as well. Some children have extreme nearsightedness, farsightedness, or astigmatism, even in infancy. This can be detected during an eye examination and result in a prescription for glasses or contact lenses.

Infants with glaucoma often have some degree of nearsightedness requiring glasses early in life. All children who have cataract surgery without IOL implantation will need glasses or contact lenses. Even with IOL implantation, many children need glasses or contact lenses to work with the IOL in order to get the right power to see clearly at a distance as they grow. In addition, reading glasses are needed for clear near vision in an eye that has undergone cataract surgery. Some forms of glaucoma surgery distort the shape of the surface of the eye, resulting in blurred vision due to astigmatism and a need for glasses to obtain clear vision.

Q. *Can my child wear contact lenses instead of glasses?*
A. The choice of glasses or contact lenses is largely one of preference and cosmetics. Contact lenses can be used to correct a wide range of vision problems. Strong glasses prescriptions often cause distortions in the view at the edge of the lenses. Patients with such powerful prescriptions usually prefer vision with contact lenses as compared to thick glasses. As children proceed into grade school, contact lenses are also more cosmetically acceptable and less likely to result in teasing by peers.

There is no minimum age for wearing glasses or contact lenses. If an infant has cataract surgery, the visual rehabilitation usually involves contact lenses that are put in and taken out by the parents at an interval selected by the contact lens provider.

When choosing between contact lenses and glasses for an older child, consider both the cost and your child's level of responsibility. Contact lens management requires cleanliness and attentiveness to the regular insertion and removal of the lenses. If a child is not able to handle these responsibilities and the parents are not able to do so, then glasses are a more appropriate solution. Another factor to consider is the activity level involved in your child's lifestyle. If your child is engaged in many sports, contact lenses may be much more practical than glasses.

Some eye conditions preclude the use of contact lenses. In some cases, there may be a higher chance of complications occurring if something is placed directly on the eyeball. In others, something about the condition causes eye irritation or otherwise makes it difficult to wear the lenses for long periods of time. Conditions that disrupt the surface of the eye, such as corneal disease and corneal transplants, or certain eye surgeries, especially trabeculectomy with mitomycin, may cause particular trouble.

Q. Can my child see when he/she is not wearing his/her contact lenses or glasses?
A. A child with subnormal vision who does not have cataract or glaucoma sees a blurry image if he/she does not wear his/her glasses or contact lenses. He/she is not completely blind. If the child has had cataract surgery, or for some other reason wears very strong glasses or contact lenses, then the image is extremely blurry when they are not worn. Children who have very strong prescriptions may have vision that is so blurry without their glasses or contact lenses that it would qualify them as legally blind (less than 20/200 vision), even though they can still see.

Infants who are legally blind behave normally. If an infant or young child had cataract surgery and had his/her contacts out or glasses off, he/she will function almost the same as when the contacts are in or glasses on, even though his/her vision will be blurry. This does not mean the child can go without glasses or contact lenses, as the focusing they provide is needed so his/her vision develops optimally.

Q. Does my child need glasses or large print books if he/she reads by holding things very close?
A. Many children like to hold things close when they read or sit close to the television. This is often a form of concentration that may be seen in normally-sighted, healthy children. These are not harmful activities, though they may be a sign of nearsightedness or an adaptation to low vision.

If an eye examination reveals nearsightedness, glasses or contact lenses may be all that are needed to correct the problem. Even with glasses or contacts, your child may still prefer the habit and concentration advantage of being near to the reading material or the television.

Children with low vision tend to adapt by holding objects close to get extra magnification. Although glasses which can magnify things, or a handheld magnifier, may also work, some children prefer not to use these devices. This refusal may either be for cosmetic reasons or due to inconvenience. Glasses do not make a child's eyes healthier. If your child prefers to adapt by holding reading material close, then this will not harm his/her eyes.

Large-print books are not generally necessary unless your child is unable to see better than 20/60 (6/18) up close. Some children with low vision prefer to use normal size print materials in order to be like other kids, even if they have to hold things closer. Large print books also do not improve the health of the eye. They are simply a matter of convenience some children may not wish to have. The decision should be left to the child and the school, based on the child's comfort level and school performance.

Q. Since my young child functions like any other child without using his/her glasses/contact lenses/low vision aids, are they really necessary?
A. In the first four to six years of life, visual demands are actually quite small. Infants have all their care provided, so they have no particular visual needs. Even a legally blind infant may be indistinguishable from an infant with normal vision.

As children begin to walk and notice more in the world around them, very little vision is needed to see the big objects that attract their attention. Infants and toddlers who have had cataract surgery can function remarkably well without their aphakic glasses or contact lenses, yet these corrective devices are extremely important. Without the clarity they provide to the images the brain receives, proper visual development cannot occur.

Once your child reaches school age, his/her vision demands will increase (for example, reading a blackboard from the back of a classroom). At that point, the need for vision correction will become much more apparent.

Q. Will the surgery correct my child's vision so that he/she no longer needs to wear glasses or contact lenses?
A. In certain situations, your child may no longer need glasses or contacts, but this is not so in the majority of cases. Surgery to treat glaucoma or cataract does not cure nearsightedness, farsightedness, or astigmatism, but your child's prescription may change after surgery. Some children who have an IOL implanted during or after cataract surgery may not need glasses or contact lenses, especially if the cataract was only in one eye.

B. GLASSES

Q. When should my child wear his/her glasses?
A. Glasses are prescribed for many different reasons. When your child should wear his/her glasses depends on why they were prescribed.

If the primary reason glasses were prescribed is to improve your child's vision, then the glasses should generally be worn whenever he/she is awake. This is particularly true in children less than 9 to 11 years old, when the visual system is still developing, and especially so if the prescription is strong. Glasses simply bend light to fit the shape of the eye. By doing this, images fall correctly on the retina at the back of the eye to be in proper focus. Without glasses, the image is blurred and visual development will not take place properly. Young children with less powerful prescriptions may still develop acceptable vision without wearing glasses full-time because the visual image may still be good enough to encourage proper visual development and function. If glasses are prescribed because your child has amblyopia due to unequal glasses prescription and unequal vision between the eyes, then full-time wear becomes more important. Your child's eye doctor can best tell you how important it may or may not be for your child to wear glasses all the time.

After the first decade of life, when vision is fully mature, a child can choose whether to wear or not wear glasses. A child with mild *myopia* may only want to wear glasses to help see the blackboard at school. To go without glasses at other times will not be harmful to this particular child. A teenager or adult can go without glasses for many years without any harm, provided that he/she does not mind having blurry vision. Once the glasses are reinstated, his/her vision will be clear again.

Glasses may also be prescribed for eyes that are either crossed (*esotropia*) or turned out (*exotropia*). The lenses in these glasses are designed to keep the eyes aligned, but they do not necessarily improve vision. They simply do focusing work that the eyes could normally do on their own. It is important for an individual whose glasses were prescribed to correct misaligned eyes to wear his/her glasses whenever he/she is awake. If they are worn only intermittently, it becomes more difficult for the glasses to straighten the eye.

Lastly, a child with good vision in only one eye may be prescribed glasses with lenses that have no power but are made of break-resistant polycarbonate. These are designed to protect the good eye from accidental injury. They should be worn full-time, as it is impossible to predict when an accident will occur.

Q. Why does my child refuse to wear his/her glasses?
A. There are four main reasons why children will not wear glasses.

- The glasses may not fit properly. If your child is not wearing his/her glasses, go back to the store where you bought them and make sure the fit is correct.
- The glasses prescription is incorrect. Your child's eye doctor should recheck the prescription to make sure it is not making the child's vision worse rather than better. Sometimes a simple writing mistake can occur in the eye doctor's or optician's office. Although these types of prescription errors are usually not harmful, the worsened vision they provide will give the child a disincentive to wear his/her glasses.
- The glasses prescription does not give the child an appreciable benefit. This is particularly likely in developmentally delayed children or very young children, where an increase in their vision does not change their perception or appreciation of the world around them. Infants and very young children do not have great visual demands and can get by with blurry vision quite easily. They function equally well with or without glasses and, therefore, have no incentive to wear them.
- Some children refuse to wear glasses simply because they do not want to wear them. This is particularly true of teenagers who dislike or fear the change in appearance caused by the presence of glasses. If the child is beyond the first decade of life, then there is little or no impact to vision development in the child going without glasses and he/she may be allowed to do so. If this is the difficulty, consider whether switching from glasses to contact lenses is a workable option. Some children are so obstinate that they may not wear glasses even when it causes them to have trouble seeing the board. Even without glasses, most normal children have little or no difficulty reading up close and may be able to get by in school.

Q. What can I do if my child will not wear his/her glasses?
A. A parent's role goes beyond the selection process and fitting of eyeglasses. When high-powered lenses are worn, a child's appearance is altered significantly. Infants and young children will not regard a change in appearance as negative or positive. Young children respond to the parent's clues. A positive reaction from a parent is helpful in getting him/her to accept wearing glasses.

Cable ear pieces (*temples*) that wrap around the back of the ear are recommended, though these should not extend past the earlobe. This style of temple will help keep the lenses, especially those that are heavy, positioned correctly in front of the child's eyes. If the lenses remain correctly positioned, they will allow your child to see better, which will also encourage him/her to continue wearing the glasses. A strap that goes around the back of the head can also help make it more difficult for the glasses to be removed.

For older children, and especially teenagers, your child should be involved in the decision-making process wherever possible. His/her self-esteem and self-image are important. The more involved he/she is, the more likely your child is to accept the presence of glasses in his/her life. Be sure to be shopping for glasses at a place that is familiar with fitting children. A good eyeglass professional can explain the features and benefits of each frame, and help you and your child make informed eyewear decisions.

Perhaps most importantly, if your child is not wearing his/her glasses, then check with the eye doctor. He/she can help figure out why the problem is occurring.

Q. Why don't glasses make my child see 20/20?

A. The eye is similar to a camera. If one buys the most expensive camera available and attaches the most expensive lens available to it, but loads it with bad film, the pictures still come out blurry. In the same way, the best glasses in the world cannot make an eye see perfectly if there is something intrinsically wrong with it. If glasses are prescribed to focus images correctly on the retina but the retina is sick or damaged, then the image the brain sees will still be blurry. If glaucoma damages the optic nerve, it may be impossible for the optic nerve to carry a clear image to the brain, even with the best glasses focusing the sharpest image imaginable.

If a child's vision has failed to develop properly, the problem lies in the brain's ability to perceive a well-defined image. In this situation, even if all other conditions are perfect, the brain will not be able to perceive the image clearly.

Q. Why were glasses not prescribed for my child?

A. Glasses are only prescribed when the physician feels that they will be useful to the patient. One situation in which glasses may not be prescribed is when the prescription would be very mild and unlikely to make a significant change in your child's vision. Another would be when glasses are unlikely to improve his/her vision because there is something wrong with the eye itself or the child is old enough that his/her amblyopia cannot be successfully treated. If a child is developmentally delayed or too young to appreciate the change in vision in a way that will have functional significance, glasses will not be useful and may not be prescribed.

Q. If my child begins wearing glasses as a toddler, will he/she become dependent on them?

A. Glasses are prescribed if they are important for your child to obtain the best vision. The idea that people become dependent on glasses by starting to wear them when very young is a myth. When people get glasses, they tend to use them more because they can see better when wearing them. There is no addiction or dependency.

Q. Should my child wear glasses for protection?

A. During the first few weeks after cataract surgery, the eye is more at risk for injury. Once the eye is completely healed, it may still be a bit more sensitive to a serious trauma. The same rules that apply for protective glasses after glaucoma surgery would then apply.

Protective eyewear is a good idea for most children who participate in sports that involve racquets, balls, or physical contact. If one eye sees poorly, full-time glasses are essential to protect the good eye from an injury.

Q. What should my child and I consider when choosing frames?

A. Eyeglass frame selection is virtually unlimited for children. Frames are chosen to fit the child's face and to be cosmetically pleasing. Some style limitations may occur if a child requires particularly thick lenses.

Another factor to keep in mind is how likely a particular frame is to break during your child's normal activities. Flexible frames that can withstand the traumas of normal childhood activities are particularly good. Plastic frames tend to be stronger than wire frames. This may be an important factor if the possibility of frequent breakage is a concern.

Virtually unbreakable frames are often a good choice for an active or athletic child. If a child participates in sports, plastic frames are the most desirable. Forceful contact with a metal frame can cause it to invert and cut the skin around the eyes. Spring hinges will absorb a lot of abuse, but they may cause injury to the skin or eye if the hinges invert when the glasses are hit by an object or during a fall.

Regular daily glasses should never be used as sports protection, especially for sports involving balls, sticks, racquets, or physical contact. Always purchase plastic lenses rather than glass.

Q. What factors should be considered when choosing sunglasses?

A. Sunglasses provide one of the best sources of protection from UV radiation. Although some UV-absorbing contact lenses are available, they do not provide as much protection. Sunglasses also cover the eyelids and surround the entire eye. There are a number of factors to be considered when choosing sunglasses.

Sunglasses are available in a wide variety of styles. Many manufacturers have numerous frame and lens designs. Both metal and plastic frames are available for children's sunglasses. For children who wear glasses with particularly thick lenses, such as aphakic glasses, clip-on sun filters may be a more economical and readily available option. These can be cut to fit the glasses of a small child.

Optically, the best lenses for sunglasses are distortion-free and allow a degree of light reduction that provides comfortable vision in bright light without squinting. Not everyone needs the same light-blocking level to achieve visual comfort. For example, children with aniridia and albinism often need to use darker sunglasses than other children would require. Wraparound sunglasses, or those with side shields, prevent bothersome light from entering around the glasses.

Dark lenses do not always provide the best UV protection. The chemical coating applied to the lens is responsible for UV protection, not the tint or color.

Polarized lenses are very effective at blocking reflected glare. The advantage of polarized lenses is that they effectively reduce or eliminate reflected light, which accounts for the majority of bothersome glare in sunlight.

Photochromatic lenses darken when exposed to UV and then lighten when not in direct sunlight. Gray or amber-brown are the most common colors of photochromatic lenses. These transitional lenses are available in plastic, and may be appropriate for some children.

Do not make your choice based on price alone. Highly priced sunglasses do not always provide better UV protection than less expensive models.

C. CONTACT LENSES AND THEIR CARE

Q. How do I insert the contact lens?
A. At first, you may find that it takes two adults (four hands) and some experimentation to arrive at just the right routine for successfully inserting and removing your child's contact lenses.

Most parents find it easiest to insert the lenses when their children are lying down. If your child resists the insertion of his/her contact lenses, it may be necessary to wrap him/her in a sheet or blanket in order to immobilize his/her arms. One way to accomplish this is for one person to hold the baby on a changing table or the floor, or while seated and cradling his/her head. Another method is for one adult to hold the child's arms above each side of his/her head, stabilizing both the arms and the head, while the other adult inserts the lenses.

Once the child is in position, the person inserting the lens should hold it between his/her thumb and index finger, sliding the edge of the lens onto the eye under the upper lid. One adult may need to gently roll or pull the upper lid toward the child's forehead. Once the edge of the lens has slid under the upper eyelid, follow through with an upward thumb or finger motion until the lens is completely on the surface of the eye. You should be able to feel the eyeball under your finger. The pupil does not have to be centered for lens insertion to be successful. A video demonstrating this process is available on the PGCFA website (*http://www.pgcfa.org*).

Q. What should I do if the lens curls when I try to insert it into my child's eye?
A. The lens may curl under when inserted, especially if using a soft, non-silicone lens. Either take the lens out and start over or move the lens around with your finger till it flattens. If this is a continual problem, sometimes a change to a harder contact lens material may be helpful.

Q. What should I do if the lens sticks to my fingers when I try to insert it in my child's eye?
A. If a lens sticks to your fingers and will not release onto your child's eye, put a drop of saline solution to the lens and keep your finger a bit moist.

Q. How can I tell if the contact lens is in the right place?
A. A contact lens should generally fit over the iris. It will sometimes drift a little from one to either side, or up or down. This is usually not a problem as long as is the lens remains fairly well centered most of the time. If you are having trouble seeing the contact lens, simply shine a flashlight from the side of your child's eye. This should cause the contact lens to become more visible.

Q. How can I keep my child's contact lens from popping out as soon as I put it in?
A. Once you have inserted the lens, take a quick look to ensure that it is seated on the surface of your child's eye before he/she is allowed to move about. For smaller eyes, the lens may pop out easily if the lower lid is not over the edge of the lens. It may be necessary to pull down the lower eyelid during the insertion process to make sure that the lid is over the bottom edge of the lens.

Q. How will my child react to wearing contact lenses?
A. All children react differently to the process of inserting and removing contact lenses. Some will accept the lenses easily, while others will react to the process and resist your attempts to insert or remove the lenses. It is important to realize that, no matter how your child reacts, insertion and removal do not hurt and the contact lenses are essential for proper development of your child's vision. It may take as long as two to four months for you to gain the skills and confidence necessary

to deal with the insertion and removal of the lenses. These processes will eventually become part of your daily routine.

As they get older, many children are so appreciative of the better vision they have in contact lenses that they resist having them removed. Some varieties of contact lens are designed to stay in for more than a day. Talk to the doctor who gives you the contact lens about this option.

Q. What if my child will not let me put the contact lens in?
A. It takes every parent some time to gain the skills and confidence necessary to deal with the insertion and removal of his/her child's contact lenses. It is important to realize that, no matter how your child reacts, this process does not hurt and is essential for the proper development of his/her vision.

It is possible that some restraining of your child may be necessary. Having another adult hold him/her still, or using a blanket to swaddle the child so he/she cannot flail with his/her arms, is helpful.

The biggest obstacle to lens insertion is usually that the child is squeezing his/her eyelids tightly together. You can counteract this by placing your thumb or fingers on the skin over the bone around the eyeball (*orbital rim*) and gently but firmly pushing down towards the bone. The eyelid muscles are weakened and the lids can be separated. This is not painful for the child. Then, insert one edge of the contact lens under the upper eyelid and slide it onto the eye with your finger. Only a slight crack between the eyelids is needed to get the leading edge of the contact lens in far enough to push it onto surface of the eye.

If behavior issues become difficult to manage, discuss the matter with your child's ophthalmologist and pediatrician.

Q. What can I do if my child will not wear his/her contact lenses?
A. What can be done depends on the reason your child refuses to wear the lenses. There are several possible factors.

Contact lens intolerance may be caused by improper fit or other causes of discomfort. If this seems to be the case for your child, return to his/her contact lens provider to discuss whether an alternative brand or fit of contact lens may alleviate the problem.

Some children just cannot get used to having lenses put in and taken out of their eyes. These children may get better results from glasses or IOL implantation.

As with glasses, if your child does not experience an appreciable change in his/her visual function or if the prescription makes his/her vision worse, he/she will have no incentive to wear the contact lenses. If this seems to be the situation, discuss these factors with your child's eye doctor to determine if contact lenses are a necessary and appropriate solution.

Q. How do I remove the lens?
A. The method for contact lens removal depends on the type of contact lens. If your child is using a gas permeable rigid contact lens, you may be instructed on how to remove the lens using a small plunger that has a suction cup on the tip.

For silicone lenses, the most commonly used method is to use both of your thumbs to pull the upper and lower eyelids apart. Make sure they cover the upper and lower eyelashes. Dip your thumbnails towards the surface of the eye and use them as a lever against the edge of the lens to pop it out. The eye needs to be relatively centered to remove the lens. This method also works well for small eyes.

An alternate method is to use the thumb and forefinger of one hand to pinch the lens off the surface of the eye. This can be done with silicone lenses and is especially useful for soft contact lenses.

Q. What position is best for removing the contact lens?
A. You will likely find it easiest to remove the lens if the child is in the same position you use to insert the lenses. Many parents find it most convenient when the child is lying down.

Q. What should I do if the contact lens will not come out of my child's eye?
A. First, verify that the lens is in fact in your child's eye prior to trying to remove it. If the lens is truly there and you cannot get it out, take a break and let things settle down. Try again later. If it continues to be a problem, call your child's eye doctor or the doctor who gave you the lens.

Q. Is there anything I can do to lessen the stress of placing or removing my child's contact lenses?
A. Ask for help! Learning to put lenses in your baby's or young child's eyes can be a stressful time. Others have gone through it. If you need support in any way, do not hesitate to contact your child's eye doctor, contact lens provider, or the PGCFA (*http://www.pgcfa.org*). Other parents are often willing to offer moral support and may have helpful suggestions.

Q. How can I prevent my child from losing his/her contact lenses?
A. All children lose contact lenses, usually from rubbing their eyes with their fists. Contact lenses should not be easy to rub out and should not fall out spontaneously. If either of these things happens, it is usually a sign that the lenses need to be refit.

Check occasionally to ensure that the lens is in your child's eyes. It may be more difficult to see it if your child has dark eyes, but you will get used to looking for it. If a lens is missing, check his/her clothes first. A flashlight may be useful in searching, as it can cause the lens to glint.

Contact lenses dry out very quickly. If you do find a lost lens, allow it to soak in saline solution for a couple of hours. Clean and disinfect it and check for marks or tears before reinserting it into the eye. If using a rehydrated lens that was discovered after more than a few hours, check with your contact lens doctor about whether it is still usable. Sometimes long periods of nonuse will cause the lens to change power, even after it is rehydrated.

Q. Can a contact lens slide around to the back of the eye or move into the brain?
A. These common myths are factual impossibilities. The eyeball surface is lined with conjunctiva, which goes up to the inside of the upper lid and down onto the inner surface of the lower eyelid. This forms a barrier to the contact lens moving to the back of the eye.

A contact lens does not sit directly on the surface of the eye. It floats on the tear film over the eye. Some movement of the lens is necessary. It is more worrisome when the contact lens does not move at all. A fit that is too tight can deprive the eye's surface of much-needed oxygen.

It is possible for a contact lens to come completely off the cornea and move up, down, or to either side, over the iris. The lens will usually find its way back to center of the eye on its own. If necessary, you can use your finger to nudge it in the right direction.

Contact lenses should not slide excessively. If your child's lenses often move around off the center of his/her eye, consult his/her contact lens provider.

Q. Is it acceptable to put eyedrops in the eye while wearing contact lenses?

A. Whether or not you can put eyedrops in your child's eye while he/she is wearing contact lenses depends on the type of contacts he/she is using. If your child is wearing gas permeable contact lenses, drops can be used while the contacts are in place. If he/she had cataract surgery, especially if it occurred early in life, he/she may wear silicone contact lenses. Drops can be administered while the lenses are in place. This is not harmful to the eye, but it may shorten the lifespan of silicone contacts. If your child wears soft contact lenses made from something other than silicone, drops cannot be used while the contacts are in.

If you have questions, talk with your child's contact lens provider for more information. Also talk to your child's eye doctor. He/she may be able to change the eyedrop schedule so that contacts can still be worn. For example, twice daily dosing may allow for drops to be put in before the contacts are inserted and after they are removed each day.

Q. Can my child take a bath or shower with the contact lenses in?

A. Routine bathing is fine, and should not be a problem unless your child rubs his/her eyes a lot when being washed or shampooed. It is unlikely that your child will get a significant amount of water in his/her eyes, so it should not wash away the tear film that the lenses usually float on. You should not plan to take the contact lenses out immediately after a bath or shower. The contacts tend to stick to the eye a bit more after bathing. While it is still safe to remove them, it is often more difficult to do so.

Q. How long can my child wear contact lenses without damaging his/her eyes?

A. There does not appear to be a limit to the number of years of contact lens may be used with no ill effects. Just think of the number of adults you know who have been wearing them since childhood. By the time your child is an adult, there will likely be many new options available from which he/she can make his/her own informed choice.

There are limitations on how long daily or extended wear contacts may be used before they need to be removed and/or replaced. Talk to your child's contact lens provider to learn how long each day, or for how many days at a time, your child can wear his/her specific kind of contact lens.

Q. If my child gets pink eye (conjunctivitis), can he/she still use the lenses during and after the infection?

A. Always stop using the contact lens if the eye is red for any reason, and especially when conjunctivitis is suspected. Do not start using them again until your child's eye doctor verifies that it is all right to do so. If your child has conjunctivitis caused by a virus or bacteria, be sure the contacts are sterilized before using them again.

Q. What kind of care do contact lenses require?

A. Cleaning and disinfection of contact lenses is almost as important as obtaining the proper fit. If the cleaning and disinfectant regimen is not correctly followed, blinding corneal infection can result.

Contact lenses are also unlikely to provide the comfort and vision for which they were prescribed if not maintained properly. This holds true for anyone who wears contact lenses, whether for cosmetic or therapeutic reasons.

Contact lenses can be generally categorized as rigid (gas permeable), soft, or silicone-based. Each material is compatible with certain solution care systems. The care system prescribed by your contact lens provider is the one to clean and disinfect that variety of lens without causing eye irritation.

At one time, heat was used to sterilize contact lenses. This process has not been promoted for several years due to the unreliability of the sterilizing units. Contact lens care systems in use today are classed as cold disinfection, meaning that some form of chemical or combination of chemicals in the storage or cleaning solution acts as an antibacterial agent. The active ingredient in the solution may be the preservative, which serves a double purpose. It prevents deterioration of the solution while also disinfecting the lens.

Different cleaning and disinfecting systems are available for different types of lenses. Rub systems involve manual manipulation of lenses in a chemical solution. Each lens is rubbed for a minimum of five seconds to clean debris from the surface and kill bacteria. These kits include a bottle of fluid that is used to clean the lens before it is soaked overnight in the chemical disinfectant. Disinfection may also be achieved by using a cleaning or starting solution that contains isopropyl alcohol. The lens is then rinsed and stored in a saline solution that may be preservative free, if recommended. This type of system may include enzymatic cleaning and can be used on all soft and silicone lenses. The rubbing or cleaning step is an integral part of the disinfection process. The physical cleaning of the lens removes most of the bacteria and contaminants, making it easier for the disinfectant solution to be effective against those that remain on the lens surface.

Multipurpose, or all-in-one, solutions for soft lenses are commonly available. Unfortunately, while these systems can be very effective and convenient, they generally contain preservatives that may cause some low-level eye irritation. These solutions generally work best when used with disposable or frequently replaced soft lenses. Versions of the all-in-one type that do not require the lenses to be rubbed are available, but the amount of rinsing required is significantly greater than is necessary for the rub, rinse, and soak versions of the same solutions.

Rigid lens care systems require that lenses be soaked in the storage or conditioning solution for a minimum of four hours prior to lens wear. The solutions used for storing and conditioning rigid lenses may not be used on soft lenses, as they will be damaged by the solution.

Oxidizing or hydrogen peroxide-based systems are particularly effective in disinfecting soft lenses, and do not use chemical preservatives. These types of solutions must be neutralized with a catalytic tablet or disc that is placed in a cassette with the contact lenses. It usually takes a minimum of six hours to disinfect the lens while neutralizing the peroxide. Peroxide will cause severe burning and redness if put in the eye without being neutralized. These systems usually include a daily cleaner, saline rinse, and weekly enzyme cleaner.

Hydrogen peroxide-based systems may be used for most other soft lens materials, though they may shorten the lifespan of silicone lenses, causing them to break down prematurely. Unfortunately, the oxidization process of this type of system will also cause a bleaching effect on tinted soft lenses, causing the color to fade. Peroxide-based systems cannot be used for the gas permeable rigid lenses, as they do not provide the necessary surface wetting for the material.

The specific solutions and care systems which have been prescribed are the ones that should always be used with your child's lenses. By using alternate solutions, your child may experience eye irritation or allergic reaction, or his/her lenses may be damaged. Always consult with your child's contact lens provider regarding any changes to your contact lens care system.

Q. How can I tell if a contact lens is clean?
A. A clean contact lens is crystal clear and transparent. The lens is not clean if you see whitish deposits or it appears cloudy. Such deposits may cover the entire center of the lens or just form a ring around the edge of the stronger central zone of the lens. If the lens does not appear to be clean, consult your contact lens provider and do not use it.

Q. What should be used to rinse a contact lens?
A. Saline is the best rinsing solution for contact lenses, and the only one designed specifically for this function. Multipurpose solution may be used to rinse prior to insertion of the lens, but it is more intended to be used for storage and disinfection. Saline should be used to rinse contact lenses that have been stored in cleaning and disinfecting solution, have been treated with a cleaning rub solution prior to soaking, and especially before putting a contact in the eye after using a hydrogen peroxide system. Never use tap water to rinse contact lenses. Tap water contains bacteria and other germs that can cause eye infection. Saline can also be used to rinse rigid lenses in order to reduce the chance of contamination.

Saline is available with mild or no preservatives. In either form, it has no disinfecting ability and should not be used as such. Both varieties are available in squeeze bottles. Saline that is packaged in an aerosol container contains no preservatives and is excellent for patients who suffer from allergies to preservatives found in contact lens solutions. Be careful when using the aerosols. The jet that comes out can be quite strong and blow the contact lens out of your hand.

Q. How long will my child's lenses last?
A. It is important to remember that contact lenses have a finite life. Younger patients develop heavier deposits on their contact lenses faster than adults. As a result, their lenses may require more frequent replacement through normal wear. Non-disposable lenses may require replacement as often as every three to six months in spite of excellent care and cleaning. Each child is an individual and will require replacement lenses based on his/her specific needs. Your child's contact lens provider or eye doctor is the best source of information regarding his/her contact lens fitting and management. If a contact lens appears to be cloudy, a new lens is almost always needed. Never use a contact that is torn, missing a piece of the lens, or is otherwise visibly damaged.

Q. Should my child have spare lenses?
A. Contact lenses may be too expensive to allow for the purchase of spares. If you can afford to purchase extra lenses, it is usually advisable to do so. Having extra lenses on hand allows lost lenses to be replaced immediately instead of waiting while new lenses are ordered. If you keep the spare lens in the sealed bottle in which it is received and your child's prescription changes before it is used, most contact lens providers will allow you to exchange the sealed bottle for a lens having the new prescription without any additional cost.

Q. Can my child leave his/her contact lenses in overnight?
A. It is always safest to take contact lenses out before sleeping overnight. Doing so reduces the risk of infection. The choice of overnight wear versus daily wear is one that should be discussed with your child's eye doctor. Napping while wearing contacts is not a problem.

For some children and families, overnight wear is necessary. Extended wear silicone contact lenses are the safest for overnight use. They can be left in for a week or longer, if necessary. It is not advisable for your child to wear regular soft contact lenses made from other materials overnight.

Gas permeable contact lenses are made out of a hard material and are usually not comfortable for overnight wear. They may be tried, but only under the supervision of your child's eye doctor.

Q. If we find a lost contact lens, can it be used again?
A. If a lens simply falls out momentarily during contact lens insertion, it may be used again. In this situation, it is advisable to sterilize it with the usual cleaning procedure before inserting it into the eye.

If your child is using a soft or silicone contact lens, it may be dried out and hard when it is found. If the lens is soaked overnight in the cleaning solution, it will return to its original shape. Once the lens is sterilized, it can be used again. If the lens has dried out and been remoistened in this way, you should check with your child's contact lens provider to make sure that the prescription has not changed from drying out.

Gas permeable contact lenses do not dry out. They can be used again once cleaned and sterilized.

Q. Should my child's contact lenses be removed during long flights so his/her eyes do not get dry?
A. Long flights typically dry the eyes of any contact lens wearer. The type of contact lens worn will determine how much drying effect a long flight will have. Another concern is the increased chance of losing a lens during the flight if dryness causes the need for the lenses to be removed. If you are concerned, it is not unreasonable to remove the lenses before a flight or during the flight if your child becomes uncomfortable. He/she can use glasses during the flight, instead. Many children will spend large portions of flight time asleep, reducing the need for lenses. No harm will come to your child's vision if he/she does not use contacts, even during a long flight.

PART VI: OTHER CONDITIONS RELATED TO BOTH GLAUCOMA AND CATARACT

A. AMBLYOPIA AND OCCLUSION THERAPY

Q. What is amblyopia?
A. When one eye is not focusing equally with the other, or when one eye is not straight (strabismus), the brain can turn off its awareness of the image received from the weaker, less used eye. If this process remains untreated for several weeks in a child whose vision is still developing, the vision in that eye can worsen as the brain fails to pay attention to the eye. This condition is sometimes called lazy eye. The term lazy eye is also sometimes used to refer to misalignment of the eyes, even if the vision is normal.

A child's brain and eyes are wired together in a way that causes the brain to readily prefer interpreting vision from the better eye, particularly during the first six years of life. The brain will use this eye more, and begin to ignore the visual development of the other eye. By ignoring the vision in one eye, the brain is actually forgetting to develop the vision, causing blurring of sight. If left untreated, this can lead to permanent visual loss.

When a child's eye develops a cataract or glaucoma, the resulting unclear image can lead to amblyopia in addition to the loss of vision from the disease itself. Treating the cataract or glaucoma problem may not, by itself, restore good vision. Treatment for amblyopia, such as patching, may also be needed.

Q. What is occlusion therapy?
A. Occlusion therapy is simply a fancy term for blocking, or occluding, vision from one eye to force improvement of vision in the other eye. Occlusion therapy often involves the child wearing a patch over the eye that has better vision. A black contact lens is occasionally used instead of wearing a patch.

Q. How does patching work?
A. By patching the good eye, the brain is forced to use the worse eye. If caught early enough, amblyopia can be reversed and vision restored. If the optic nerve has been damaged by glaucoma, or the amblyopia is long standing, the eye may not be capable of seeing perfectly normally. As children get older, they are more resistant to *occlusion amblyopia*, but it is also harder to reverse the amblyopia in the worse eye.

Q. What are the benefits of patching?
A. Patching is perhaps the most important treatment for children with cataract and/or glaucoma who also develop amblyopia, but patching is only needed when amblyopia is present. Young children with glaucoma or cataract in one eye (unilateral) almost always have some amblyopia at some time and, therefore, need patching. Without patching, young children who have cataract surgery and amblyopia are destined for poor vision, even though the cataract has been removed.

Q. Will patching adversely affect the eye that is covered?
A. It would certainly seem that obstructing the vision in the good eye would cause the brain to ignore it, in the same way that it ignores vision from the worse eye and causes the amblyopia. Interestingly, it seems that the better eye is protected from the effects of patching in most

circumstances. Most dramatically, in children with a cataract in only one eye who have surgery, it seems that the good eye is hardwired to resist the development of amblyopia despite extensive patching that may occur on an around-the-clock basis for years.

In general, the more patching, the better the end result. In patients with glaucoma or cataracts in both eyes who have one eye that is stronger than the other, patching may rarely cause a temporary reduction in vision. This is almost always easily reversed by decreasing the number of hours spent patched, temporarily stopping the patching altogether, or switching the patch to the other eye. This possibility, though rare, is one of the reasons why regular follow-up visits with your child's eye doctor are important during occlusion therapy. During these visits, the doctor will check for improvement in the bad eye and also test the good eye for any harmful effects from patching.

The chance of a child developing amblyopia in the better eye (occlusion amblyopia) is higher for an infant. As a result, some doctors prefer to patch infants and toddlers for fewer hours and/or schedule follow-up visits more frequently. If a child is patching during all hours when he/she is awake, the follow-up is generally needed in increments of one week per year of age. For example, a 1-year-old should be seen every week. No child undergoing full-time occlusion therapy should go more than four weeks without seeing his/her doctor for a follow-up visit. If the child spends some waking hours without the patch every day, then the follow-up visits can be spaced farther apart.

Q. How much time should my child spend patched each day?

A. There is no standard amount of patching that has been determined to be effective. Infants in the first three months of life are often patched for shorter periods than older children. The decision on how much time a particular child should remain patched each day is made by his/her physician based on the child's age, practicality and convenience, how well the child tolerates being patched, the acuity of vision in each eye, and the alignment of the child's eyes. Your child's ophthalmologist will help you determine the patching schedule.

In general, studies suggest that patching a child with severe amblyopia, where vision in the amblyopic eye is somewhere between 20/100 and 20/400, for six hours per day, or possibly less, may be equivalent to patching full–time although it may take longer to get the amblyopia reversed as compared to patching full time. For children with moderate amblyopia, where vision in the amblyopic eye is between 20/40 and 20/100, studies have suggested that two hours per day of patching may be just as effective as patching six hours per day. Most of these studies were not done on children with cataract or glaucoma. More patching may be required in these more difficult situations.

Q. How long will my child have to continue patching?

A. The goal is to patch until the vision is approximately equal in both eyes. It is impossible to predict how long this will take. Patching may be required for months, or even years.

After the vision is equal, some children need continued patching to keep it that way. Your child's visual development may stop when he/she is as young as 6 years old or it may continue into his/her early teen years. As long as visual development is ongoing, amblyopia can occur. For that reason, he/she may still need to continue patching.

Patients with amblyopia due to causes other than cataract or glaucoma have shown some improvement up to age 12 or 13. If your child is 12 or 13 years old and has never undergone occlusion therapy before, it might be worth trying to see if his/her vision can be improved. Keep in mind that patching teenagers is very difficult, largely because of social concerns, the vigorous ways in which they can protest, and their need to have vision that is better than what will be available using only the worse eye when the patch is on.

It tends to be more difficult to successfully treat amblyopia in children with cataract and glaucoma. Their improvement may be limited. Patching can become ineffective in improving vision in these patients when they are as young as 5 or 6 years old.

Q. When should my child stop patching?
A. Your child's ophthalmologist will advise you when he/she is to stop patching. The amount of time spent patched is often gradually tapered in order to prevent recurrence of the amblyopia. The goal is to patch until the vision in both eyes is equal, but most ophthalmologists will consider patching to have failed if the prescribed regimen has been followed but the vision has not improved after two or three follow-up visits. The decision to stop patching takes into consideration the vision, the reason for the amblyopia, the response of the child and family to patching, and the child's age.

Q. Is a pirate patch acceptable to use for occlusion therapy?
A. In general, pirate-style patches held in place by an elastic band or string around the head should be avoided. Since this type of patch is not adhered to the skin, your child can easily move it and look around it. This completely negates the whole purpose of the patching exercise.

Q. Do I put the patch on my child's glasses or his/her skin?
A. The patch should be applied to the child's skin. If it is placed on the glasses, it is much too easy for the child to peek around the glasses. This is why certain other forms of occlusion using glasses, such as fingernail polish applied to the lens or blurring of the lens, are less desirable than patching on the skin.

If a child already wears glasses, there are cloth patches designed to go over the lens that extend beyond the frame so that the child cannot look past them. Another option is a suction cup occluder, which sticks to the inside of the glasses lens and extends back to cover the eye, leaving no room for the child to peek.

Q. What if the patch causes irritation to my child's skin?
A. Removing the patch sometimes results in minor damage or irritation to the skin. Porous paper tape, which can be purchased in any pharmacy, may be useful in alleviating this problem. It is designed to allow the skin underneath to breathe so it can heal. Place the paper tape on the irritated skin. Use the patch over the tape (see figure 16). The patch sticks to the tape rather than the skin and is less painful to remove. Leave the tape on 24 hours a day until it falls off on its own.

Redness and irritation of the skin under the patch may also result from minor allergic reaction to the patch adhesive (see Figure 17). If this occurs, allow the redness to subside, then try switching to another brand of patch.

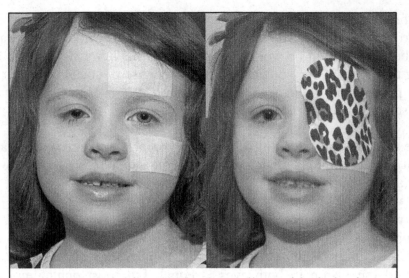

Figure 16: Patching method to relieve skin irritation caused by patch adhesive. Porous paper tape is placed directly over areas of skin irritation on the forehead and cheek (left). The patch is then applied to the tape (right) so that the patch adheres to the tape rather than the skin.

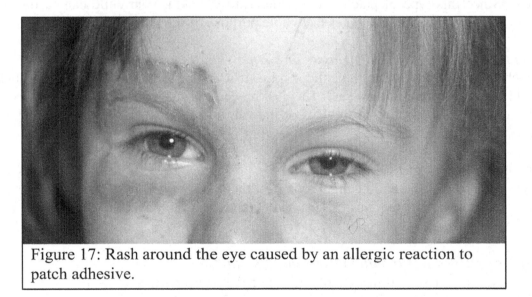

Figure 17: Rash around the eye caused by an allergic reaction to patch adhesive.

Q. How can I make the patch hurt less when it is pulled off?
A. Most children do not like the sensation when the patch comes off. It tends to hurt, just like any sticky dressing on the skin. To make removal less painful, try using a washcloth soaked with warm water to gently massage the patch off. In some countries, over-the-counter wipes designed to make removing adhesive dressings easier and less painful are available. If you choose to use these, be careful not to get the chemicals on the wipes in your child's eye.

Q. How will my child cope with wearing a patch in school?
A. There are two potential obstacles to patching during school. Firstly, if the vision in your child's bad eye is not good enough to allow proper performance in school, then it may be necessary for him/her to only patch when not in school. Secondly, other children may make fun of a child with a

patch. If this is happening, try having a show and tell session, where your child talks to the class about his/her patch and helps classmates understand why it is necessary for him/her to wear it. Some teachers have even had the whole class go through a day of patching so that others can feel what the child is going through. Once the mystery is removed, the teasing may stop. If not, it may be worth considering a compromise and discontinuing patching during school hours. Young children who are in preschool, kindergarten, or the first years of elementary school may actually comply more with patching in school than at home.

Q. What can I do if my child will not wear the patch?
A. Here are some suggestions:

- Start slowly. Starting by patching for long periods is likely to induce frustration early in the course of treatment. Ask your child's doctor if you can start at a lower level and gradually add time, perhaps at the rate of one additional hour a day each week.
- Treat skin irritation early.
- Use positive reinforcement. Linking rewards or activities your child enjoys, such as watching a movie, to compliance with patching are usually more successful than negative reinforcement. Patching is often more of a behavioral issue than a visual issue. Most children, particularly those in the first five to six years of life, can function perfectly normally even with vision as low as the level of legal blindness (20/200). The objections to using the lesser eye, having a patch adhered to the skin, and being told to do something he/she does not want to do, are the obstacle. We often tell our children to do things they do not like or want to do. Getting them to comply is one of the behavioral challenges of parenting. Most published studies have shown that positive reinforcement tends to have a more successful influence on behavior.
- Avoid negative reinforcement. If patching becomes a battle between parent and child, it is almost guaranteed to be one that the parent loses. This result is particularly likely with children 2 years old and older. If patching has become a series of arguments, then it may be helpful to back off to shorter periods of patching in combination with positive reinforcement to regain compliance, and then gradually build up to the prescribed level.
- Tincture of Benzoin. This over-the-counter product is a type of skin glue that is commonly used in hospitals when bandages or tape need to be applied. Using a cotton swab, apply some of this liquid to the skin on the areas around the eye. Be sure not to get it in the eye. Wave your hand in the air over the area to help dry the solution, then apply the patch. This makes it harder and a bit painful for the child to remove the patch. When you are ready to take the patch off, simply use a warm, wet washcloth to help massage it off.
- Use distraction. Shifting your child's attention to a more pleasurable interest might help him/her forget that the patch is on.
- Make your child king/queen for the day that patching begins. Getting off to a good start often goes a long way. If there are other children in the home, perhaps they can spend a day or two at a babysitter's or the home of a friend or family member. This way, all attention can be focused on the child being introduced to patching. Filling his/her day with special privileges and attention may distract the child from the rigors of patching and help get him/her off to a good start. It may be advantageous to start patching on the weekend, when all adult caretakers are at home, rather than leaving the initial task to a babysitter or daycare center.

- Be creative. Many parents have found that a little bit of creativity can go a long way. Some parents put a bow or a picture on the patch. You may also be able to purchase patches that come with child-friendly pictures printed on them. Other parents create elaborate games for patching, such as pirate games. Believe it or not, some families are even successful at making patching fun. Visit *http://www.pgcfa.org* for more information on patching.
- Physical restraints are sometimes necessary to keep a child from removing his/her patch. Here are some suggested techniques you may find useful.
    - Hand socks: Placing a sock over both of an infant's or younger child's hands, with or without taping around the wrists, can make it more difficult for him/her to peel the patch off.
    - Water wings: Inflatable water wings, often used as flotation devices around the upper arms of young children learning to swim, can be placed around the elbows. Your child will have enough arm motion for play and the daily tasks of living while the water wings make it impossible to bend his/her arms enough to reach the patch to remove it.
    - Rigid arm restraints: Arm restraints that prevent your child from bending his/her arm at the elbow are commercially available. Some physicians feel this technique is too punitive, but others have had success using it to get a child to accept wearing a patch.

The most important thing you can do is not give up too soon. Talk to your child's eye doctor or the support staff at his/her office if patching is not going well. Describe what the actual problem is. It may be possible to adjust the patching schedule to better fit your child's lifestyle. Perhaps an alternative treatment can be considered. Some children will fail at patching despite all of the best intentions and hard work, but do not give up!

Q. How can atropine be used to treat amblyopia?

A. Studies have shown that daily use of atropine eyedrops in the non-amblyopic eye can be equivalent to patching when used to treat moderate amblyopia. Atropine works by blurring the vision in the good eye so that it becomes worse than that of the amblyopic eye. This may be a good option if patching becomes too difficult. These studies were not done on children with cataract or glaucoma. As children with these problems tend to have worse amblyopia, atropine may not be strong enough. Atropine cannot be used if the lens has been removed from the good eye during cataract surgery, as the drug works by paralyzing the focusing ability of the natural lens.

Side effects of atropine are uncommon. They include pupil dilation, increased heart rate, flushing, inability to pass urine, dry mouth, and psychiatric disturbances. All are temporary and will subside when the medication is stopped.

Q. How can black contact lenses be used to treat amblyopia?

A. A contact lens with a black center can be placed in the non-amblyopic eye to treat amblyopia. These lenses block the vision in the good eye and force the child to use the amblyopic eye. They are not easily noticeable when looking at the child because the black spot rests where the natural pupil would be seen. Some ophthalmologists may be concerned that contact lenses should not be used on the good eye because there is a very small risk of the lenses causing a potentially blinding infection. Proper hygiene and care can reduce this already small risk even further.

B. STRABISMUS

Q. How do the eyes work together to produce normal vision?
A. A child born with normal vision has the capacity for clear focusing by both eyes simultaneously. In addition, the eyes are parallel to each other (straight). When the child wishes to look in different directions, both eyes move in tandem so that their lines of sight remain parallel to each other at all times. When both eyes see well, are positioned parallel to each other, and move in tandem, the individual images seen by the each eye are unified into one clear image by the brain. This process also leads to vision in three dimensions, known as stereoscopic vision. Any problems that upset the alignment or balance of the eye muscles, or compromise the vision in one or both eyes, can lead to a decrease or complete loss of stereoscopic vision. A child's visual system is especially sensitive to such problems, as it is not fully developed until perhaps as late as early adolescence.

Q. What is strabismus?
A. Strabismus is the medical term for eyes that are not parallel to each other. An eye can turn in either the horizontal or vertical direction. If it turns inward, it is often called a crossed eye. The medical term for this is esotropia. If the eye turns outward, it is sometimes called a wall-eye. The medical term for this is exotropia. The medical term for one eye appearing to be higher than the other is *hypertropia*. An eye can drift in such a manner that it is misaligned in both the horizontal and vertical directions at the same time.

Q. What causes strabismus?
A. Strabismus may develop for a number of different reasons. Some children are born with strabismus. In this situation, the parents generally notice that the child's eyes are misaligned within the first few weeks of life. This misalignment is often intermittent, transient, and self-resolving. It is more common for strabismus to develop several months or years after birth. This may occur as either as a result of problems with the focusing mechanism of the eyes or disorders of vision or the muscles.

Strabismus can be caused by the following:

- Focusing problems: All eyes have a muscle (ciliary muscle) that is used for focusing. If a child is very farsighted (*hyperopic*), this muscle is more active. This excessive focusing stimulates the eyes to cross because there is a link between the focusing mechanism and the messages to the eye muscles, which causes the muscles to turn the eyes toward the nose. If a child is nearsighted (*myopic*), sometimes the eyes will drift outward. If the two eyes do not focus equally, the image from one eye may be blurred. As a result, the eye that sees the blurry image may wander because the brain will turn off its awareness of the signal from that eye and may no longer send the signals to the eye muscles to keep the eyes aligned. For these conditions, patients are initially treated with glasses to help their eyes focus. In some cases, patching of the better eye is also needed to equalize the vision in both eyes. If these measures do not lead to a straighter eye, then eye muscle surgery is performed in order to put the eye muscles back into balance.
- Disorders within the eyes: A problem such as glaucoma or cataract can reduce the vision in an eye to such an extent that the brain ignores the image from that eye and concentrates only on the one received from the good eye. The eye with poor vision may then begin to wander.

- Eye muscle imbalance: Children may be born with an inability to move the eyes together because the muscles are not properly balanced. They may also develop this problem as they grow and develop. The reasons muscle imbalances develop are not always understood. Examples of diagnoses related to eye muscle imbalance include congenital esotropia and exotropia, intermittent exotropia, and oblique muscle dysfunction.

- Inability of an eye muscle to work: Some children are born with various anomalies of the extraocular muscles or the nerves that control them. One example of this situation is Duane syndrome, where the muscle that moves the eye outward (*lateral rectus*) is controlled by the nerve that moves the eye inward. This leads to an inability to move the eye outward and retraction of the eye with attempts to look towards the nose.

- Trauma: Fracturing of the bones around the eye can permanently damage the eye muscles or the nerves that control them. This can lead to strabismus and an inability to move the eye in certain directions.

- Neurologic problems: Damage to either the central nervous system or the nerves that control the eye muscles can cause strabismus. Causes may include strokes, brain tumors, congenital anomalies, and brain damage after severe trauma.

Q. How is strabismus treated?

A. If the strabismus is a result of blurry vision, then the treatment involves attempting to resolve whatever is affecting the vision. If one eye has amblyopia, then patching of or atropine in the good eye may solve the problem. If the poorer-seeing eye has a cataract, the lens must be removed and rehabilitation enacted to improve the vision. If the vision is blurred because of glaucoma, then either medications or surgery are often needed to control the pressure in the eyes.

Contact lenses or glasses, and often patching of the good eye, may be needed to restore the vision in the abnormal eye. If these measures do not lead to a more parallel alignment of the eyes, then eye muscle surgery can be performed put them into a more normal position.

If the strabismus is due to farsightedness or nearsightedness, then glasses would be the first line of treatment. If the glasses do not successfully treat the strabismus, then eye muscle surgery may be needed.

Q. What is the link between strabismus and amblyopia?

A. Amblyopia is often associated with strabismus in children. Both problems involve disruption of the visual signals that normally come into the brain equally from both eyes. When a child has strabismus, a misaligned eye may stop being used, as it cannot look straight ahead while the other eye is being used. As a result, the brain may ignore the signals coming from that eye, which can lead to amblyopia of that eye. Conversely, if an eye develops amblyopia, the brain receives less visual input from that eye than the other. This may result in the brain reducing the intensity of messages it sends to the muscles surrounding that eye, leading to strabismus.

Fortunately, if amblyopia and strabismus are diagnosed and treated during childhood, the chances for recovery of vision and proper alignment of the eyes are very good. It is important for family doctors and pediatricians to check the eyes for signs of strabismus, amblyopia, cataract, and glaucoma during all routine visits, starting immediately after birth.

Q. Why would glaucoma or cataract cause my child to tilt his/her head sideways and tuck his/her chin down to focus on things?

A. Children with glaucoma and cataract often also have eye muscle problems. Sometimes children will use a head position to compensate for the visual challenges created by those issues. If a child's eyes are misaligned when looking straight ahead but are aligned when looking up, he/she may tuck his/her chin down to keep the eyes gazing upward while looking straight ahead. Eye muscle surgery can align the eyes so that the child does not need to adopt this type of abnormal head position.

The presence of nystagmus can also cause a child to hold his/her head in an abnormal position while attempting to see straight ahead. Children with cataracts or glaucoma who have poor vision are more likely to suffer from nystagmus. When the vision is poor, it is as if the image is not clear enough for the brain to keep the eyes still. The nystagmus might be less, and the vision clearer, if the child looks in certain directions. For example, if the nystagmus is less when the child looks up, he/she might then keep his/her chin down to cause the eyes to be aimed in a relatively upward position when looking straight ahead. If the nystagmus is less when the eyes are looking to the left, the child will tend to turn his/her face to the right while looking straight ahead in order to keep the eyes in the left position.

Eye muscle surgery can be used to reposition the eyes so that they shake least when looking straight ahead while the child's head is in a normal position. Eye muscle surgery can sometimes reduce the nystagmus and may even increase vision a bit.

Less commonly, if a child loses some of his/her central vision due to glaucoma damage to the optic nerve, he/she may have blind spots (scotomas). He/she may try to see around the blind spot by either looking off-center while facing straight ahead (*eccentric fixation*) or using an adjusted head position.

Q. When should a child who has had cataract surgery in one eye and developed strabismus have eye muscle surgery?

A. It is very common for children who have had a cataract in only one eye to develop strabismus due to the decreased vision in that eye. If a child is tolerating patching of the normal eye on a regular basis, some surgeons will choose to try to straighten the eyes fairly early to allow them to work together sooner. The theory is that the child might gain some binocularity that would be less likely with later surgery. Other surgeons prefer to wait until a child is closer to school age, in the belief that the chance of him/her achieving complete binocularity is quite small and that the position of the eyes might be more stable later. Patching alone, with the resultant improved vision, may result in reduced strabismus. Some surgeons will wait until the vision is optimized by patching before doing eye muscle surgery. In general, surgeons favor waiting until the amount of strabismus is fairly stable, not changing from one visit to the next.

PART VII: LOW VISION

Despite the best treatment, some children with cataract and/or glaucoma will have vision outcomes that are subnormal, perhaps even at a level qualifying as low vision or legal blindness. It is beyond the scope of this book to cover the many issues that will come up in the life of a child with visual challenges. Fortunately, there are many sources for such information, including the PGCFA website. If your child has low vision or is blind, you should consult with your child's school and low vision support organizations in your community, such as a blind commission or school for the visually impaired, to learn more. What follows are some highlights that you may find useful.

A child with normal vision in one eye will generally function normally in every way, including sports and education. Low vision interventions are not needed. If the child is sometimes patching his/her good eye to reverse amblyopia in the bad eye, the child may have low vision issues while the patch is on.

Q. Will my child's vision limit his/her ability to participate in common activities?
A. It is the type and amount of usable vision a child has, along with any other medical issues, that will determine the function and activity restrictions, if any.

A child who has good vision in one eye but poor vision in the other eye, regardless of the cause, may be limited from pursuing certain professions that require excellent vision in both eyes. These professions vary from country to country, but generally include military and commercial air piloting. In some jurisdictions, individuals with poor vision in one eye may be barred from operating commercial trucks, becoming police officers or firefighters, or practicing certain surgical medical subspecialties or dentistry. Children who have one stronger eye and one eye that does not see as well should always wear appropriate protective sports glasses when participating in outdoor and sports activities.

Even when vision is reduced in both eyes, there is no way that a parent can decide what a child is capable of accomplishing, as the parent cannot see what the child sees. Let your child find his/her own comfort level with activities.

Q. When does a child qualify for low vision services in school?
A. When you have a school-aged child who has a visual impairment, locating the appropriate support in school can be overwhelming. Keep in mind that every district school board is different. For specific information related to obtaining services, it is best that you begin by contacting the special education department. Here are some general steps to follow that will make the process smoother.

Your first step is to obtain a medical eye examination report. This information is helpful both to gain a referral to obtain vision support for a child in the school system and to help those who care for your child understand his/her vision problems and their cause. The report should include:

- the name of the eye condition/diagnosis and
- a statement that your child has either
  - a visual acuity less than a certain amount in the better eye after best correction (the specific level is different for each state); or
  - a field abnormality (i.e., loss of side vision or blind spots).

Typically, a child whose visual acuity is worse than a certain specified level or who has a severe visual field restriction meets the medical criteria for a referral to the vision services portion of the special education department. If your child does not meet the medical criteria, he/she can still be referred, but support within the classroom may or may not occur. It is up to the discretion of the individual school board as to how much support to provide, if any, to a child who does not meet the medical criteria.

Once you have the medical documentation, contact your local district's school board and ask to speak with a person in the special education department to learn more about the process and options for obtaining low vision support.

Q. How do school districts provide low vision services to students?
A. Depending on the size of the school district, there may or may not be itinerant vision teachers (specially certified teachers who are trained to work with children with visual impairments and travel from school to school) employed by that school district.

If the district does not have teachers who have been specifically trained to work with children who are visually impaired, you can contact the closest school for the blind. Some schools for the blind employ resource teachers of the blind that travel throughout the province or state. These individuals conduct assessments on children who are visually impaired and may provide support to classroom teachers. In addition, any state or province government agencies for the blind or disabled should be able to help you uncover any additional resources available for your child.

Parents and their children with low vision have various rights regarding the way the children are treated, the opportunities afforded to them, and the identification and placement recommendations that the parents should be informed about. These standards are specific to each state/province. Learn about these and do not be afraid to advocate for your child.

Q. Can a visually impaired child be integrated into a regular classroom?
A. Integrating children who are visually impaired into a regular classroom while meeting their needs can be accomplished with some creativity, simple adaptations, and the use of adaptive technology. Some students may only need a simple accommodation, such as sitting with their backs to the window. Others may require more extensive, and expensive, accommodations, such as computers with screen enlargement software.

Accommodating students' needs and providing modifications to the environment to meet their needs have very different educational implications. Accommodations are things that school personnel can do to make the visual environment more accessible to the student who is visually impaired without making changes to the academic expectations or standards for that student. They may include special equipment or alternate teaching methods. Examples of accommodations include:

- allowing the child to use a closed-circuit television (CCTV) that enlarges regular print to a size that is easier for him/her to see;
- allowing the child to sit closer to the chalkboard to better allow him/her to see what the teacher is writing;
- having the teacher speak information aloud as it is written on the chalkboard to help the child take down notes;
- providing task lighting, enlarged handouts, high contrast materials, or black-lined paper and pens to allow the child to more easily see assignments;

164

- assigning fewer questions as homework; and
- allowing extra time to complete assignments or tests.

Modifications are changes made to a child's educational program that cause it to be different from the regular stream. Examples include:

- A child who is in grade six but is assigned his/her math work from a grade two textbook is on a modified math program.
- A child who spends part or all of the school day in a special education classroom is usually on a modified academic program.

If a student is on a modified program in high school, he/she may not obtain academic credits for some courses. The policy may vary from one school district to another.

Q. Is it important to start education interventions early?

A. Yes, it is important that school personnel know that your child has special needs. The earlier those needs are identified, the earlier support can be provided in school. For young children entering the school system for the first time, early intervention has proven to be essential to early literacy skill development. For older children with established literacy skills, special education support can help them continue to meet curricular expectations.

Q. If my child's vision is not very poor, do I need to still tell the school about his/her eye condition?

A. Even if the specialized support a child needs is minimal, it is still important that his/her teachers know he/she has glaucoma and/or cataracts. Keeping the school informed allows for the optimum partnership between the staff, the child, and the parent to achieve the best educational outcomes. Minor classroom accommodations, such as changing the lighting conditions, seating a child facing away from the main light source, enlarging print, or seating him/her in the front row may be sufficient to meet his/her needs.

It is also helpful if the teacher and school know in advance that a child might need to be absent for doctor appointments or surgery. In these situations, completing school work from home may be an option. There may also be periods when a child needs additional accommodation or resources because his/her vision is intermittently more blurry, such as after surgery.

Many districts now have restrictions on who can administer medications during school hours. If a child has medications that need to be used during the school day, the school's nurse and/or administrators need to be informed of the details as early as possible.

PART VIII: GENETICS

Q. What is a genetic counselor?
A. A genetic counselor is a medical professional trained to offer information to patients, parents, and prospective parents about what caused a disease to occur and the likelihood that other family members carry or could also get the disease. Genetic counselors help families make important health decisions related to their genetic disorders. They specialize in taking the family history and drawing the family tree (*pedigree*), showing any family history of occurrence of the disease, while looking for clues to help understand the patient (known as the index case or proband) understand his/her disease better. They also talk to families about prenatal testing options (options for finding out if an unborn baby may have the disease) and genetic testing of other family members who may or may not have the disease. Genetic counselors work with individuals of all ages who may have a disease, a family history of genetic disease, or otherwise are at an increased risk of having an affected child.

Q. Why should we see a genetic counselor?
A. If your child's cataract is a result of a genetic anomaly, a genetic counselor can explain how the abnormal gene occurred and how it caused a cataract. He/she can also help you and your family to understand the implications of other genetic abnormalities your child may have.

Genetic counselors may be able to help you arrange DNA blood testing to find the exact gene responsible for causing the cataract. This type of testing is not yet readily available for most cataracts due to the huge number of genes that can be related to cataract, but it may be helpful in some specific kinds of cataract. A genetic counselor can also offer information regarding the chances of having another affected child and prenatal counseling.

Q. Is glaucoma or cataract genetic?
A. Not all varieties of childhood glaucoma or cataracts are hereditary, but a significant subgroup of each is. By recognizing the type of glaucoma or cataract a child has, the doctor can often tell if it is genetic or not. Table 7 lists the genes known to cause glaucoma when mutated. There are far too many genes that may cause cataract to list. Each also tends to be less specifically linked to a certain type of cataract. The same gene can often cause several different kinds of cataract.

Remember that, even if your child's glaucoma or cataract is genetic, there does not have to be a history of someone else in the family who has it. All genetic diseases have to start somewhere, and any child could be the first in a family to get a genetic form of glaucoma or cataract. One or both parents could be *carriers*, meaning that they do not have glaucoma or cataract themselves but carry genetic factors which, alone or when combined, cause it in their child. It could also be spontaneous, meaning that the gene abnormality just happened to occur in that child.

If either or both parents are carriers, then they might have other children who also have glaucoma or cataract. Therefore, all other children born to either parent should have an eye examination to ensure they do not have glaucoma or a cataract that may be undiagnosed. Both parents should also be examined for glaucoma and cataract.

Even if the siblings or parents of a child with genetic glaucoma or cataract do not have the disease, the affected child may have the risk of having children with glaucoma or cataract. If the siblings are carriers, then they may also face a similar risk.

| Table 7: Genes Known to Cause Glaucoma When Mutated ||
Gene (Protein produced)	Type of Glaucoma*
MYOC (myocillin)	JOAG or POAG
OPTN (optineurin)	POAG (often NTG)
WDR36	POAG
NTF4 (neurotrophin 4)	POAG
OPA1 (dynamin)	NTG
CYP1B1	Congenital or infantile glaucoma
FKHL7/FOXC1	Congenital or infantile glaucoma
LTBP2	Congenital glaucoma
GJA1	Axenfeld-Rieger spectrum
FKHL7/FOXC1	Axenfeld-Rieger spectrum
PITX2/RIEG1	Axenfeld-Rieger spectrum/ Partial aniridia/Peters/ Sclerocornea
FKHL7/FOXC1	Iridogoniodysgenesis anomaly
PITX2	Iridogoniodysgenesis syndrome
PITX2/IRID2	Iris hypoplasia
PITX3	Anterior segment mesenchymal dysgenesis (ASMD) with anterior polar cataract
COL4A1	Axenfeld-Rieger spectrum
GPDS1	Pigment dispersion syndrome
NPS/LMX1B	Nail-patella syndrome
FOXE3	Peters anomaly
CYP1B1	Peters anomaly
PITX2	Peters anomaly
FKHL7/FOXC1	Peters anomaly
NDP (norrin)	Peters anomaly
PAX6	Peters anomaly
B3GALTL	Peters plus
SHOX/SOX3	Peters plus
PAX6	Aniridia
FOXC1	Aniridia
PITX2/RIEG1	Aniridia
LOXL1	Pseudoexfoliation glaucoma
Key: *Use of a / indicates alternate terminology POAG = adult primary open angle glaucoma JOAG = juvenile open angle glaucoma COAG =chronic open angle glaucoma (adults) NTG = normal tension glaucoma (adults)	

Q. How hereditary are pediatric glaucoma and cataract?

A. The risk of having a child with glaucoma or cataract depends on the type of glaucoma or cataract and the family history. For certain types of glaucoma or cataract, such as those caused by trauma, the risk of having an affected child is no greater than it is for the general population. Other forms may have a transmission risk of zero, 50 percent, or somewhere in between. The risk of having another child with persistent fetal vasculature may be remote, since this is generally not considered a genetic form of cataract.

For varieties of glaucoma passed genetically based on an autosomal dominant pattern, such as JOAG, and some forms of cataract, an affected individual has a 50 percent chance of having an affected child with each pregnancy, regardless of the child's gender.

Other forms, such as congenital or infantile glaucoma, and certain forms of cataract, are usually autosomal recessive (both parents are usually carriers). Carriers generally do not have glaucoma or cataract themselves and often have no idea that they are carriers. Everyone is a carrier of several abnormal genes that he/she does not know about. The only circumstance in which an individual with the autosomal recessive gene can have a child with the disease is if he/she has a child with someone who also happens to be a carrier. The disease develops because the child has received a copy of the abnormal gene from each parent. If one parent's gene does not have the abnormality, then that overrides the one with the abnormality and the child will not have the disease. There is a 25 percent chance of two carriers having an affected child for each pregnancy. For the same type of recessive glaucoma or cataract to be passed to the following generation, the affected child would have to have a child with another carrier. This is very rare unless the affected individual marries a relative or someone from the same tightly knit community.

A particular form of cataract occurs as part of the Nance-Horan syndrome. This syndrome is also associated with characteristic teeth abnormalities in addition to the cataract. Both the syndrome and the cataract are X-linked. This means that it affects boys more often and more severely than girls because the affecting gene is located on the X chromosome. There is no X-linked form of glaucoma. As a result, glaucoma is equally likely to affect males and females.

A definitive risk assessment can only come from genetic testing. Genetic testing is available for many forms of glaucoma. It is only available for cataracts when the cataract occurs as part of a specific eye or body syndrome.

Q. Does glaucoma or cataract skip generations?
A. Although abnormal genes cannot skip generations, it is possible for a person carrying a glaucoma or cataract gene to remain unaffected. We call these people "nonpenetrant" for the disease, as they have the abnormal gene but not the disease it causes. They can still pass on the abnormal gene and their children can still be affected.

Genes do not act alone. They interact with the products of other genes. As a result, some individuals have their glaucoma- or cataract-causing gene modified by the counteraction of another gene, leaving them with normal eye pressure and clear eye lenses. Not all family members would carry this modifier gene, causing the pattern of inheritance to make it appear that the disease has skipped generations.

One method to identify relatives at risk of developing glaucoma or cataract is to study the family tree. By determining who is affected and who is not, it is sometimes possible to discover the pattern of inheritance occurring in each family and determine whether there may be someone who has the gene but not the disease.

Q. Are there gene tests for glaucoma or cataract?
A. Many genes have been identified which, when mutated, cause glaucoma or cataract. It is possible to use a blood test to identify individuals at risk of developing glaucoma if a relative is known to have one of the specific genetic defects. To do this, the gene causing the disease in the affected person must first be found. There are too many genes that can cause cataract to make blood testing

to find the mutated gene practical unless the cataract is part of a specific eye or body syndrome. As technologies improve, it is likely to become more practical to do so.

When glaucoma or a cataract is found in a child with other body abnormalities, special tests may be conducted to look for missing or extra pieces of DNA. One of these tests, a karyotype, allows the doctor to look at the actual chromosomes from blood cells under a microscope. In a microarray test, the doctor looks for tiny extra or missing pieces of DNA that cannot be seen even when using a microscope. When glaucoma or cataract is found in a child with other body abnormalities, the presence of the eye condition can help the doctor to identify a syndrome. This, in turn, indicates what specific diagnostic gene testing might be useful.

Obtaining results from gene testing depends on selecting the appropriate test. The tests are costly, and sometimes are not readily available or only available on a research basis. They are also sometimes complex to interpret. A negative test does not necessarily mean the person does not have genetically-caused glaucoma or cataract. Rather, it may be that the lab could not find a hidden abnormality in the gene or that the individual's glaucoma or cataract is caused by another gene, perhaps one that has not yet been discovered. Likewise, a positive test does not prove the patient will develop glaucoma or cataract. Sometimes abnormalities in more than one gene are needed for a particular disease to develop. Consultation with an ocular geneticist, medical geneticist, or genetic counselor is usually very helpful.

Q. Is there a prenatal test for glaucoma or cataract?

A. If the gene and the exact gene mutation that runs in a family and causes glaucoma are known, it is possible to conduct a prenatal test, such as *amniocentesis* or *chorionic villus sampling*, early in the pregnancy to determine if the child has that mutation. Even if the fetus is found to carry the gene mutation, it does not necessarily mean the child will develop glaucoma. Sometimes, due to the unique genetic mix of each individual, the protective effects of other genes (variable expression) may prevent glaucoma from developing. Such tests are not yet available for cataract unless the cataract is part of a specific syndrome for which the gene is known.

Some eye disorders can be detected by special prenatal ultrasound. Although the eyes can be visualized by ultrasound at 12 to 16 weeks of a pregnancy, buphthalmos commonly seen with congenital glaucoma is generally not visible until the third trimester. Abnormally small eyes (microphthalmia), which are often associated with cataract, can be detected by ultrasound early during pregnancy, but the child may or may not have cataract. The use of ultrasound to detect cataract is not always reliable. As a result, ultrasound tends not to be frequently used as a tool in prenatal glaucoma or cataract detection.

The topic of prenatal testing for glaucoma or cataract also raises some ethical issues. One of the most contentious of these is the question of abortion. Abortion is legal in some countries. Prenatal testing for certain diseases, such as glaucoma or cataract, may lead a family to consider this option. Should a woman be permitted to abort a child due to test results that show it has or may develop glaucoma or cataract—diseases that are largely treatable and are not severe in their association with or impact upon other bodily systems? On the other hand, if prenatal glaucoma or cataract testing becomes inexpensive and readily available, early identification of infants at risk for developing glaucoma or cataract would be possible. This would lead to more frequent screening, which would in turn lead to earlier diagnosis and potentially better glaucoma control or cataract surgery with less vision loss.

Currently, prenatal molecular genetic testing for glaucoma or cataract is not performed routinely. As science advances, this kind of testing will certainly become more available, and the ethical challenges of whether or not it should be provided will have to be addressed at that time.

Q. If I have one child with glaucoma, what is the chance that I might have another affected child?
A. Table 8 shows the risks of having a child with the various types of glaucoma in two scenarios: if one parent is affected and has not yet had any children; and if the parents are unaffected, already have one affected child, and no other family members are affected. Where the figure "0%" appears in this table, it does not mean there is no risk of having a child who has or will develop glaucoma. It simply means that the risk is the same as the risk for anyone else in the general population. The risk is never truly zero percent. These risks refer to the risks for each pregnancy, not the total number of children. If the risk to a family of having an affected child is 50 percent, this does not mean half their children will or will not be affected. With each pregnancy, the risk of the child being affected is 50 percent.

Keep in mind that some parents and children may not realize they have glaucoma or conditions that predispose them to it. If one child develops glaucoma, it is very important for the eye doctor to examine the other family members to ensure that no one else in the family is also affected.

Q. If I have one child with cataract, what is the chance that I might have another affected child?
A. This question is more difficult to answer than for glaucoma since there is no clear correlation between the type of cataract and the risk. The risk may range from zero to 50% for each additional pregnancy, depending on the cause of the first affected child's cataract. If one child has cataract resulting from persistent fetal vasculature, it is extremely unlikely that his/her parents will have another child who is similarly affected. Each son of a woman with Nance-Horan syndrome has a 50 percent chance of being affected. The risk is less for any daughters. The sons of a man with Nance-Horan syndrome will not have the syndrome or related cataract, though each of his daughters would be affected. Affected females usually have a milder form of the syndrome and cataract than affected males. These examples illustrate how complicated it is to determine the risks, as well as the importance of consulting your physician, geneticist, or genetic counselor to best determine the type of cataract and pattern in your family to give you an answer.

Q. Does the chance of having another affected child depend on the gender of the child?
A. In general, pediatric glaucoma and cataract are not linked to the gender of the child. The one exception is cataract resulting from Nance-Horan syndrome.

Q. If I have another affected child, will he/she be affected to the same degree as this child?
A. Unfortunately, it is impossible to predict whether another affected child will be affected to the same degree as the first affected child. Genetic disorders may express themselves differently in different individuals, even within the same family. The second child may have a more mild, more severe, or similar clinical picture than your first affected child.

An abnormal gene does not exert its effect in isolation, but in the context of the entire unique genetic make-up of an individual. The effect of that gene in each unique individual may be more or less severe than in another individual. Likewise, responses to various drugs or surgeries may be different for different members of a family. Vision outcome may also be different. If it is known that an individual carries the gene for the disease, then early screening would lead to early detection. In turn, early detection could potentially prevent the disease from reaching a more severe stage.

Table 8: Risk of Having Another Affected Child		
Type of Glaucoma	**Parents affected, no children yet**	**One child affected; no other family members affected**
Congenital or infantile glaucoma	0 to 50%	0 to 50% (average 8%)
Aphakic glaucoma	0%	Risk to the next child only if that child has cataract(s) and surgery. Each family member who has cataract surgery has his/her own individual risk of developing glaucoma. Some types of cataracts that run in families are associated with higher risks of glaucoma developing in individuals who have cataract surgery.
Sturge-Weber syndrome	0%	0%
Anterior segment dysgenesis (e.g., Axenfeld-Rieger; Peters, aniridia)	0 to 50%, depending on specific abnormality	0 to 50%
Traumatic glaucoma	0%	0%
Steroid-induced glaucoma	Risk in the general population unknown, but risk of glaucoma developing in exposed family members may be higher in some families.	
Juvenile open angle glaucoma (JOAG)	50%	0% if new gene just in child, 50% if inherited from parent.
Iritis	Although some forms of iritis may be due to diseases that have a genetic predisposition in some families, the risk for getting glaucoma as a complication of iritis in any given individual is probably unique.	
Persistent fetal vasculature	0%	Not usually a genetic disease. If both eyes are affected, disorder may be the result of a syndrome that could be genetic and affect other children.
Neurofibromatosis	Risk of neurofibromatosis being passed from parent to child is 50%. The risk of developing glaucoma is unique to any individual with neurofibromatosis within a family.	

Q. Why would my child's doctor recommend that my spouse and I get our eyes examined?

A. Sometimes examining a parent can offer clues to the diagnosis of a child. If a parent is carrying a gene but not showing signs of the disorder he/she is aware of, he/she may still show changes. These will usually be most apparent in the iris, if the child has glaucoma, or the lens, if the child has a cataract. These findings can help determine the cause and inheritance pattern in his/her child. The changes may have been present, yet undetected, throughout the parent's life. These signs may not be picked up on a routine eye examination, as they can be so subtle that they would not be recognized by an eye doctor who was not familiar with what to look for. Eye doctors specifically interested in pediatric glaucoma, pediatric cataracts, or eye genetics may be more alert to such changes.

It is also possible that a parent has a milder form of glaucoma or cataract without any symptoms. If a child has a genetic form of glaucoma or cataract, it is helpful to know that neither parent is affected. Conversely, diagnosing glaucoma or cataract in a parent would allow appropriate treatment, and hopefully help prevent glaucoma- or cataract-related vision loss in that parent.

Although examining parents may be useful, a parent might have an entirely normal examination yet still carry a gene mutation that is related to the disease in his/her child. A normal examination does not rule out the possibility that a genetic cause of the child's glaucoma or cataract is present or that a parent could pass this disorder on to another child in a subsequent pregnancy.

Q. Why would my child's doctor want to draw blood for genetic testing on lots of family members, even those without glaucoma or cataract?

A. There are two general reasons for genetic testing. If the exact gene for a type of glaucoma is known, then a single individual who has the disease can be tested for mutations of that gene. Unfortunately, this type of testing is not currently available for cataract unless it is the result of a recognizable syndrome. There are too many possible genes that could cause cataract to make it practical. If a mutation or other abnormality in that specific gene is found, then other members can be tested to see if they carry the same gene abnormality.

The other reason for testing comes into play if the specific gene causing the glaucoma or cataract is unknown. Most genes for glaucoma and cataract have not yet been discovered. In this case, special investigative testing is performed to try to find the gene causing the disease. By drawing blood from both affected and unaffected family members, DNA can be compared in an effort to try and find which chromosome is carrying the abnormal gene. The errant gene will only be found in individuals who have the disease. Once the small piece of DNA is identified, researchers can look further into that piece to find the affected gene.

Q. If I have an adult relative who has glaucoma or cataract, could it be related to my child's glaucoma or cataract?

A. This is currently a very active area of glaucoma and cataract research. There is currently no firm answer. In general, current accepted understanding is that a family history of late-onset adult glaucoma (after 40 years old), in the absence of any other body or eye abnormalities, does not mean that young children in that family are at risk of developing childhood glaucoma. Much less is known about the genetic implications of age-related cataract occurring in older people, but cataracts that develop in adulthood are usually totally unrelated to the pediatric forms. It is unlikely that there is any added risk of children related to an individual with adult-onset cataract developing pediatric cataract.

There is mounting evidence that there may be genetic factors that predispose certain individuals to get POAG. If these factors run in the family and a child also had another coincidental genetic risk factor, the chance of him/her getting glaucoma later in life would be higher than that of someone in the general population.

Q. What side of the family did the glaucoma or cataract come from?
A. Different types of genetically-caused glaucoma or cataract can be inherited in different ways, usually autosomal dominant (inherited from one parent) or autosomal recessive (both parents are carriers). Like all genetic diseases, glaucoma and cataract can also arise in a child with no family history. Even if neither parent has glaucoma or cataract, the parents may still carry a gene that causes it in their child. There are also more complicated inheritance patterns. Certain genetic tests are available that may be able to determine whether one parent or both, and which parent, carries the gene responsible for pediatric glaucoma. Unfortunately, similar tests are not currently available to determine inheritance for cataract unless the cataract is part of a recognizable eye or body syndrome. A consultation with a clinical or eye geneticist can be useful in sorting this out in your particular family.

Q. If the blood test is positive for a glaucoma-causing gene, do I have to tell my insurance company?
A. When a patient is already symptomatic and then has genetic testing, the condition is considered to be preexisting and the positive test has no effect on future coverage. The bigger issue is when a patient is presymptomatic and has a positive gene test. In the United States, the *Genetic Information Nondiscrimination Act (GINA)* was enacted in May 2008. This law prohibits health plans or employers from denying coverage or charging higher premiums when a healthy patient has a gene test that reveals the likelihood of developing a disease or other medical condition. This information does not have to be reported to insurance companies. Additionally, if the insurance company knows about a positive result, it cannot have a negative effect on the individual's coverage. Even if a patient is symptomatic prior to testing, there is still no requirement to share genetic test results with the insurance company.

Q. Should I have my other children checked?
A. If you have one child with glaucoma or cataract, your other children would only need to be checked if it is a type that has a genetic cause. If your child developed glaucoma or cataract for another reason, such as due to an injury, your other children would not have to be checked.

If one of your children is diagnosed with a form of glaucoma or cataract that his/her doctor indicates may have a genetic basis, then all of your children should be checked at once to make sure they are not at risk. This is particularly important for the younger children. In addition, any children born after the first child's diagnosis should be examined within the first week of life. Even if the risk is low, early detection is critical to avoid damage to the child's vision.

If a sibling's eye examination is normal, follow-up for the development of glaucoma or cataract may still be necessary, even if he/she is older than the child who was first diagnosed with glaucoma or cataract. Children in the same family can develop glaucoma or cataract at different ages. For example, if you have a child whose cataract was first detected at 3 years old, his/her 5-year-old sibling still needs to be checked and followed, for he/she could develop cataract at a later age.

These are simply guidelines. Check with your child's eye doctor to get specific recommendations based on the type of cataract that your child has.

AFTERWORD

This book represents the culmination of tireless work of many people dedicated to helping children and their families living with eye diseases. Of particular note is Dr. Alex Levin, the committed and dedicated founder and leader of the PGCFA. Dr. Levin has a deep personal commitment to all of the children and families he cares for and recognizes the benefit of families being educated and actively involved in care and treatment.

The PGCFA is primarily composed of parents and families affected by childhood cataract or glaucoma. We understand how scary and confusing the initial diagnosis can be and that you may have many questions. Why my child? How did this happen? What next? This book strives to provide answers to these questions by helping you understand the often complex medical details of these childhood eye diseases.

Although your journey will be unique, a greater understanding of your child's condition will allow you to advocate on his/her behalf and play an active role on his/her health care team. The medical system can feel overwhelming, but this book can help, as can the PGCFA. We encourage you to visit our website at *http://www.pgcfa.org*. We provide ongoing support through education via our newsletter and our "Ask the Expert" forum. Once again, we thank Dr. Levin and the team of global experts he worked with closely to make this book a reality and for their commitment to helping children see the sun, the moon, and the stars.

    Dave Prowten, Chair, PGCFA

GLOSSARY

5-fluorouracil (5-FU): A drug used in glaucoma surgery (mainly trabeculectomy) to reduce scarring, which is the most common reason for surgery failure.

acanthamoeba: A germ that can cause severe cornea infection. Risk factors include swimming in fresh water, such as lakes or streams, and poor contact lens care, such as sleeping while wearing contacts not made for overnight wear, using homemade contact lens solution, or using tap water on contact lenses.

acetaminophen: An over-the-counter medication for pain relief.

acute: Sudden.

add: See *bifocal*.

advocate: A person who acts and speaks in support of another person.

ALK: See *anterior lamellar keratoplasty*.

alpha-agonist: An eyedrop that is used to lower intraocular pressure. Brimonidine and apraclonidine are examples.

amblyopia: Loss of vision or incomplete vision development, usually only occurring in one eye, because the brain prefers using vision from one eye more than the other. Amblyopia can be caused by going without a strong glasses prescription that is needed or glasses prescriptions that are unequal between the two eyes. When structural defects, such as cataracts, glaucoma, or other conditions that block vision in one eye, are also present, amblyopia will often make the vision even worse. (Commonly referred to as lazy eye.)

amniocentesis: A procedure that can be used to test a baby for a variety of conditions, usually genetic disorders, before he/she is born. A small amount of the fluid surrounding the baby in the womb is removed for examination by using a needle that goes through the belly of the pregnant mother.

anesthesia: Medicine used during surgery to put patients to sleep. See also *gas anesthetic*.

anesthesiologist: A physician who specializes in giving anesthesia during surgery.

anesthetic: A numbing medicine that can be administered in a variety of ways and for different reasons. A gas or intravenous form of anesthetic may be given to a patient to cause him/her to sleep during surgery. Anesthetic gel, eyedrops, and injections can be used to numb just one part of the body.

angle closure glaucoma: A closure of the drainage system of the eye, often sudden (acute), but sometimes more chronic, that can cause high eye pressure. When acute, it is typically painful. This form of glaucoma is uncommon in children. This is also sometimes referred to as closed angle glaucoma.

angle of the eye: The area where the cornea and iris meet. This is where the fluid inside the eye drains from the eye, regulating the eye's internal pressure. This term is often shortened to angle.

angle recession glaucoma: A form of increased eye pressure caused by damage to the drainage system of the eye from an injury.

angle surgery: Any of a variety of surgical procedures performed on the draining system of the eye in order to facilitate increased outflow. Examples include goniotomy and trabeculotomy.

aniridia: A congenital lack of iris tissue.

anisocoria: A difference in pupil size between the two eyes.

anomaly: A body part that was formed differently than normal.

anterior capsule: The front part of the membrane that surrounds the lens of the eye. An opening is made in the anterior capsule when performing cataract surgery.

anterior chamber: The space between the cornea and the iris that is filled with fluid (aqueous humor).

anterior lamellar keratoplasty: A partial corneal transplant, where only the front layers of the cornea are transplanted. This procedure is often referred to by the acronym ALK.

anterior pyramidal cataract: A type of congenital cataract that is shaped like a pyramid with the point coming through the pupil from the front surface of the lens.

anterior segment: The front half of the eye, including the lens, iris, anterior chamber, and cornea.

anterior uveitis: Inflammation of the iris.

anterior vitrectomy: Removal of the front part of the vitreous. It is commonly performed in children who undergo cataract surgery. This procedure is sometimes referred to as core vitrectomy.

antibody: A chemical made by the body to fight against infection or anything else it senses to be foreign. Sometimes the body incorrectly creates antibodies that attack its own tissues. This results in disease rather than the normal protection that antibodies are supposed to provide.

antimetabolites: Drugs, such as 5-FU and mitomycin, that inhibit or reduce scar tissue formation after surgery.

antinuclear antibody (ANA) test: A blood test used to determine if a particular type of antibody is present. This test is commonly used in children with juvenile idiopathic arthritis (JIA). The presence of these antibodies indicates a higher likelihood that the eyes of a patient with JIA will be affected and a need for more frequent screening.

anti-TNF drugs: See *tumor necrosis factor*.

anti-VEGF drugs: See *VEGF-blockers*.

aphakic: Lacking the natural lens of the eye. This is the state of the eye after cataract surgery if a lens implant is not put in the eye.

aphakic accommodation: The ability of the eye to change its focusing ability, even without the presence of the natural lens, which usually performs this task.

aphakic glaucoma: Increased pressure inside the eye that occurs after cataract surgery. The cause is not known. Aphakic glaucoma can occur days, weeks, months, or many years after the surgery.

apnea: A temporary stoppage of breathing.

aqueous humor: The fluid that fills the front part of the eye over the pupil and iris (anterior chamber).

aqueous shunt device: See *seton*.

arrhythmia: A group of conditions in which the electrical activity of the heart is abnormal and causes the heart to beat irregularly.

artificial eye: See *ocular prosthetic*.

A-scan ultrasound: A device that uses sound reflections to measure the length of different parts of the eye or the whole eye length.

aspiration: Use of suction to remove a cataract or fluid.

assent: To agree to something. Children who may not be mature enough to give full informed consent may be asked to give their assent to a procedure or research.

astigmatism: An abnormal curvature of the cornea that causes blurring of vision. Astigmatism is generally correctable with glasses or contact lenses.

autosomal dominant: A genetic pattern of inheritance in which only one abnormal gene copy is necessary to produce a disease. A person with this form of genetic disease has a 50 percent chance that each child that he/she has will also have the disease.

autosomal recessive: A genetic pattern of inheritance in which two abnormal gene copies are necessary to produce a disease state. Since a person can only pass on one copy at a time to his/her children, a person with an autosomal recessive disease cannot have a child with the disease unless the other parent of the child has the same disease or is a carrier. This is more likely to occur if the other parent is a relative or from the same small community.

avascularity: Lacking blood vessels.

Axenfeld anomaly: See *posterior embryotoxon*.

Axenfeld syndrome: Axenfeld anomaly with glaucoma. This term is no longer commonly used, as it is now recognized to be part of Axenfeld-Rieger spectrum.

Axenfeld-Rieger spectrum: A congenital abnormality of eye development characterized by the presence of one or more of the following conditions: malformations of the iris, abnormal pupil position or number, posterior embryotoxon, and/or abnormal attachments between the iris and cornea (iridocorneal adhesions). Individuals with Axenfeld-Rieger spectrum are at high risk for developing glaucoma. Some patients may also have abnormal teeth, redundant skin around their belly buttons, and/or characteristic facial appearance.

bag: See *capsule*.

band keratopathy: Calcium deposits on the cornea that are usually caused by chronic inflammation.

beta-blockers: Medications that block receptors in the eye that are involved in producing aqueous humor. Eyedrop forms of these medications are used to treat glaucoma. Examples include timolol, levobunolol, and betaxolol.

bifocal: A segment of a contact lens, eyeglass lens, or an IOL that has extra power, to allow an individual to view things both up close and at a distance.

bilateral: Occurring on both sides. A bilateral eye disease affects both eyes.

binocular vision: Using both eyes to look at the same thing at the same time; using both eyes together.

bionic: Using electronic or mechanical parts to assist the body in performing certain tasks. An electronic chip on the retina to improve sight is an example of a bionic device.

bleb: The bubble of fluid under the conjunctiva that is caused by the flow of aqueous fluid out of the eye through a trabeculectomy or glaucoma tube.

buphthalmos: Increased eye size caused by childhood glaucoma.

capsule: The thin membrane that covers the front or back of the lens of the eye. Sometimes referred to as the bag. This term is also used to describe a form of oral medication, often designed to release its dose over a specified period of time.

capsulotomy: Surgical opening of the posterior capsule.

carrier: A person who does not have a genetic disease but has the abnormal gene which causes the disease.

catalyst: A chemical that causes a reaction to occur more easily and promptly. For example, the disc in a contact lens cleaning solution works as a catalyst to activate hydrogen peroxide liquid, cleaning the contact lens and then turning into harmless saline.

cataract: Any opacity of all or part of the lens of the eye.

CCTV: Acronym for closed-circuit television, a device that uses video cameras to project reading material onto a screen with much enlargement to assist the visually impaired.

central retinal artery occlusion: A blockage of the artery that supplies the eye with blood; a form of stroke that occurs only within the eye.

chelation: A process by which calcium deposits (band keratopathy) are removed from the surface of the cornea using a liquid that binds to the calcium.

chloral hydrate: A drug used for sedation.

chorionic villus sampling: A procedure that can be used to test a baby for a variety of conditions, usually genetic disorders, before he/she is born. A small amount of the placenta in the womb is removed for examination by using a needle that goes through the vagina of the pregnant mother.

choroid: The layer between the retina and the white of the eye (sclera). The choroid plays a role in supplying the retina with blood.

choroidal hemangioma: A benign tumor of the blood vessels in the choroid. Choroidal hemangiomas are not cancerous and cannot metastasize, but they can sometimes leak and cause fluid to accumulate under the retina.

choroiditis: A form of uveitis localized to the choroid.

chromosome: The structures in cells that contain DNA and genetic information.

ciliary body: Located behind the iris, this area includes the ciliary processes, underlying tissues, and the muscle inside the eye used for focusing vision at near range.

ciliary epithelium: The cells lining the ciliary processes of the eye. These cells play a significant role in producing aqueous humor.

ciliary muscle: A ring of muscle in the eye, behind the iris, that controls changing the eye's focus for viewing objects at different distances.

ciliary processes: The finger-like projections of the ciliary body, located behind the iris, that produce aqueous humor. The region of the eye that contains the ciliary processes is called the pars plicata.

closed angle glaucoma: See *angle closure glaucoma*

closed-circuit television: See *CCTV*.

CME: See *cystoid macular edema*.

CMV: See *congenital cytomegalovirus*.

Coats disease: An uncommon, nonhereditary eye disease in which abnormal blood vessels leak large amounts of fluid into the retina. It is usually found in only one eye.

coloboma: A congenital absence of or defect in a part of one of the structures of the eye. Colobomas can occur in the iris, retina, choroid, lids, or optic nerve.

congenital: A condition present at birth.

congenital cytomegalovirus: A virus that can be transmitted from the mother to the fetus during pregnancy, potentially resulting in brain damage and eye abnormalities, including cataract, iritis, and inflammation of the retina and optic nerve. Sometimes abbreviated to CMV.

congenital glaucoma: Glaucoma that is present at birth.

congenital rubella syndrome: A group of findings present in an infant whose mother contracted rubella while pregnant. These findings may include eye effects, such as cataracts, glaucoma, and retinal problems. Affected children may also have developmental delay, heart problems, and hearing loss.

congenital unilateral cataract: Born with a cataract in only one eye.

conjunctiva: The tissue that covers the white of the eye (sclera).

conjunctival hyperemia: Inflammation of the conjunctiva that causes the white of the eye (sclera) to appear reddish.

conjunctivitis: Inflammation or infection of the conjunctiva. Conjunctivitis can be caused by viruses, bacteria, allergies, or chemical irritants.

core vitrectomy: Removal of the center part of the vitreous.

cornea: The clear, front part of the eye over the pupil.

cryotherapy: Freezing treatment used to treat glaucoma and other eye disorders.

cup of the optic nerve: See *optic cup*.

cupping: Loss of optic nerve tissue secondary to glaucoma. Cupping appears as an enlargement of the central canal in the optic nerve. This effect is sometimes referred to as optic nerve cupping.

cycloablation: See *cyclodestruction*.

cyclodestruction: A treatment for glaucoma that involves destruction of some of the ciliary processes in order to reduce production of aqueous humor. This process is sometimes referred to as cycloablation or (when done with a laser) cyclophotodestruction.

cyclodialysis cleft: A tear at the peripheral edges of the iris that allows aqueous humor to leave the anterior chamber, resulting in eye pressure that is too low.

cyclophotodestruction: See *cyclodestruction*.

cystoid macular edema: Swelling of the area of the retina that provides central vision. Cystoid macular edema can occur after cataract surgery or be caused by drugs or inflammation. Sometimes abbreviated to CME.

deletion: All or part of a gene is missing.

Descemet stripping endothelial keratoplasty: See *DSEK*.

Descemet's membrane: One of the inner layers of the cornea.

dilate: To become bigger.

direct ophthalmoscope: A handheld instrument used to examine the optic nerve, retinal blood vessels, and parts of the retina.

dislocated lens: Complete displacement of the lens from its normal anatomic position to the vitreous or in front of the pupil.

diurnal curve: A procedure in which the eye pressure is measured at different times throughout the day to check for high points or larger than normal variations. Both are possible signs of glaucoma and could be missed if the pressure is checked only once each day.

DNA: Acronym for deoxyribonucleic acid, the material inside cells that contains genetic information (genes).

drainage surgery: Any of several procedures performed to create new drainage sites to help filter aqueous fluid from the eye, such as trabeculectomy. Drainage surgery is also sometimes referred to as filtration surgery.

DSEK: Commonly used acronym for Descemet stripping endothelial keratoplasty, a surgical procedure in which the back layers of the cornea are removed and replaced by similar layers from a donor eye.

Duane syndrome: A congenital eye muscle disorder that causes an inability of one or both eyes to move to one or both sides.

dysgenesis: Defective development of an organ or part of an organ.

eccentric fixation: When an eye looks slightly off-center to see straight ahead. This occurs when the area of the eye that is responsible for straight ahead vision is not working properly, causing the eye to try to see around the defect.

ectopia lentis: Movement of the lens of the eye away from its normal anatomic position. See also *dislocated lens* and *subluxed lens*.

edema: Swelling of a body tissue due to accumulation of fluid.

electric cautery: An instrument that uses small electrical currents to stop minor bleeding during surgery.

encapsulation: An action by which the body encloses or encases an object or area in scar tissue. After glaucoma surgery, scar tissue can encapsulate the plate of a glaucoma tube or the area where aqueous humor is draining through a trabeculectomy.

endophthalmitis: Infection of the inside of the eye.

endoscope: A small camera that can be placed inside the eye to provide magnified views and guide surgery.

endoscopic diode cyclophotoablation: An endoscope-guided use of a laser to destroy ciliary processes and decrease aqueous humor production. This procedure is used in the treatment of glaucoma.

enucleation: Surgical removal of an eye.

enuresis: Inability to control urination. Also known as bedwetting.

epiphora: Excessive tearing from the eyes.

episclera: The area in between the sclera and the conjunctiva.

episcleral veins: Blood vessels in the episclera that drain blood from the eye. Also referred to as episcleral vessels.

episcleral vessels: See *episcleral veins*.

epithelium: The lining of a tissue surface or cavity inside the body.

esophagus: The muscular tube that food passes through before reaching the stomach.

esotropia: A form of eye misalignment in which one or both eyes turn in towards the nose. Commonly referred to as crossed eyes.

evisceration: Surgical removal of the inner structures of an eye while leaving the sclera intact.

exotropia: A form of eye misalignment in which one or both eyes turn out towards the ear. Commonly referred to as wall-eyes.

eye pressure: See *intraocular pressure*.

eye socket: See *orbit*.

farsighted: See *hyperopic*.

fibroblast: A cell that plays an important role in tissue and wound healing.

filtration surgery: See *drainage surgery*.

finger tension: Estimation of the eye pressure by gently touching the eye through the eyelids.

FISH : Acronym for fluorescence in situ hybridization, a test used to detect a specific missing piece of a chromosome.

fluorescein: A liquid substance that glows bright green when blue light shines on it. Fluorescein has several uses in ophthalmology, including identifying corneal abrasions and problems with the retinal blood vessels.

fluorescence in situ hybridization: See *FISH*.

fluorouracil, 5- (5-FU): See *5-fluorouracil (5-FU)*.

fovea: The central part of the retina, which is specially structured to allow for straight ahead vision.

functional vision: An individual's ability to use the vision he/she has for specific tasks, as determined by a professional assessment.

gas anesthetic: An inhaled medicine used during surgery to put patients to sleep.

gene: The molecular unit of inheritance. Genes carry all the information on how to build all the parts of the body and coordinate their function.

Genetic Information Nondiscrimination Act (GINA): A law passed by the United States Congress that stops the use of genetic information in health insurance and employment.

glaucoma: A disease that causes damage to the optic nerve due to increased pressure inside the eye.

glaucoma drainage device: See *seton*.

glaucoma tube: See *seton*.

goniotomy: A procedure in which a small incision is made in the drainage system of the eye to facilitate increased flow of aqueous humor from the eye. Goniotomy is performed to treat certain types of glaucoma.

graded responsibility: Granting increased responsibility to medical trainees after they show basic knowledge and progressive skill development.

granulomatous iritis: A form of iritis in which the cells in the anterior chamber form large clumps (keratoprecipitates) on the inner surface of the cornea. This is more commonly seen in certain disorders, such as sarcoidosis and tuberculosis, but may be seen in any case of severe iritis.

granulomatous uveitis: Severe uveitis with larger clumps of keratoprecipitates (called mutton fat keratoprecipitates).

half-life: The amount of time that it takes for the amount of drug in the body to fall to half its initial level.

hemorrhage: Bleeding.

HOTV test: A method used to measure visual acuity in patients who may not recognize all the standard letters or may be too shy to speak the answers to vision testing. Patients are asked to match the letter shown – H, O, T, or V – with a card that shows the same letter.

hyperopia: An eye that naturally focuses better at a distance than at close range. People with this type of vision are commonly referred to as farsighted.

hyperopic: An individual with hyperopia in one or both eyes.

hypertonic saline: Water that has a high concentration of salt. It is sometimes used to treat swelling of the cornea. The extra fluid causing the swelling flows from the cornea into the high salt solution.

hypertropia: A form of strabismus in which one eye is higher than the other.

hyperventilation: Breathing more rapidly and deeply than normal.

hyphema: Blood inside the eye, in the space between the cornea and the iris.

hypoplasia: Underdevelopment or incomplete development of a body part.

hypotony: Eye pressure that is too low.

idiopathic: Cause unknown.

illuminated microcatheter: A tiny cable that shines a light and can be inserted in parts of the eye.

implant: An artificial device designed to replace a missing anatomic structure or enhance a structure's function. Examples in ophthalmology include intraocular lens implants and glaucoma tube implants.

in-the-bag implantation: Placement of an intraocular lens inside the membrane that normally surrounds the natural lens.

indirect ophthalmoscope: An instrument made up of a light attached to a headband that the eye doctor wears and special eye pieces used to examine the retina, optic nerve, and blood vessels inside the eye. It provides a wider angle view of the inside of the eye than the direct ophthalmoscope, allowing the doctor to see the entire retina.

individualized education plan (IEP): The individualized objectives and plan for a child with a disability that may impact school performance. IEPs are designed to help these children reach their goals more easily.

Individuals with Disabilities Education Act (IDEA): A law in the United States that governs how public entities provide early intervention and special education to children with disabilities.

infantile: Occurring as an infant after birth.

infantile glaucoma: Increased intraocular pressure in infancy in an eye that is otherwise normally formed and having no apparent cause other than genetics.

informed consent: The process by which a doctor explains a treatment plan or procedure, including a thorough discussion of the risks, benefits, and alternatives, after which the patient or his/her substitute decision maker (often his/her parent) agrees to the plan.

inhalation anesthetic: See *gas anesthetic*.

intraocular lens: An artificial implant placed inside the eye after cataract surgery to replace the natural lens that has been removed. Commonly referred to as IOL.

intraocular pressure: The pressure of the fluid inside the eye. Commonly referred to as IOP.

intravenous: Inside a vein.

intravenous line: A small tube inserted into a vein to administer medications or draw blood.

IOL: See *intraocular lens*.

IOP: See *intraocular pressure*.

iridocyclitis: Inflammation of the iris and ciliary body. Iridocyclitis is a form of uveitis.

iris: The colored part of the eye that surrounds the pupil.

iris bombé: A buildup of pressure behind the iris that causes it to bow forward. This is usually caused by scar tissue formation between the pupil and lens.

iris claw IOL: A type of intraocular lens implant that is clipped onto the front or back of the iris instead of being placed in the bag or sulcus.

iris hypoplasia: Although this term can be used for any congenital underdevelopment or incomplete development of the iris, it is most often used to describe a specific eye condition in which the surface iris tissue is underdeveloped and there is a high risk for glaucoma.

iritis: Inflammation of the iris. Iritis is a form of uveitis.

isolated: Occurring alone, without associated eye or body conditions.

itinerant vision teachers: Teachers who specialize in helping visually impaired children learn. Their services are shared between students at more than one location.

JIA: See *juvenile idiopathic arthritis*.

JOAG: See *juvenile open angle glaucoma*.

JRA: See *juvenile idiopathic arthritis*.

juvenile idiopathic arthritis: An inflammatory joint condition of childhood which may be associated with uveitis. In the past, this type of arthritis was commonly referred to as juvenile rheumatoid arthritis (JRA) or juvenile chronic arthritis (JCA). Commonly referred to by the acronym JIA.

juvenile open angle glaucoma: Increased pressure inside the eye that occurs between the ages of 4 and 40 years old in an eye that has no other diseases and is not otherwise predisposed to develop glaucoma for any reason. Commonly referred to by the acronym JOAG.

juvenile rheumatoid arthritis: See *juvenile idiopathic arthritis*.

karyotype: A laboratory test that measures the number and structure of chromosomes.

keratometry: Measurements of the curvature of the cornea that are used to determine the correct power of IOL implants and sometimes also to fit contact lenses.

keratoprecipitates: Clumps of white blood cells on the inner side of the cornea that occur in uveitis. Sometimes referred to by the acronym KP.

Landolt C test: A method of testing vision in patients who are either nonverbal, due to youth or developmental delay, or who may not be familiar with English letters. The patient is presented with images of the letter "C" turned in different directions. He/she then indicates what direction each "C" is facing.

lap board: A flat board held on the lap and used as a makeshift desk to read, write, or communicate by matching or symbol identification. It is particularly useful for children with language delays, cerebral palsy, low vision, or other developmental or educational challenges.

laryngomalacia: A condition in which soft, immature cartilage of the voice box (larynx) collapses inward during breathing. This is more common in premature babies than older children and may make it difficult for a child to undergo general anesthesia.

laryngospasm: An involuntary contraction of the vocal cords that stops breathing. Laryngospasm may occur during general anesthesia, so anesthesiologists take special precautions to prevent it from happening.

laser iridotomy: Use of a laser to create a hole in the iris that allows aqueous humor from behind the iris to flow into the front and out the drainage system. Laser iridotomy is used to treat glaucoma which occurs due to the pupil becoming attached to the lens and blocking the normal path of fluid from behind the iris through the pupil.

laser trabeculoplasty: Use of a laser on the trabecular meshwork to decrease pressure inside the eye. Laser trabeculoplasty is used to treat certain types of glaucoma in adults and is rarely performed in children. Also referred to as selective laser trabeculoplasty (SLT).

lateral rectus: The muscle that moves the eye outward towards the ear.

lazy eye: See *amblyopia*.

lens: The clear structure behind the pupil and iris that helps focus light on the retina.

lens capsule: See *capsule*.

limbal stem cells: Cells at the edge of the cornea that are responsible for producing new corneal cells.

Lowe syndrome: A rare genetic disorder, also known as oculocerebrorenal syndrome, that can cause congenital cataracts, glaucoma, kidney problems, and developmental delay.

macula: The area at the back of the eye responsible for central vision.

macular hypoplasia: A condition that occurs when the macula, which is responsible for central vision, does not form fully. Macular hypoplasia can be found in ocular albinism, aniridia, or as an isolated phenomenon.

meninges: The membranes that envelop the central nervous system, including the brain, optic nerves, and spinal cord.

metabolic acidosis: A medical condition that occurs when the body produces too much acid or the kidneys do not remove acid from the blood quickly enough. This is sometimes a complication of using oral carbonic anhydrase inhibitors.

microarray: A test used to detect tiny variations in genes or chromosomes, such as duplicated areas, deleted areas, or even single gene mutations.

microphthalmia: A congenitally small eye.

miosis: Small pupil(s).

mires: The two semicircles, viewed through the slit lamp by the examiner, that guide measurement of eye pressure during Goldmann applanation tonometry.

mitomycin C: A medication that is used in certain glaucoma procedures to prevent scarring. Sometimes referred to as mitomycin or by the acronym MMC.

mm Hg (millimeters of mercury): The units of measurement for eye pressure.

MMC: See *mitomycin C*.

moderate: A mid-range condition, between mild and severe.

monovision: Use of one eye for distance vision and the other eye for near vision.

multifocal: An eyeglass lens or IOL that has more than one focus point, allowing a patient to see clearly at different distances.

mydriasis: Dilated pupil(s).

mydriatics: Eyedrops that are used to dilate the pupil(s).

myopia: An eye that naturally focuses better at close range than at a distance. Individuals with this type of vision are commonly referred to as nearsighted.

myopic: An individual who has myopia in one or both eyes.

narrow angle glaucoma: An intermittent closure of the draining system of the eye that can cause high eye pressure. This form of glaucoma is rarely seen in children. See also *angle closure glaucoma*.

nasolacrimal duct: The channel that allows tears to drain from the eye into the nose.

nasolacrimal duct obstruction: Blockage of the channel that allows tears to drain from the eye into the nose. Symptoms of a nasolacrimal duct obstruction include tearing and mucous discharge.

nearsighted: See *myopic*.

needling: Use of a needle to break up scar tissue that has caused trabeculectomy or glaucoma tube surgery to fail.

neovascularization: Growth of abnormal blood vessels.

neurofibromatosis type I: An inherited condition in which nerves are prone to growing tumors called neurofibromas. Patients with this condition may experience developmental delays, have tiny spots on the iris called Lisch nodules, have light brown birthmarks (café au lait spots) and possess other body abnormalities.

neurofibromatosis type II: An inherited condition in which the nerves that carry signals for hearing are prone to develop tumors. In addition, patients with this condition may have cataract and/or retinal abnormalities.

non-penetrating procedure: A glaucoma surgery that does not extend into the eye, but rather stays around it.

normal tension glaucoma: Damage to the optic nerve that appears like glaucoma, but without high pressure in the eye. This is a disorder only seen in adults.

nuclear cataract: An opacity of the lens *nucleus*. Nuclear cataract can be present before birth, at birth, or start later in infancy or childhood.

nucleus: The center of the lens. The nucleus consists of two parts, the most inner embryonic nucleus and the surrounding fetal nucleus.

nurse: A health care professional who assists doctors and focuses on the care of individuals and families.

nystagmus: A constant, rhythmic shaking of the eyes.

obstructed airway: A blockage in the breathing passage (trachea) that prevents air from entering or leaving the lungs.

occipital lobes: The parts of the brain that are responsible for perceiving vision and interpreting visual input from the eyes.

occlusion amblyopia: A rare form of amblyopia caused by patching treatment. If a patient has amblyopia in one eye, the ophthalmologist might prescribe patching of the other, stronger eye. Rarely, the patching can weaken the vision in the patched eye.

OCT: See *optical coherence tomography*.

ocular hypertension: High pressure inside the eye but without true glaucoma.

ocular prosthetic: An artificial, synthetic, hard shell painted to look like an eye that is placed over the socket after a real eye is removed (enucleation) or to cover an eye that is too small to be usable. Ocular prostheses do not give patients the capability of vision. Sometimes referred to as an artificial eye.

ocularist: A professional who create prosthetic eyes.

oligoarthritis: Arthritis that is characterized by inflammation of fewer than seven joints.

open angle glaucoma: Glaucoma that occurs when the drainage system of the eye is not blocked.

ophthalmologist: A physician who graduated medical school and performed a minimum of four years of residency who specializes in the medical and surgical treatment of the eye and vision disorders.

ophthalmology: The branch of medicine that specializes in the eye and vision.

ophthalmoscope: An instrument used to look inside the eye at the retina, optic nerve, and blood vessels.

optic cup: The canal in the center of the optic nerve, through which the blood vessels that feed the retina enter the eye. An excessively large cup can be a sign of damage from glaucoma. Also referred to as the cup of the optic nerve or optic nerve cup.

optic disc: The end of the optic nerve as it enters into the back of the eye. Also referred to as the optic nerve head or the disc.

optic nerve: The nerve that carries visual information from the eye to the brain.

optic nerve cupping: See *cupping*.

optic nerve head: See *optic disc*.

optic nerve hypoplasia: Congenitally small optic nerves.

optician: A professional who specializes in making and fitting glasses.

optical coherence tomography: A form of ultrasound that gives highly detailed pictures of the optic nerve and retina. It can be used to measure the health of the optic nerve in patients who have glaucoma. Sometimes abbreviated to OCT.

optometrist: A non-physician health care professional who specializes in the prescription of glasses and contact lenses and provides primary eye care. Optometrists attend optometry school, not medical school, after college. They do not perform eye surgery. Some optometrists specialize in care for patients with low vision.

optometry: The non-medical study of primary eye care.

optotype: A letter or symbol on an eye chart that is used to test vision.

orbit: The bony area around and behind the eye. The optic nerve, eye muscles, and other tissues are found within this bony cone. Often referred to as the eye socket.

orbital rim: The edge of the eye socket defined by the bone that can be felt surrounding the eye.

orthoptist: A professional who specializes in detecting and measuring strabismus and amblyopia. Orthoptists often assist pediatric ophthalmologists.

over-plussed: Glasses that have too much farsighted correction. This causes blurred distance vision but may result in better vision up close, especially in infants with aphakia.

PACU: Acronym for postanesthesia care unit. See also *recovery room*.

pannus: Abnormal blood vessels growing into the cornea.

panuveitis: Coexisting anterior and posterior uveitis in an eye.

parasympatholytic: A drug that reduces the activity of the parasympathetic nervous system. In the eye, this causes dilation of the pupil.

pars plana: The part of the inside of the eye between the edge of the retina and the ciliary body. It is a safe area to make an incision to access the back part of the eye because there is no retina present.

pars plana approach: Surgically accessing the inside of the eye through an incision in the pars plana.

pars planitis: A form of uveitis localized to the vitreous, ciliary body, edges of the retina, and area just behind the edges of the retina (pars plana). Pars planitis is also referred to as intermediate uveitis.

pars plicata: See *ciliary processes*.

pediatric: Pertaining to children.

Pediatric Glaucoma and Cataract Family Association: A support organization run by families for families that provides information, resources, education, and support to parents of children with cataract and/or glaucoma (*http://www.pgcfa.org*). Commonly referred to by the acronym PGCFA.

Pediatric Glaucoma Family Association): Predecessor to the Pediatric Glaucoma and Cataract Family Association (PGCFA). Commonly referred to by the acronym PGFA.

pedigree: A family tree diagram that shows how family members are related to each other and which family members have certain diseases that can be inherited.

penetrate: To pierce or pass into a structure such as the eye.

peripheral anterior synechiae: Scar tissue between the outside edges of the iris and the cornea. Sometimes referred to by the abbreviation PAS. A multitude of peripheral anterior synechiae can lead to closed angle glaucoma.

peripheral iridectomy: Removal of a piece of iris which may be performed to prevent pupillary block glaucoma or treat iris bombé.

peripheral vision: The outer edges of sight around the center of vision. Peripheral vision is sometimes referred to as side vision.

persistent fetal vasculature: A developmental disorder of the eye in which blood vessels normally present inside the eye of the baby during pregnancy fail to disappear as they are supposed to do in the last few months of the pregnancy. Sometimes referred to by the abbreviation PFV. PFV was previously known as persistent hyperplastic primary vitreous or PHPV.

persistent fetal vasculature cataract: Any opacity of the lens caused by persistent fetal vasculature (PFV, previously known as persistent hyperplastic primary vitreous or PHPV).

persistent hyperplastic primary vitreous: See *persistent fetal vasculature*

PFV: See *persistent fetal vasculature*.

PGCFA: See *Pediatric Glaucoma and Cataract Family Association*.

PGFA: See *Pediatric Glaucoma Family Association*.

photophobia: Sensitivity to light. An individual with photophobia may experience pain and squeeze his/her eyelids shut to avoid the light.

PHPV: See *persistent fetal vasculature*.

phthisis: An eye that has stopped functioning, lost eye pressure, and shrunken.

POAG: See *primary open angle glaucoma*.

polyarthritis: Arthritis that is characterized by the inflammation of more than six joints.

postanesthetic care unit: See *recovery room*.

posterior capsule: The membrane on the back surface of the natural lens of the eye. The posterior capsule is sometimes left behind after a cataract is removed and may later become cloudy, requiring use of a laser to create a hole in the capsule through which the vision is clear.

posterior embryotoxon: A white line on the peripheral edge of the inner surface of the cornea that can be seen during an examination with a slit lamp. Posterior embryotoxon does not affect vision but is a sign of a malformed drainage system of the eye. This phenomenon was once called Axenfeld anomaly but is now recognized as occurring in almost all forms of Axenfeld-Rieger spectrum. Posterior embryotoxon can occur in patients with no other eye abnormalities, people who do not have glaucoma, or individuals who have certain syndromes that are not normally eye-related, such as Alagille syndrome with liver disease. Strands of iris are sometimes attached to the posterior embryotoxon.

posterior segment: The back part of the eye, behind the lens, including the vitreous, retina, choroid, and optic nerve.

posterior synechiae: Scar tissue between the pupil edge and lens.

posterior uveitis: Inflammation of the retina, vitreous, optic nerve, and/or choroid.

power: Focusing strength of glasses, contact lenses, IOLs, or the natural lens of the eye.

preferential looking test: A method of testing vision in patients who are non-verbal due to either age or developmental delay. A card is presented to the patient and the child is observed to see whether he/she is more attentive to a series of vertical or horizontal bars on one side of the card compared with a blank area of the same size on the other side of the card.

premedication: Medication given before a procedure or surgery to make a patient sleepier and less anxious.

primary: An action performed at the first surgery, such as when a primary IOL is placed at the initial cataract surgery rather than during a second operation. This term may also be used to indicate a disease process that occurs without an inciting event (such as primary open angle glaucoma rather than glaucoma secondary to trauma).

primary open angle glaucoma: Increased pressure inside the eye that occurs after the age of 40 years old in an eye that has no other diseases and is not otherwise predisposed to develop glaucoma for any reason.

progressive: A type of bifocal eyeglass lens in which the lens power gets increasingly stronger towards the bottom instead of having an abrupt line where the power suddenly becomes stronger. Progressive lenses are also sometimes called invisible bifocals.

prosthetic: An artificial device that substitutes for a missing or defective part of the body.

pseudophakic accommodation: The ability of an eye with an intraocular lens implant to change its focusing ability, even without the natural lens that usually performs this task.

pupil: The hole in the center of the iris through which light enters the eye.

pupil dilator muscle: The small muscle inside the iris that causes the pupil to get bigger.

pupil sphincter muscle: The small muscle inside the iris that causes the pupil to become smaller.

pupillary block glaucoma: An increase in IOP that occurs when the pupil adheres to the surface of the lens, either from scar tissue due to inflammation or forward movement of the lens against the pupil, blocking the normal flow pathway of aqueous humor from the ciliary body behind the iris through the pupil. This causes the iris to bow forward (iris bombé) because the aqueous humor is trapped behind the iris. The forward movement of the iris then closes off the drainage system of the eye, causing angle closure glaucoma.

recovery room: The area where patients are brought for care after surgery is complete and they are waking up from anesthesia. Sometimes referred to as the postanesthetic care unit or PACU.

red reflex: The red reflection of light from the inside of the eye that is seen by the ophthalmologist when shining either an ophthalmoscope or a *retinoscope* at the eye. This is the same effect seen in photographs where the pupil appears red.

reflux: Flowing backwards.

refraction: Measuring to calculate a patient's glasses or contact lens prescription.

reservoir: A receptacle for holding liquid.

retina: The wallpaper-like structure that lines the inside of the back of the eye and senses light. The retina is like film in a camera, converting an image that is seen into a message for the brain to read.

retinal dystrophy: A genetic disease of the retina that causes it to function improperly.

retinoblastoma: A childhood cancer of the retina.

retinopathy of prematurity: A disease of the retina found in premature babies. Retinopathy of prematurity can cause retinal detachment and blindness if not identified early and treated. Sometimes referred to by the acronym ROP.

retinoscope: An instrument used to measure if an eye is nearsighted, farsighted, or has astigmatism. The eye doctor holds lenses in front of the eye while using the retinoscope to project a slit of light into the eye until the light is focused properly on the retina.

retract: To hold back tissue during surgery and provide a better view for the surgeon.

revise: To fix, repair, or change a previous surgery. Also referred to as revision or surgical revision.

rheumatoid: Pertaining to joints or connective tissue.

Rieger anomaly: Axenfeld anomaly with iris and pupil abnormalities. This term is no longer commonly used, as it is now recognized to be part of Axenfeld-Rieger spectrum.

Rieger syndrome: Rieger anomaly with glaucoma and systemic manifestations. This term is no longer commonly used, as it is now recognized to be part of Axenfeld-Rieger spectrum.

ROP: See *retinopathy of prematurity*.

salicylates: A class of drugs used to treat pain and discomfort. Aspirin is an example.

sarcoidosis: A disease where abnormal microscopic inflammatory nodules, called granulomas, form in multiple organs. Sarcoidosis can cause inflammation in many parts of the eye.

Schlemm's canal: A circular channel in the sclera surrounding the cornea that drains aqueous humor from the eye.

sclera: The white part of the eye.

sclerostomy: A small hole made in the sclera to allow excess aqueous humor to escape from the eye. This is a critical step in trabeculectomy surgery.

scotoma: An area of the visual field that is partially diminished or entirely gone.

secondary: An action or condition that is due to or results from, something else. This term is often used to refer to an action performed after a first surgery is completed, such as implanting an IOL during a second surgery rather than doing so during the initial cataract surgery.

sedation: Use of a medicine to produce a calming effect in order to allow an examination or to reduce anxiety before the start of general anesthesia.

selective laser trabeculoplasty: See *laser trabeculoplasty*.

seton: A tube that is put in the eye surgically to treat glaucoma by providing an alternate drainage pathway for the aqueous humor. Also referred to as a glaucoma drainage tube, glaucoma tube, glaucoma valve, tube, or tube shunt.

Sheridan-Gardiner test: A method of testing visual acuity that depends on matching letters by pointing rather than verbally naming them.

sickle cell disease: A blood disorder that causes red blood cells to become shaped like crescents instead of their usual oval shape. These abnormal blood cells can clog blood vessels.

side vision: See *peripheral vision*.

single vision: A single image that is perceived by the brain when both eyes are looking at an object. This phrase is also used to describe an eyeglass lens, contact lens, or IOL that has one power across the entire surface instead of bifocal or multifocal powers.

slit lamp: A machine used by eye doctors to examine the eye in fine detail. There are handheld versions and upright machines. This device is also referred to as slit lamp biomicroscope.

SLT: Acronym for selective laser trabeculoplasty. See also *laser trabeculoplasty*.

Snellen chart: A set of letters of several scaled sizes used to test visual acuity. It is the most commonly used vision test.

snuff: To extinguish or put an end to. This term is sometimes used to refer to sudden blindness in advanced glaucoma that occurs as a result of surgery.

solution: A mixture of two or more liquids or a liquid into which a solid is dissolved (such as crushing a medicine pill to dissolve it into a liquid).

spectrum: A range of related things, the individual features of which tend to overlap and form a continuous series or sequence of varying severity.

speculum: A metal clip used to hold the eyelids open.

squint: See *strabismus*.

steroid: A medicine that has the ability to reduce inflammation. Steroids may be administered as eyedrops, eye ointment, orally, or by injection.

strabismus: Misaligned eyes. In some countries, the term squint is used instead.

stroma: The main bulk of a tissue, usually referring to material sandwiched between the surface and the underside of an organ or body structure. In the eye, one example of this is the corneal stroma.

subluxed lens: See *ectopia lentis*.

sulcus: The area between the front surface of the lens and the back side of the iris.

sulcus implantation: Placement of an intraocular lens implant in the area between the front of where the natural lens was located before cataract surgery and the back side of the iris.

suprachoroidal space: The space between the choroid and the sclera.

surgical revision: See *revise*.

suspension: The result of mixing a solid substance with a fluid when the particles of the solid are not completely dissolved.

suture: A stitch used to close cuts from injury or surgery.

sympathomimetic: A drug that activates the sympathetic, or "fight or flight," part of the nervous system. Sympathomimetics are used to dilate the pupil.

syndrome: A group of related clinical findings that are often found together as a result of a common cause.

synechiae: Scar tissue found between the pupil edges and the lens, IOL, posterior capsule, or vitreous.

systemic: Involving the entire body.

tachyphylaxis: A decreased response to a medication when used over a long period of time.

Teller visual acuity test: See *preferential looking test*.

temples: The flattened region on either side of a person's forehead. This term is also used to indicate the side arms of eyeglasses that extend over the ears.

tension support rings: Small plastic rings placed inside the capsular bag to prevent it from moving out of position. These are most often used in cases of ectopia lentis in adults.

TNF: See *tumor necrosis factor*.

tonometer: A device used to measure intraocular pressure.

topical: Applied to the front surface of the eye, usually in the form of eyedrops or ointment.

topical anesthetic: Numbing medicine applied to the front surface of the eye. Examples include proparacaine and tetracaine.

toric IOL: An intraocular lens implant that is designed to replace the natural lens while also correcting any astigmatism that may be present.

total cataract: A complete opacity of the entire lens.

trabecular meshwork: The tissue through which aqueous humor leaves the eye. See also *angle of the eye*.

trabeculoplasty: See *laser trabeculoplasty*.

trauma: Damage to a body part from physical injury.

traumatic iritis: Inflammation of the iris caused by an injury.

tube: See *seton*.

tumbling E test: A method of testing vision in patients who are either non-verbal, due to youth or developmental delay, or who may not be familiar with English letters. The patient is presented with images of the letter "E" turned in different directions. He/she then indicates what direction each "E" is facing.

tumor necrosis factor: A natural molecule in the body involved in inflammatory responses. Often referred to by the acronym TNF. Anti-TNF medications are used by rheumatologists to treat autoimmune diseases.

ulcer: An infected tissue with thinning of the infected area. In the eye, this term is often reserved for infection of the cornea. In some countries, the term ulcer is used to refer to a corneal abrasion, which is a scratch to the surface of the eye without infection.

umbilicus: The navel, commonly referred to as the belly button.

unilateral: Medical term meaning occurring on one side. A unilateral eye disease affects only one eye.

uvea: The pigmented middle layer of the eye that is made up of the iris, ciliary body, and choroid. Sometimes also referred to as the uveal tract.

uveitic glaucoma: Increased eye pressure caused by uveitis.

uveitis: Inflammation of any part of the uveal tract of the eye, which includes the iris, ciliary body, and choroid.

uveoscleral pathway: An alternate pathway for aqueous humor to drain from the eye. Approximately five to ten percent of the aqueous humor drains through this pathway instead of following the traditional route through the trabecular meshwork and Schlemm's canal.

valve: Any device for stopping the flow of liquid through a passage. Glaucoma tubes used in surgery sometimes have valves or other flow restriction mechanisms to prevent too much fluid from going through the tube. If too much fluid goes out through the tube, then eye pressure can go too low after surgery.

variable expression: When a genetic disease affects different individuals to different levels of severity.

varicella: The virus that causes chicken pox and shingles.

vascular endothelial growth factor: A protein produced by cells that causes blood vessel growth and sometimes the growth of abnormal vessels (neovascularization). This term is often shortened to the acronym VEGF. VEGF plays a significant role in causing retinopathy of prematurity and other eye diseases.

VEGF: See *vascular endothelial growth factor*

VEGF-blockers: Medications that are used to counteract the effects of vascular endothelial growth factor (VEGF) and stop abnormal blood vessel growth. Also referred to as anti-VEGF drugs.

VEP test: See *visual evoked potential test*.

viscocanalostomy: Injection of a jelly-like substance into Schlemm's canal to open it to achieve better fluid drainage. Viscocanalostomy is used to treat certain types of glaucoma in adults and is rarely used in children.

viscoelastic: A sterile, gel-like material that is used during surgery inside the eye to help make space and protect tissue.

visual acuity: The measurement of vision at predetermined distances.

visual evoked potential test: A test that uses electrodes taped to the scalp to determine if the message from the eye has been received by the brain and whether or not that message is normal. Sometimes referred to as a VEP test.

visual field constriction: Limitation of peripheral vision by a disease process.

visual field defect: An area of the vision that is either missing or not functioning well.

vitreous hemorrhage: Blood inside the vitreous.

vitreous humor: The jelly-like substance that fills the area between the retina and the back of the lens (posterior segment). Often shortened to vitreous.

vitritis: A form of uveitis localized to the vitreous.

YAG laser: A type of laser used to remove membranes or scar tissue that can sometimes form on the back of an IOL, or even without an IOL, after cataract surgery.

zonules: Tiny fibers that hold the lens in place behind the pupil.

Alex V. Levin, MD, MHSc, FAAP, FAAO, FRCSC
Once he finished a pediatric residency at the Children's Hospital of Philadelphia, Dr. Levin completed an ophthalmology residency at Wills Eye Hospital in Philadelphia. He then completed a pediatric ophthalmology fellowship at The Hospital for Sick Children in Toronto. While there, he served as Professor in the Departments of Pediatrics, Genetics, and Ophthalmology and Vision Sciences at the University of Toronto for over 16 years. Dr. Levin is now the Chief of Pediatric Ophthalmology and Ocular Genetics at Wills Eye Hospital and the Robison D. Harley, MD Endowed Chair in Pediatric Ophthalmology and Ocular Genetics. He has a special interest in childhood cataracts, glaucoma, and uveitis. Dr. Levin is also the Medical Advisor for the Pediatric Glaucoma and Cataract Family Association and Chair of their Scientific Advisory Board. He is one of fewer than 10 pediatric ophthalmologists worldwide who is board certified in both pediatrics and ophthalmology.

Christopher M. Fecarotta, MD
Dr. Fecarotta completed an ophthalmology residency at Wills Eye Hospital and a pediatric ophthalmology fellowship at Indiana University. He was an associate editor of the <u>Wills Eye Manual: 6th Edition</u>. Dr. Fecarotta's work on this book occurred while he was an Assistant Clinical Professor of Ophthalmology & Pediatrics at Thomas Jefferson University and Wills Eye Hospital. He is now at SUNY Downstate Medical Center in Brooklyn, NY. Dr. Fecarotta has a special interest in strabismus, amblyopia, retinopathy of prematurity, and pediatric neuro-ophthalmology.

CPSIA information can be obtained
at www.ICGtesting.com
Printed in the USA
LVOW03s2238260116

472370LV00013B/222/P